Seven Rules for Social Research

Seven Rules for Social Research

Glenn Firebaugh

PRINCETON UNIVERSITY PRESS

PRINCETON AND OXFORD

Copyright © 2008 by Princeton University Press
Published by Princeton University Press, 41 William Street, Princeton, New Jersey 08540
In the United Kingdom: Princeton University Press, 3 Market Place, Woodstock,
Oxfordshire OX20 1SY

Library of Congress Cataloging-in-Publication Data
Firebaugh, Glenn.
    Seven rules for social research / Glenn Firebaugh.
       p. cm.
    Includes bibliographical references and indexes.
    ISBN 978-0-691-12546-6 (hardcover : alk. paper)—ISBN 978-0-691-13567-0 (pbk. :
alk. paper)   1. Social sciences—Research.   2. Psychology—Research.   3. Education
research.   4. Public health—Research   5. Qualitative research.   6. Quantitative research.
I. Title.
   H62.F438 2008
     300.72—dc22   2007023942

British Library Cataloging-in-Publication Data is available

This book has been composed in Sabon

Printed on acid-free paper. ∞

press.princeton.edu

Printed in the United States of America

10 9 8 7 6 5 4 3 2 1

To Sarah Elizabeth Gingrich Firebaugh—
loving daughter-in-law, engineer, athlete,
environmental activist, woman of faith—
whose life was cut short by an errant driver.
We miss you.

Contents

CHAPTER 4: *The Fourth Rule*

Replicate Where Possible   90

CHAPTER 5: *The Fifth Rule*

Compare Like with Like   120

CHAPTER 6: *The Sixth Rule*

Use Panel Data to Study Individual Change and Repeated Cross-section Data to Study Social Change   172

CHAPTER 7: *The Seventh Rule*

Let Method Be the Servant, Not the Master   207

Preface

Seven Rules for Social Research is meant to serve as a second methods textbook for students in the social sciences. It can also serve as a reference book for experienced social researchers who want to update their methodological perspectives and skills. My aim in writing this book is to contribute to the improvement of observational (that is, nonexperimental) social research by setting forth seven key rules for doing that kind of research.

This book is appropriate as a text in upper-level undergraduate methods courses and in graduate methods courses. Indeed, the rules can be useful to anyone who is doing or wants to do observational research in the social sciences, from undergraduates writing senior theses to graduate students beginning a dissertation project to seasoned veterans striving to improve their research. In elaborating the rules, I assume only that the reader has a working knowledge of standard regression analysis and of the major modes of data collection and analysis in the social sciences. The book is geared toward classroom use for methods courses in economics, sociology, political science, anthropology, psychology, geography and regional science, education research, criminology and criminal justice, public health and epidemiology, administrative science, policy analysis, and quantitative history. Whatever your discipline, there should be little repetition with your introductory methods textbook. (In fact, because I wanted a book that creates a new mold for methods textbooks, I studiously avoided looking at other methods textbooks while I was writing this one.) Nowhere in *Seven Rules*, for example, do I present a step-by-step description of the research process, as an introductory text would. Instead I focus on the rules for doing good social research.

The central message of the book is "let's do better—not just statistically fancier—research." Because I want that message to reach a broad audience, I have tried to make the book as accessible as possible. There are seven chapters, one for each rule. The chapters are self-contained, so instructors can select the ones most relevant for their purposes. To facilitate classroom use, each chapter concludes with a set of data analysis exercises for students.

In teaching this material, I have found that one chapter each week is a good pace, except for chapters 5 and 6. Those chapters might require two or three weeks each for instructors to cover the material adequately and for students to complete the assignments at the end of the two chapters.

Although chapters 5 and 6 (covering rules 5 and 6) are the most challenging chapters in the book and could be omitted in some undergraduate courses, the persistent reader will be rewarded since rules 5 and 6 reflect the current turn of social research toward issues of causal inference (rule 5) and the analysis of longitudinal data (rule 6).

The rules are liberally illustrated with applications from economics, political science, sociology, and related fields. I sometimes rely on examples from my own work in sociology, since I know that research best. Equations are necessary, but I keep them to a minimum, and in any case I present arguments and examples that rely more on intuition than on formal proofs. The book is much heavier on examples and thought experiments than on formal statistics. Although the book is geared toward quantitative methods, the rules (and certainly the principles behind them) apply to qualitative research as well.

It is fair to say that, for the most part, I learned the seven rules either in the process of my own research or from my experiences as a journal editor. I did not learn them in graduate school—at least not in a codified form. I expect to hear from other social scientists who are in a hurry to tell me about the rules that I missed. I concede the point: It would be foolhardy to claim that the seven rules here are exhaustive. (So send me your additional rules, in case there is a second edition of this book.) What I do claim is that the seven rules are timely and important. Adherence to these rules would materially improve current research in the social sciences.

The idea for this book was hatched after a week-long series of lectures I presented to faculty and others at Academia Sinica (Taipei, Taiwan) in January 2005. The theme of the lectures was "Let method be the servant, not the master." At the end of the week several participants in the course encouraged me to publish the lectures. My first thought was to carve out several journal articles from the lectures. Upon further reflection, however, it became apparent that a series of articles would not do—I would need a book. I resisted the idea at first but later warmed to it, in part due to the encouragement of Tim Sullivan at Princeton University Press. And so this book was born.

An early draft was written in sabbatical facilities kindly provided by Harvard University. I thank Peter Marsden and Mary Waters for inviting me to spend the 2004–05 academic year at Harvard, and for providing me with an office with such a grand view of Cambridge. I thank the other occupants of William James Hall, and Christopher Winship in particular, for stimulating conversations about matters sometimes relevant (and sometimes not) to the issues of this book. I also thank Susan Welch, dean of the College of the Liberal Arts at Penn State, for her efforts in providing a timely and welcome sabbatical to focus on a number of research projects.

Several other individuals also deserve my thanks for contributing to this book in significant ways. Tony Tam invited me to give the lectures at Academia Sinica and then suggested that I should consider publishing those lectures. As the book began to take shape, I received initial encouragement and suggestions from Richard Felson, George Farkas, Stephen Matthews, and Sal Oropesa. The following colleagues and friends read and provided comments on one or more of the chapters: Paul Amato, Satvika Chalasani, David Code, Dalton Conley, George Farkas, Michelle Frisco, David Johnson, Michael Massoglia, Steve Morgan, Wayne Osgood, Alan Sica, and Eric Silver. The comments of Christopher Winship were especially detailed and helpful. The anonymous reviewers at Princeton University Press provided gentle but probing comments that forced me to speak more directly and clearly on some points.

Finally, I would like to thank my wife, Judy Rae. She has not read the book, but her support and encouragement have come in other ways, too numerous to mention.

CHAPTER 1

The First Rule

THERE SHOULD BE THE POSSIBILITY OF SURPRISE IN SOCIAL RESEARCH

Social research differs fundamentally from advocacy research. Advocacy research refers to research that sifts through evidence to argue a predetermined position. Lawyers engage in advocacy research in attempting to prove the guilt or innocence of defendants. Special interest groups engage in advocacy research when trying to influence the vote of lawmakers on a particular bill. The aim of advocacy research is to convince others (juries, lawmakers) to think or act in a given way. Hence advocacy research presents evidence selectively, focusing on supporting evidence and suppressing contrary or inconvenient evidence.

Social research, in contrast, does not suppress contrary or inconvenient evidence. In the social sciences we may begin with a point of view, but (unlike advocacy research) we do not want that point of view to determine the outcome of our research. Rule 1 is not intended to suggest that you need to check your idealism at the door when you embark on a social research project. Far from that—if you don't want to change the world for the better, you might not have the doggedness needed to do good social research. But rule 1 is intended to warn that you don't want to be blinded by preconceived ideas so that you fail to look for contrary evidence, or you fail to recognize contrary evidence when you do encounter it, or you recognize contrary evidence but suppress it and refuse to accept your findings for what they appear to say.

You must be ready to be surprised by your research findings. It is the uncertainty that makes social research exciting and rewarding. If you always knew the answer beforehand, what is the point of doing the research?

For first-time researchers, the surprise very often is in the finding of small effects where large effects were expected. Rarely do new researchers obtain findings that were as strong as they anticipated. Sometimes results are even opposite to expectations. Perhaps you were absolutely certain, for example, that in the United States women are more likely to approve of abortion than men are (not true: see exercises at the end of this chapter), or that younger adults tend to be happier than older adults are (which is also false: see exercises at the end of chapter 2).

Although you might at first be disappointed in your results, it is important to keep in mind that a *noneffect* is not a *nonfinding*. Any result is a finding. Finding no effect could be more interesting than finding a big effect, especially when conventional wisdom holds that there is a big effect. Often the most interesting results in social research are those that fly in the face of conventional wisdom. So you should not be disappointed when you do not find the big effect you expected, or when your results are inconsistent with "what everyone knows."

SELECTING A RESEARCH QUESTION

The first step in a research project is to decide upon a research question. A research question in the social sciences is a question about the social world that you try to answer through the analysis of empirical data. The empirical data may be data that you collected yourself, or data collected by someone else.

There are two fundamental criteria for a research question: interest and researchability. In selecting a research question, your aim is to find a question that is (1) researchable and (2) interesting to you and to others in your field.

RESEARCHABLE QUESTIONS

Some research questions in the social sciences are not researchable because they are simply unanswerable (see Lieberson 1985, chap. 1). In that respect economics, political science, psychology, and sociology are the same as astronomy, biology, chemistry, and physics. Some questions—such as the existence of God—are inherently unknowable with the scientific method. Other questions might be unanswerable as the questions are currently conceived. Other questions might be unanswerable with the knowledge and methods we currently have.

If you are a student, some questions that are answerable in principle might nonetheless be beyond your reach. The Minneapolis Domestic Violence Experiment, for example, sought to determine whether repeat incidents of domestic violence would decline if police arrested accused abusers on the spot (Sherman 1992; Sherman and Berk 1984). Typically students do not have the time, resources, or credentials required to carry out an experiment of this magnitude. The possibilities for student projects are not as restricted as one might think, however, because there are a surprising number of data sets that are available to students for analysis (the student exercises at the end of this chapter use just such a data set, the General

Social Survey). Even if you plan to collect your own survey data, you should consult such prior surveys early in your project, if only for guidance on how to word your questions.

Other research is ruled out because it is unethical. To jump ahead to an example that is central in a subsequent discussion of causality (chapter 5), we did not know, until a few decades ago, whether or not smoking causes lung cancer—some experts said it did, some said that the evidence was inconclusive. Scientifically, the best way to settle the dispute would have been to assign individuals randomly to one of two groups, a smoking group and a nonsmoking group. In terms of science, then, the question could be answered by doing an experiment. In practice, however, such an experiment would have raised serious ethical questions regarding an individual's right to smoke (or not smoke). The important point here is that ethical considerations are important—important enough to render some types of research undoable.[1]

What, then, does a researchable question look like? Researchable questions in the social sciences tend to be questions that are neither too specific (for example, about a specific individual or event) nor too grand ("Why are there wars?"). The question "Why is my uncle an alcoholic?" is not a good research question because in the final analysis it is impossible to predict the behavior of a given individual; social laws are not deterministic. (Besides, the question isn't very interesting to anyone outside your family.) It is possible to make that question researchable by generalizing it to alcoholics in general. We could ask, for example, why some people tend to be more prone to alcoholism than others are. To address that question, we first ask what characteristics distinguish alcoholics from nonalcoholics. In other words, we ask what individual or community traits *correlate* with alcoholism.

In the social sciences *what* questions generally are easier to answer than *why* questions. As Lieberson (1985, p. 219, italics removed) puts it, "Empirical data can tell us what is happening far more readily than they can tell us why it is happening." Consider alcoholism again. With appropriate data it is a straightforward matter to find the correlates of alcoholism, that is, to find the characteristics that distinguish alcoholics from others. Whether these correlates are *causes* of alcoholism is another matter (we take up the causality question under rule 5, "Compare like with

---

[1] In large part because of famous (or infamous) experiments over the past century that harmed human subjects or placed them at risk of harm, universities now maintain guidelines regarding any investigation involving human subjects. At the outset of your research you should contact your university's institutional review board (IRB) for the procedures to follow in your own research. The central principles are that participation by human subjects should be voluntary, that anonymity or confidentiality of subjects should be maintained, and that the benefits of the research should outweigh any foreseeable risks to the subjects.

like"). But that does not make the correlates uninformative. Even if we want to determine causes, generally the first step is to find correlates, since knowing the *what* gives us clues about the *why*.

Because "mere description" is sometimes devalued in the social sciences, it is important to underscore the point that "what" questions come before "why" questions. Facts come first, as Sherlock Holmes stated famously in his warning to Dr. Watson that "It is a capital mistake to theorize in advance of the facts" ("The Adventure of the Second Stain"). To punctuate the detective's point, later I describe an instance where social theorizing went astray by attempting to account for "rising global inequality" when in fact global inequality was not rising. Obviously we need to get the facts right about what there is to explain before we concoct an explanation. As the first maxim of Galileo's *Discors* states, "description first, explanation second" (see Pearl 2000, pp. 334–35).

Getting the facts right is critical, second, because accurate description sometimes is itself the end goal. Consider the problem of motion. Medieval attempts to understand motion grappled with the nature and origins of motion. Current understanding takes motion as given and attempts to describe it precisely and accurately. As Andrew Abbott (2003, p. 7) points out:

> [Isaac Newton] solved the problem of motion by simply assuming that (a) motion exists and (b) it tends to persist. By means of these assumptions (really a matter of declaring victory, as we would now put it), he was able to develop and systematize a general account of the regularities of motion in the physical world. That is, by giving up on the *why* question, he almost completely answered the *what* question.

In this instance progress was stalled until the question was switched from the unknowable (why things move) to the knowable (how they move). We have returned, then, to the central point of this section: that a research question must first of all be answerable. The second requirement is that it is interesting.

INTERESTING QUESTIONS

Besides finding a question that is answerable, you want a question that is interesting—to you and to others. Research involves entering into a conversation. The issue is how your research will contribute to that conversation. A research question might be interesting because of its scientific relevance: In addressing this issue, you join an ongoing discussion in the social sciences. Or a question might be interesting because it is socially important;

perhaps it bears on some important local or national social problem. Or a question might be interesting because of its timeliness; a question relating to Americans' attitudes about gun control might be particularly interesting, for example, when important legislation is pending on the subject.

"The heart of good work," Abbott (2003, p. xi) writes, "is a puzzle and an idea." An interesting research question encompasses both. The puzzle is the issue about the social world that bears investigation. The idea is the new twist that you bring to the investigation.

How do you find an interesting research question? Often personal experiences, or the experiences of others we know, provoke our curiosity about some aspect of human behavior. You can also obtain ideas by reading the research of others. New findings often lead to new questions, and research reports often conclude by noting further research that is needed, or by suggesting directions that subsequent research might take.

Unfortunately, there is no foolproof recipe for cooking up an interesting research question. In that light, it is important to keep in mind that the ideas below are intended to stimulate your thinking, not to provide a roadmap to discovery. No one knows where lightning will strike, but it is still a good idea to avoid sitting on a high metal roof in a thunderstorm. Inspiration is the same way: We cannot be certain where it will strike, but we know that the probabilities are greater in some places than in others.

If you have trouble thinking of a good question for a research project, most likely the problem is either that you have an idea that you like but others don't, or you cannot come up with an idea in the first place.

Suppose you have an idea for a project that enthuses you but no one else. One reaction—perhaps most common among students doing their first research project involving actual data analysis—is to ignore what others, such as your professors, think. That is generally not a good idea. The interest criterion for a research question dictates that you find an issue that is interesting to you and to others in your field. The "others in your field" requirement is important because the "so what?" question is the first challenge you will face when writing up the results of your research. Early in the report you must be able to explain, in a few sentences, why your results are of interest to your readers. Perhaps the question you address relates to an ongoing discussion in your field. Perhaps it extends prior research in new directions, or replicates findings using a new population. Or perhaps it sheds light on an empirical puzzle. The point is that you need some rationale for doing your research. The fact that you cannot get anyone else interested in your research is a telltale sign that you need to rethink the project. Rethinking the project does not necessarily mean that you need to abandon your idea. But it does mean that you need to rework your question to make it interesting to others.

The issue, then, is how to revise your research question to make it more interesting to others. (I assume here that you have done the necessary preliminary review of other research on the topic, so you have a basic idea of what others have found before you.[2]) First you should discuss the project with others to find out why it is uninteresting to them. Most likely they will say that your question is uninteresting either because we already know the answer, or because we would not care about the answer even if we knew it. That is:

- **The no-surprises objection**: We won't learn anything from the research because the answer either is already well documented by prior research or is preordained by the research method. In other words, the research is gratuitous, since we know the answer before we do the research.
- **The "so what" objection**: The answer to the research question either has no relevance for social science theory or for everyday life, or matters to such a small handful of people that the question is trivial.

"Why is my uncle an alcoholic?" is a good example of a trivial research question. No matter how important the answer might be to you, the question is trivial to social scientists because the answer matters to such a small handful of people. To make the question interesting we must generalize it. Instead of asking why your uncle is an alcoholic, we ask what general traits distinguish alcoholics from others. So the triviality problem generally is solved by casting a wider net in the research question.

Irrelevance is also solved by casting a wider net. In truth, of course, few questions are completely irrelevant; relevance is a matter of degree. As editor of the *American Sociological Review* I found that one of the most frequent complaints of reviewers was "Why should I care about the results of this paper?" As social scientists we care about research when the results speak to ongoing conversations and debates in our field. The more such connections we can make, the more interesting our results tend to be. So it is important to show how our research question links to theories and other empirical work.

The other objection (no-surprises) is consequential because, as rule 1 states, surprise is a hallmark of social research. It is the possibility of

[2] In early stages of your literature search you should look particularly for review articles. A good review article will provide (1) a theoretical grid or template for thinking about the important issues in the field, (2) an overview of key findings and key unresolved issues, and (3) a description of the most influential and important studies in the area. The *Journal of Economic Perspectives* and the *Journal of Economic Literature* are valuable sources of summary articles of the latest findings in particular areas of economics. In the other social sciences review articles are available in the *Annual Review* series (e.g., *Annual Review of Sociology*). When beginning a new research project it is a good idea to scan the table of contents of the *Annual Review* to see if recent summary articles are available, and go from there.

surprise that distinguishes social research from advocacy research. So if your social research project is uninteresting because it lacks the element of surprise, you need to make the case that the answer is *not* known beforehand. Sometimes results can be known ahead of time (making the research uninteresting) because the results are built in by the way concepts are measured. So if others say your project is uninteresting, you first need to make sure that your method is not to some degree preordaining your result. In examining the effect of marital satisfaction on overall life satisfaction, for example, it is important to find independent measures of the two concepts, so that the measures used do not guarantee a positive relationship between the two.

Alternatively, perhaps the possibility of surprise has been eliminated by prior research; you've been "scooped." Lest you be too hasty in that judgment, however, it is important to distinguish *well-established research* from *well-established findings*. Lots of research does not necessarily mean that researchers have reached a consensus. Indeed, because controversy itself can stimulate research, an extensive research literature might signal the opposite. Because research in the social sciences sometimes yields mixed, inconclusive, or controversial findings, there are issues of import where research is well established but findings are not. If your research falls into that category, then it does not run afoul of the no-surprises objection, since prior findings do not tell you what you will find. In the happiest of circumstances, you will devise a critical test that reaches a definitive conclusion and shows why prior research has been inconclusive. So there is great potential for a significant research contribution where there is much research but little in the way of established findings.

That situation is quite different from the situation where there is general consensus on research findings. Unless prior research is seriously flawed, well-established findings from prior research rule out the possibility of surprise. So if you believe, for example, that prior research has amply demonstrated that married people in the United States tend to be happier than unmarried people, there is little point in another study of the association of marital status and happiness unless the new study extends that finding in some new direction (examples below). Note the critical qualifier here: *if you believe prior research has amply demonstrated*. Some of the most interesting and significant research in science has overturned the findings of prior research. There is nothing wrong with challenging well-established findings in the social sciences *if you can show that there is reason to doubt those findings*.

In short, if you want to investigate a topic with (apparently) well-established findings, you have two options: *challenge the findings* or *clarify/extend the findings*. Challenging prior research involves both deductive and inductive work: First you demonstrate the logical or methodological flaw in prior research (deduction), then you show, empirically, that the flaw matters (induction).

The other option is to clarify or extend established findings. The *clarification* of findings is deductive (or largely so), involving further conceptualization and theorizing. The *extension* of findings is inductive, involving further data analysis. I consider each of these options in turn.

Challenging Prior Research

In challenging the findings of prior research, the burden of proof rests with you to identify some shortcoming or flaw that is serious enough to raise questions about the reliability of earlier results. Personal anecdotes are not enough in this regard. For example, with regard to the established finding that married people tend to be happier, it won't do to say "I'm not married and I am happier than most married people I know" or "I know lots of unmarried people who are happy and lots of married people who aren't." If you believe prior results are off the mark, you need to focus on the relevant research itself and identify precisely where it has gone astray. Perhaps key concepts are not measured adequately, or the statistical methods are misapplied, or there are problems with the sample or the data.

Box 1.1 gives an example of a presumably well-established social science finding that was effectively challenged by new research. Early accounts suggested that global income inequality shot up dramatically in the last decades of the twentieth century. Using more appropriate data and methods to analyze the trend over that period, however, recent research now finds that global income inequality did not grow at all over that period, and most likely declined somewhat.

The example in box 1.1 is not typical. Not all research is easily challenged. In the first place, you must find something clearly dubious about earlier research, and explain how your suspicions could account for the observed findings. You might, for example, question the finding about marriage and happiness on the grounds that the finding is based on self-reported happiness, and you have good reason to believe that self-reported happiness is an unreliable measure. Your argument might be that, because American culture places a premium on being married, the married are more likely to say they are happy whether they are or not, and the unmarried are more likely to say they are unhappy whether they are or not, and it is that bias in the measurement of happiness that accounts for the association between marriage and happiness.

The next step is to devise a test to show that your critique matters empirically. In the example of marriage and happiness, you would hypothesize that the association between marriage and happiness disappears when happiness is measured in (presumably) more reliable ways, such as how *others* rate you on level of happiness. Very possibly you will be wrong—you may find that marriage is associated with happiness no matter how you measure happiness. Your study nonetheless contributes by showing that marriage is related to happiness even when we measure happiness in different ways. In other words, when you use a new approach to challenge an old finding, you add to knowledge whether you are right or

---

Box 1.1
Case Study: Rethinking the Findings of Research on Global Income Inequality

Contrary to some earlier research, recent studies of global income inequality find that, when China and India are given their due weight, global income inequality is not rising (Bourguignon and Morrisson 2002; Firebaugh 2003; Goesling 2001; Melchior and Telle 2001; Sala-i-Martin 2006; Schulz 1998). (To be clear, there is massive global income inequality in the world today—but it is not growing rapidly, as once feared.) The "yes it is/no it isn't" story of rising global income inequality provides a good example of the importance of knowing what it is that you are trying to explain before you try to explain it. In a number of popular articles and books, inequality has been linked to economic globalization, one of the hottest topics in social science, to fashion a growing literature on globalization and the "explosion" of global income inequality. But the argument that globalization is the cause of rising global income inequality is wrongheaded—it tries to explain a "fact" that isn't.

It is instructive to see where the earlier research went wrong. Income inequality refers to the disproportionate distribution of income across individuals or households. Social scientists have devised ways to measure disproportionality in income (Allison 1978). By applying these measures to income data over time we can determine whether income inequality is rising or falling for a country—or even the whole world.

Global income inequality refers to the disproportionate distribution of income across all the world's citizens, where each citizen is given equal weight. With regard to the discussion here, the important point to note is that the claim of rapidly growing global income inequality in earlier research was subject to challenge because it rested on a series of dubious assumptions and incomplete analyses. These included:

(continued on next page)

wrong. If you are right, your results pose a challenge to conventional findings. If you are wrong, your results extend the conventional findings, albeit that was not your intention.

Probably the most common outcome is that challenges serve to refine rather than dislodge established research findings. Of course, the refinement

(continued from previous page)

- *Extrapolation from results for the tails of the income distribution.* Some earlier studies concluded that global income inequality is rising rapidly on the basis of a comparison of income trends for the very richest and very poorest countries. But the vast majority of the world's people live somewhere else. We cannot reach defensible conclusions about the inequality trend for all the world's population by examining income trends only for those who live in the very richest and very poorest regions.
- *Unequal weighting of individuals.* Early studies often weighted all countries equally. However, because global income inequality refers to the unequal distribution of income across *individuals*—and many more individuals live in poor countries (e.g., China) where incomes are growing rapidly than in poor countries where incomes are growing slowly (Firebaugh 2003)—the failure to weight countries by their population produced misleading results in those studies.
- *Extrapolation from historical trends.* Global income inequality rose rapidly over the nineteenth century and the first half of the twentieth (Bourguignon and Morrisson 2002), as the West took off economically and Asia and Africa lagged behind. Global income inequality rose rapidly because the richest regions of the world were the world's growth leaders and the poorest regions tended to grow slowly, if at all. In recent decades, however, the world has changed. Now many of the fastest-growing economies are in poorer regions of the world (Garrett 2004)—a point not fully taken into account in some early studies. Because income inequality is now declining across countries, the longstanding growth in global income inequality has halted. (At the same time, income inequality has increased *within* many countries. Declining inequality across countries and rising inequality within them implies a "new geography of global income inequality" in which countries are receding in importance as economic units: see Firebaugh [2003].)

of prior research could serve as your starting point. In that case you do not set out to challenge prior research, but to clarify or extend prior research. Indeed, unless the flaws in prior research are obvious, important, and easily correctable, clarification and extension are the most promising strategies for avoiding the no-surprises objection, especially for new researchers. In the next two sections I describe the principal ways that you might clarify or extend prior research.

Clarifying Concepts in Prior Research

You might discover that the problem with prior research is not that the findings are wrong, but that the implications are unclear because of conceptual fuzziness in the model or the variables. Eliminating the fuzziness might not lead to new results, but it could lead to new understanding about what the results mean. In this case the element of surprise in our research involves the implications of our findings, not necessarily the findings themselves.

It is especially important to be clear about the meaning of our dependent variable, the variable we are trying to explain. Richard Felson (2002, pp. 209–10) gives examples from theory and research on crime. As Felson notes, the first step in explaining crime is to determine what sorts of behavior we are trying to explain. Some types of crime involve deviant acts (for example, illegal drug use), whereas other types involve aggression as well as deviance (for example, assault). Appropriate explanations of illegal drug use may be very different from explanations of aggressive behavior. To test various theories of crime, then, Felson suggests the use of what he calls "discriminant prediction" (for example, theories of aggression should better predict assault than illegal drug use, whereas theories of deviance should predict both assault and illegal drug use).

Extending Prior Research

Suppose you have no good reason to doubt the accuracy or conceptual framework of prior research bearing on your research question. In that case you should use prior findings as the point of departure for your own research project. To make the research interesting—to permit surprises— one possibility is to extend that research in new directions. Here are some general ideas along that line.

- *Focus on a key subpopulation.* The idea here is to see whether or not earlier research findings are reproducible for some strategic subset of the population. Suppose prior research shows that college seniors tend to be more liberal politically than freshmen are. You attend a parochial school, and in your review of the literature you find that no one has examined that issue separately for parochial schools, which (you suspect) tend to be more conservative than other colleges. In that case you might design a survey for freshmen and seniors in your school to see if you find the same result for your college (better yet, administer your survey in a broad range of parochial colleges in addition to your own). Because no one has studied this issue for parochial schools, you can be surprised by the results. The results of your study likely would be of interest to a number of people, including administrators and others in parochial schools, educational sociologists, and those who study how political attitudes are formed. (A word of warning here: subpopulations such as "my friends" or "my sorority sisters" are too narrow. You might begin by pretesting your survey on your friends, but you do not want to end there. Not many people are interested in the political attitudes of your friends or those in your sorority. But a number of people are interested in the political attitudes of students in parochial colleges, a much more substantial subset of the general college population.)

- *Use a new population.* In this case the issue is whether or not earlier research findings apply to some new population. You might want to know whether there is an association between marriage and happiness in the case of arranged marriages. To find out, you could investigate the effect of marriage on happiness in societies where arranged marriages are more common than they are in the United States.

- *Use a different time period.* Here the issue is whether or not prior research findings apply to a different era. In some studies that new time period might be historical: Was there a positive association between marriage and happiness in the nineteenth-century United States, or has that association come about more recently? Historical data to address such questions often are lacking, however, so most replication studies of this type are updating studies—studies that seek to update earlier research with more recent data. For example, studies of racial attitudes in the United States have consistently found that white southerners are more likely than whites outside the South to disapprove of marriage between blacks and whites, to disapprove of racial integration of schools, and so on. Many of those studies were done in the 1970s and 1980s (for example, Middleton 1976; Tuch 1987), however, so periodically new studies appear (for example, J. S. Carter 2005) to determine how quickly regional differences are disappearing (if at all).

- *Use a new population or subpopulation to test a specific hypothesis.* In this case you choose a population or subpopulation that provides a test of some hypothesis. For example, you might hypothesize that the positive relationship between marriage and happiness is based on companionship, so you expect little or no effect of marriage on happiness where long periods of separation are common. You might test this hypothesis by estimating the effect of marriage on happiness among those in the navy (where long periods of spousal separation are commonplace) and comparing that effect with the marriage effect in branches of the military where separation is not the norm. Note that in this instance a *noneffect* (no association between marriage and happiness among those in the navy) provides support for your companionship explanation of the general marriage-happiness relationship.

In short, one possibility for well-established research results is to see whether or not old results apply in new contexts (strategic subpopulations, new populations, or different time periods).

Another possibility is to extend or refine the *causal explanations* of the observed empirical patterns found in prior research. The social sciences are pregnant with claims about what causes what. The evidence we have for these causal claims, however, is often very weak. A critical task in the social sciences is more and deeper research on causal relations. There are several general strategies for doing so. The major possibilities are discussed below.

CAUSAL CHAINS: INTRODUCE MEDIATING VARIABLES TO ACCOUNT FOR RESULTS OF PRIOR STUDIES

The idea here is to develop theories that identify the mechanisms or pathways by which some independent (explanatory, exogenous) variable X affects some dependent (outcome, endogenous) variable Y. One way to account for the effect of X on Y is to find some set of variables Q that mediate the effect of X on Y, that is, $X \to Q \to Y$. This strategy is often employed in social science to account for the effects of ascribed traits such as gender or race on outcome variables such as earnings. It is well known, for example, that women tend to earn less than men in the United States. Explanations of this gender gap in earnings typically focus on mediating or intervening variables Q in this chain: gender $\to Q \to$ earnings. In this chain Q might include things like interrupted careers (women are more likely to have interrupted work careers, and that's one reason for gender differences in earnings) and hours worked (men are more likely than women to work full-time). One way to make a research contribution, then, is to find important mediating variables that have been missed or undervalued in prior research.

The mediating variables strategy works best when reverse causation can be ruled out. That is why the strategy is often popular for explaining the effects of ascribed traits such as gender and race. In the illustration above, for example, it is clear that gender affects hours worked, not vice versa.

Sometimes causal direction is not so obvious. In the case of marriage and happiness, it is not clear which comes first, marriage or happiness (see reverse causation below). In other words, there could be a kind of selection effect in which those who are selected into marriage tend to be happier than those who are not selected into marriage. Even if marriage is not selective with respect to happiness per se, marriage could be selective with respect to possible *correlates of happiness*, such as physical attractiveness, or *causes of happiness*, such as physical health. If in fact the beautiful and the healthy are more likely to marry *and* more likely to be happy, then at least some of the association of marriage with happiness is due to the association of marriage with attractiveness and health. Thus marriage could be associated with happiness even if marriage has no *causal* effect on happiness.

This observation—that *nonmediating* variables could account for the empirical association between marriage and happiness—leads to another possibility for extending prior research.

INTRODUCE NONMEDIATING VARIABLES TO ACCOUNT
FOR RESULTS OF PRIOR STUDIES

The idea here is the same as in the mediating variables case: We want to develop theories that explain why we observe an association between X and Y. In the case of nonmediating variables, though, the mechanisms are not causal. Sometimes the term *spurious association* is used to describe associations between X and Y that can be accounted for by their associations with other variables, where those other variables are not causal mechanisms linking X and Y. (For example, X and Y might be associated because some third variable Z causes both of them. Or X and Y might be associated because X is associated with other variables that are causes of Y.) The term *spurious* here means that there is *no causal link* from X to Y. It does not mean that the association of X and Y itself is a mirage. When we say, for example, that the association of marriage and happiness is spurious, we do not mean that, on second thought, married people aren't happier after all. What we mean is that getting married typically won't make you happier. (If the distinction is unclear, it should become clearer with the discussion of causality in rule 5, "Compare like with like.")

Often an association between X and Y is partly causal and partly not, so some of the so-called *control variables* that are added to a model to account for an association of interest are mediating and some are not. Whatever the situation—whether the association of X and Y is due to mediating variables or nonmediating variables or a combination of the two—it is nearly impossible to overstate the importance of careful conceptualization and theorizing in determining what control variables to add. To assist in this theorizing, you should draw a path diagram that depicts your model (chapter 5 provides examples). In a path diagram, variables are nodes, and arrows connect the variables. A straight arrow from X to Y indicates that X causes Y, and a curved double-headed arrow between X and Y indicates that X and Y are associated, with no causal direction assumed. If there are no reciprocal effects among the variables, path analysis methods (Alwin and Hauser 1975) can be used to estimate the model. The important point here, however, is to draw the model so that you can see at a glance how all the variables are interconnected.[3]

Finally, it is important to stress that you should not add control variables willy-nilly to a model to find out if that affects your results. You need to justify the variables theoretically before you add them. More control variables are not always better than fewer control variables, as Lieberson (1985, chap. 2) emphasizes in his discussion of the dangers of what he calls "counterproductive controls" and "pseudocontrols." Careful theorizing is the best protection against such dangers.

INTRODUCE MODERATING VARIABLES TO ACCOUNT FOR, AND QUALIFY, RESULTS OF PRIOR STUDIES

A *moderating variable* is a special kind of nonmediating variable that conditions the effect of one variable on another. For example, if the effect of education on income is greater for whites than it is for nonwhites, then we say that race *moderates* or *conditions* the effect of education on income. The effect itself is called an *interaction effect* (Jaccard and Turrisi 2003).

By introducing moderating variables, Scott Myers turns a common observation—that religious parents tend to have religious children—into an interesting research project. After noting that "Religiosity, like class, is inherited," Myers (1996, p. 858) theorizes that there are factors that would "condition the ability of parents to transmit their religiosity." In other words, he theorizes that there are interaction effects. He finds that the transmission of religious practices (such as praying, reading the Bible, and attending church) is stronger when parents are happily married and do not divorce, when parents agree on religious beliefs, when parents show affection toward their children and are moderately strict in rearing their children, and when the husband works in the paid labor force and the wife is a housewife. In short, Myers finds a number of interesting interaction effects.

[3] Path diagrams also help you to see which variables are exogenous (determined outside the model) and which are endogenous (determined by other variables in the model). It is important to find exogenous variables, since you cannot estimate a model when all variables are endogenous.

We encountered the concept of interaction effects earlier, most notably in our hypothesis that the effect of marriage on happiness will be reduced in navy marriages (as opposed to marriages among those in other branches of the military). In fact, if we think again about comparing the findings of new populations with findings for other populations, we see that such comparisons are best carried out in a moderator-variable framework, that is, by combining data for the old and new populations and using interaction terms. In the case of comparing students in parochial colleges with students in other colleges, for example, we could append the data collected on parochial schools to existing data on other colleges and employ "type of school" (parochial/other) as the moderating variable. (Merging the parochial school data with the earlier data should not be a problem if the replication was done properly.) Or, to determine whether the effect of marriage on happiness is weaker in the case of navy marriages than for marriages in general, we could combine data from two samples—a sample of those in the navy, and a sample of those not in the navy—and use "in navy" (yes/no) as the moderating variable.

CHECK FOR REVERSE CAUSATION

The extension of prior research might also turn on the issue of *which variables are dependent* (called the *endogeneity problem*). You might concede, for example, that the married in fact tend to be happier (no matter how happiness is measured), but not because marriage leads to happiness. As noted earlier, the association could reflect the fact that happier people are more likely to attract a mate, so happiness increases the likelihood of marriage instead of the other way around. If prior research interprets the marriage-happiness association as reflecting only the effect of marriage on happiness, you can make a contribution by designing research to separate the effect of marriage on happiness (marriage → happiness) from the effect of happiness on marriage (happiness → marriage). If the conventional interpretation is that marriage causes happiness and you show that happiness causes marriage instead, then you have found an example of reverse causation: There is a causal effect, but prior research has the arrow going in the wrong direction.

BROADEN THE RESEARCH QUESTION BY EXPANDING IT ACROSS SUBFIELDS

The idea here is to reframe old issues by synthesizing perspectives, concepts, or methods from more than one subfield. Synthesizing studies are hard to do, but successful studies can have high payoff in terms of new insights. Consider again the issue of the transmission of religiosity across generations. Social class is also transmitted across generations, and there is a huge sociological literature on class inheritance. It is useful to think about how the study of religious inheritance could be linked to the study of class inheritance, which has been studied in much greater depth. Are the processes of class inheritance and religious inheritance similar? Are parents in the United States more effective in transmitting their class standing or their religious beliefs? To my knowledge no one has tackled that question (I suppose because it is difficult to find a common metric for comparing the two types of inheritance). The attempt to span the two fields could have high payoff, however, in terms of both substance and method. We could generalize the issue more—and make it even more interesting—by asking what overarching principles govern the transmission of beliefs, attitudes, values, and statuses across generations. For example, are parents generally more successful in transmitting their beliefs and values (political, religious, and so on) or their material statuses (such as their social class) to the next generation? In synthesizing studies of this sort, prior findings for particular fields of inquiry become the touchstones for more general theories and research about human behavior.

In short, the answer to the question of concern here—What if your research idea is not interesting because it has been thoroughly researched before?—is: Don't give up on your idea too easily. You might be able to update previous findings with more recent data, or extend findings back in time with historical data. Or you might try to replicate prior research by focusing on a strategic subpopulation, or by using a new population altogether.

Alternatively, you can use the same population as in prior research, and look for ways to extend that research by accounting for well-documented associations in terms of either mediating variables, nonmediating variables, moderating variables, or reverse causation (or some combination of the above). Your project can be especially interesting if it bears on *empirical regularities* in societies—fundamental associations that are well documented and appear to be generally true of most societies (for example, the inheritance of social class across generations). In general, the more tightly you can link your research to key empirical regularities, the more interesting it is for social scientists.

In offering these suggestions about how to build upon the foundation of prior research, I am assuming that there is prior research on the issue you want to study. Of course you do not need to worry about prior research if there is no prior research. So it is tempting to try to think of a novel research idea, something that no one else has investigated before. That often poses a dilemma. Recall that interest and researchability are the key requirements for a research topic. Yet if we find a topic that is interesting and researchable, very likely the issue has been studied a number of times, so there is extensive research on it already. It is generally difficult, then, to find a feasible research question that is important yet has not been studied.

That dilemma probably explains why researchers-in-training sometimes struggle to find a research topic. They try in vain to find an interesting question that no one has investigated before. The examples above are intended to make the point that the best social research most often is research that brings fresh perspectives and new insights to old and continuing areas of concern.

Selecting a Sample

After determining *what* you want to study, you need to determine *whom* to study. First you need to determine what target population your results are meant to describe (see chapter 4). Are you interested in drawing conclusions about all college students worldwide? (That could be overly ambitious, as obtaining a sample of college students worldwide would be difficult.) Or only American college students? Or only American college students in parochial schools? To know whom to sample, you need to identify your target population carefully and precisely.

After determining your target population, you need to determine a strategy for selecting a subset of individuals—called a *sample*—from that population. Because you attempt to draw conclusions about the entire population on the basis of results from a subset of that population, it is critical that your sample be representative of your population (or the subpopulations that you want to compare: see the third principle of sampling, below). The most straightforward way to obtain a representative sample, conceptually, is to think about selecting individuals completely at random from the population, so each individual in the target population has an equal probability of being selected for the sample. A sample selected in this way is called a *simple random sample*. In practice, though, a simple random sample usually is hard to obtain, and other sampling methods have been devised for obtaining samples that are representative, or virtually so, for target populations. Full descriptions of these methods are available elsewhere (Kalton 1983; Kish 1965), and I see no need to cover the same ground here. What I want to do instead is emphasize some overarching principles.

First principle of sampling: You don't need to eat the whole ox to know that it is tough.

Samuel Johnson is often credited (probably incorrectly) with this colorful way to express the idea—later applied to the sampling of human populations—that characteristics of the whole can be inferred from characteristics of the part. All sampling is based on this principle.

The same laws of probability that underlie the first principle of *sampling* also lead directly to the first principle of *sample size*.

First principle of sample size: For practical purposes, very large populations do not require larger samples than smaller populations do.

Suppose we want to know, with a certain degree of precision, which of two candidates will carry the states of California and Wyoming in a presidential election. If the race is equally competitive in both states, we do not need a larger sample for California than we do for the state of Wyoming, even though California has seventy times more people than Wyoming does.[4] In fact, if the race is closer in Wyoming than it is in California, then we would need a larger sample to predict the winner in Wyoming.

The first principle of sample size implies an important corollary.

Sample size corollary: We can make confident generalizations about a large population from a sample containing only a tiny fraction of that population.

Although students generally have little trouble grasping the first principle of sampling, they often are surprised by the first principle of sample size and its corollary. It seems to defy common sense that anyone could determine what millions of Americans are thinking by talking to merely 1,500 of them. Yet that is exactly what pollsters try to do.

George C. Wallace, four-term governor of Alabama and unsuccessful third-party candidate for president in 1968, provides the most memorable attacks on the reliability of political polls and the logic of polling.

---

[4] Note that the principle states *for practical purposes*. Strictly speaking, all else equal, we would need a slightly larger sample in California, due to the finite population correction $\sqrt{(N-n)/(N-1)}$, where n is sample size and N is size of the population. (This correction is needed because the standard error approaches zero as n approaches N.) In practice n is usually so small relative to N that the correction is trivial. According to U.S. Census Bureau estimates for 2003, California had 35.48 million people and Wyoming had 0.50 million people. Thus for a sample size of 1,000, the finite population correction factor is 0.999986 for California and 0.998999 for Wyoming. In other words, because a sample of 1,000 constitutes a larger fraction of the population in Wyoming than in California, the standard error shrinks more in Wyoming (by a factor of 0.998999) than in California, where the standard error is reduced only by a factor of 0.999986. The practical implication is that, all else equal, we would need a sample size of 1,001 for California to match the precision of the results for a sample of 1,000 in Wyoming.

Wallace's populist "Stand up for America" campaign resonated with large segments of the U.S. public,[5] and polls showed surprising support, particularly in the South, for his third-party candidacy. However, when polls showed his support slipping in the final weeks of the 1968 election, Wallace attacked the polls themselves. In an article "Wallace Assails 'Lying' Election Polls," the *New York Times* (October 27, 1968) reports:

> George C. Wallace delivered a blistering attack on national political polls today in response to one that indicates support for his Presidential campaign has slipped substantially in the last week. Informed of the results of the latest Gallup Poll, which shows that the American Independent party candidate dropped 5 percentage points, he said: "They lie when they poll. They are trying to rig an election. Eastern money runs everything. They are going to be pointed out the liars that they are."

Two days later Wallace dismissed political polls as "comic strips" and charged that the polls represent "a deliberate and desperate attempt on the part of the other two parties to deceive the American people" ("Wallace, Irritated by Polls, Insists He Is Doing Well," *Washington Post*, October 29, 1968, p. A7). In a campaign rally in Hannibal, Missouri, on October 28, 1968, he posed this famous question, as described the next day in the *Washington Post*: " 'The Gallup poll and the Harris poll—they talked to 1600 people in the country and say they can decide how the election's coming out,' the former Alabama Governor sniffed. 'Well, how many of you have been talked to by the Harris poll and the Gallup poll?' he demanded. 'Not a one of you, not a one of you.' "

Governor Wallace's views notwithstanding, reputable preelection polls of likely voters have been fairly accurate in forecasting the results of recent elections, even though the polls typically are based on a sample of only a dozen or so respondents per *million* voters. On the eve of a presidential election, for example, most national polls rely on a sample of 1,500 or so likely voters. Over 122 million Americans voted in the 2004 election—so a sample size of 1,500 works out to a ratio of one person sampled for every 81,000 voters, or 0.0012 percent of the voters.

How then are we to account for the fact that we can use 0.0012 percent of the population to predict so accurately the behavior of the remaining

---

[5] Wallace's campaign brochure describes him as "the undisputed leader in the fight for personal and property rights, and against excessive taxation and the takeover of personal rights by the 'great society.' " Regarding the Vietnam War, Wallace is quoted as follows in the brochure: "These few people today who are out advocating sedition and raising money and clothes and supplies for the Viet Cong—these college professors who are making speeches advocating victory for the Viet Cong Communists—I would deal with these people as they ought to be dealt with, as traitors." (http://www.4president.org/brochures/wallace1968brochure)

99.9988 percent? This principle is demystified somewhat by the second principle of sampling.

Second principle of sampling: How cases are selected for a sample is more important than *how many* cases are selected.

In other words, the *representativeness* of the sample is more important than the size of the sample. Of course I do not mean to suggest that a sample of two or three is all right, so long as those people are selected properly. But I do mean to suggest that a sample of only a few hundred can give a surprisingly accurate picture of a population of many millions, so long as the individuals in the sample are representative of the individuals in the target population. Obviously a larger sample is better than a smaller sample, other things equal—but the superiority of larger samples over smaller ones is itself due to the fact that (for a given sampling method) larger samples are more likely to be representative. Consider the extreme case of a single individual. A sample of one cannot be very representative of the entire population, unless individuals in the population are all alike. At the other extreme, a census is clearly representative of the population, since it contains everyone in the population.

It is important to understand two points here: first, that a representative sample of a few hundred people can be remarkably accurate; second, that a nonrepresentative ("biased") sample of a few million people can be remarkably inaccurate. Failure to appreciate fully the second point has led to some infamous blunders in the polling business. In the United States, "the poll that changed polling" occurred in the 1936 presidential election between Democrat Franklin D. Roosevelt and Republican Alfred M. Landon. In its October 31, 1936, issue, the venerable magazine *Literary Digest* predicted—on the basis of a sample of *over two million*—that Landon would win the election in a landslide. Three days later, Roosevelt won in a landslide. The error by the *Literary Digest* was caused by their sampling method, which oversampled Republicans and those favoring change in the government (Roosevelt was the incumbent). On the basis of a more representative sample of just 5,000 people, a little-known pollster named George Gallup correctly predicted Roosevelt's landslide victory. Not long after the 1936 election, the *Literary Digest* went out of business. The polling methods perfected by Gallup are still in use today.[6]

Because scientific polling has come a long way since the 1936 presidential election, it is hard for individual researchers to match the general

---

[6] Controversies over the results of reputable polls (such as Roper, Harrris, or Gallup polls) rarely center on sampling issues any more. Most of the focus today is on validity issues—on what respondents really mean by their responses (see Sudman, Bradburn, and Schwarz 1995; Tourangeau, Rips, and Rasinski 2000).

quality of data collected by professional firms. Most social scientists, then, rely on survey firms for the collection of the survey data they use. That is one reason for the popularity of *secondary analysis* in the social sciences, that is, the analysis of data collected by someone else. Of course, with secondary analysis of national data you cannot tailor the data to very specific or local populations—you would not, for example, be able to study the political attitudes of students in your own college with national survey data. National survey data on the attitudes of college students do, however, provide a benchmark for the attitudes of students in your own college. In short, secondary analysis of national survey or census data very often is called for even in studies where researchers collect their own data, since the national data provide a point of comparison for the more local or specialized data.

Large survey data sets have become increasingly accessible and user-friendly over recent decades. Many of these data sets have been underwritten by government money, and researchers who use public funds to collect data generally are required to place their data in the public domain for others to use. Major social science data sets are located in several data archives in the United States and other countries. Probably the best-known U.S. social science data archive is housed at the University of Michigan, at the Inter-University Consortium for Political and Social Research (ICPSR), web site http://www.icpsr.umich.edu. Undergraduate and graduate students typically have access to the national data sets most commonly used in social research.

Third principle of sampling: Collect a sample that permits powerful contrasts for the effects of interest.

If you are interested in the effects of cohabitation, for example, then make sure you have enough cohabiters in your sample to permit the comparison of cohabiters with others. If you are collecting your own data, you will want to *oversample* cohabiters. You can oversample cohabiters by using a method called *stratified random sampling*: First stratify on the basis of union type (cohabiting versus married); then randomly sample within each group. To oversample cohabiters, simply select a larger fraction of cohabiters than marrieds.

As this example suggests, simple random sampling of the overall population is not always the best method. Sometimes it is better to divide the population into homogeneous groups and oversample the minority groups. If there are G groups, we can think of G samples, one for each group. So long as you randomly sample within each group, each sample is representative of that group, and there is no problem in making comparisons *across* groups. But the G samples merged are *not* representative of the overall population. Suppose, for example, that a preelection poll heavily oversamples African Americans. To predict results for each candidate, you would need to downweight the African American sample to reflect the proportion of voters who are African American, or your predictions will be entirely too rosy for Democratic candidates (since African Americans tend to vote overwhelmingly for Democrats, and whites do not). I discuss these issues in more detail in the next section.

Finally, note that the probability of selection into a sample should not depend on potential outcomes. Typically you stratify on the basis of explanatory variables. By doing so, and oversampling cases from the minority groups, you increase the variance on your explanatory variables (demonstrated in the next section). Because you can't explain a variable with a constant (chapter 2), it's a good idea to boost the variance on your explanatory variables. Increasing the variance of your explanatory variables is especially important when you have a small sample, as we now see.

SAMPLES IN QUALITATIVE STUDIES

The third principle of sampling provides a nice bridge to the discussion of sampling in qualitative studies, since samples in qualitative studies generally are much smaller than samples in quantitative studies. All the sampling principles above apply to qualitative studies: You don't need to eat the whole ox; large populations do not require larger samples than smaller populations do; how cases are selected is more important than how many cases are selected; and you might need to stratify your sample.

What *is* different, usually, about qualitative studies is the limited number of cases studied. To understand what difference that might make regarding sampling strategy, we need first to identify more precisely the advantages of large samples over small samples. By identifying those advantages, we can think about sampling strategies that qualitative researchers might use to compensate for small sample size.

Unless the sample size is very small (say 50 cases or fewer), the chief limitation of a small sample is *not* that it fails to provide a modestly reliable description of key features of a population. A small representative sample of 100 generally yields fairly accurate *point estimates* (to use statistical parlance) of a population, where that term refers to a sample statistic that summarizes some important population characteristic, such as average income, the ratio of men to women, the percentage married, or (as in the George Wallace example) the percentage of the electorate who will vote for a particular candidate.

Instead, the chief limitation of a small sample is its lack of analytic power—its lack of leverage for separating the effects of multiple causes. The problem is especially acute when causes have little variance and (as is most often the case) covary with other causes or correlates of the dependent variable. In general, *the more highly correlated the causes, the more cases we need to separate their effects.*

To illustrate, suppose you want to test a theory about only-children. Your theory argues that children reared in a home without siblings grow up in a very different environment from that experienced by children with siblings, and that the difference in childhood environment implies different adult outcomes—perhaps only-children tend to be more self-confident as adults, and more likely to assume leadership positions. You want to examine this theory by doing a qualitative study of 100 American adults, some of whom have siblings and some of whom do not. We assume that $N = 100$ is a fixed upper limit—time and budget constraints will not allow you to collect data on more than 100 individuals total.

One issue you must worry about is obtaining enough variance on your explanatory variable. The problem arises because only about 5 percent of American adults are only-children. So in a random sample of 100 adults, you expect about 5 only-children—hardly enough to make confident inferences about the differences between only-children and others. The solution, as before, is to use stratified sampling: Divide the population into those who are only-children and those who are not, and randomly select 50 adults from each group. In other words, you deliberately oversample only-children. In that way you increase the variance on your independent variable (let's call it **no-sibs**) more than five-fold, from 0.0475 to 0.25 (the variance for a dichotomy is $\pi(1-\pi)$, where π is proportion in one of the categories).

By increasing the number of only-children from 5 to 50, you increase the reliability of your estimates of Y (your dependent variable) for only-children. Of course, you also reduce the reliability of your estimates of Y for others, since you have reduced the sample of others from 95 down to 50. But the gain in reliability in moving from 5 to 50 cases more than offsets the loss in reliability in moving from 95 to 50. You can have more confidence in your estimates of *group differences* where the groups consist of 50 each than in estimates where $N = 5$ for one group and $N = 95$ for the other.

But, you ask, does not oversampling fly in the face of the notion of representative sampling? It was the oversampling of Republicans that led to the infamous *Literary Digest* blunder on the 1936 presidential election. How are we to reconcile the advice here to oversample with the earlier discussion about the importance of using representative samples?

The key is to note that the aim of the *Literary Digest* poll was to draw inferences about a single population (voters in the 1936 election), whereas the aim of the only-child research is to draw inferences about *differences* between two populations, a majority population (adults who had siblings) and a minority population (adults who were only-children). For the best estimates of differences between populations, we want a representative sample of cases from each population. The sample does not need to be representative for the populations merged unless we want to draw inferences about that overarching population—then we need to reweight our samples to make them representative of the overarching population. To illustrate, imagine we find, in our 50/50 sample of only-children and others, that adults who were only-children attain 14 years of education on average while other adults average 12 years. Then our estimate of the educational difference is two years, but our estimate of the average education for all adults is $12(.95) + 14(.05) = 12.1$ years, reflecting the relative weights of the two groups in the overarching adult population.

In short, the use of stratified random sampling to oversample smaller populations is often strategic for comparing minority groups to majority groups, particularly in the case of qualitative research, where the total sample size may be modest. In the final analysis, though, purposive oversampling of this type cannot alleviate a fundamental problem with small samples: the lack of power to adjudicate competing explanations.[7] Consider alternative explanations for an association between the variable **no-sibs** (no siblings) and some outcome variable Y. A birth-order theorist, for example, might argue that any only-child effect that you find is a first-born effect in disguise. In other words, what matters is not the absence of siblings, but being born first. And **no-sibs** is inherently correlated with the variable **first-born**, since only-children are also first-born children. The correlation nonetheless is not perfect, since some first-born children are only-children and some are not—so it *is* possible to separate the birth-order effect from the only-child effect empirically, at least in principle. But to do that we need to divide our sample further into three groups, not two—only-children, first born among those with siblings, not first born—and compare the outcome variable Y for the three groups. If it is **no-sibs** that matters for the outcome, then Y for the only-children group should differ from Y for the other two groups. On the other hand, if it is **first-born** that matters for the outcome variable, then the difference should be between the first born and others: Y should be the same for first born with or without siblings, and differ for those who are not first born.

---

[7] Some methodologists and philosophers of social science conceptualize cause as deterministic rather than probabilistic, so a purported cause can be eliminated by a single exception. If so, then small samples could be analytically powerful, since each case has the potential to eliminate a different explanation for some phenomenon. In that tradition, as Lieberson (1991) points out, small N's can lead to "big conclusions." I do not pursue that approach here because I believe there is an alternative view of causality that holds more promise for social research (see rule 5).

The important point here is the demand placed on data by the need to examine alternative explanations, even when we stratify on explanatory variables. The more explanations there are, the more such comparisons we need to make; the more comparisons we make, the more finely we must stratify; the more finely we stratify, the smaller the subsamples upon which our comparisons are made. The solution to this dilemma is a large overall sample. That is what I mean when I say that a larger sample has greater "analytic power"—a larger sample permits more comparisons, and with more comparisons you can investigate more explanations.

Without the luxury of a large sample to provide the basis for one comparison after another, qualitative researchers very often must decide which comparisons are strategic, and select a sample accordingly. It helps to stratify on explanatory variables and oversample the smaller populations within those strata, but a stratified sample helps only up to a point: In the final analysis there are limits to the number of strata you can use when the overall sample is small. As a result, qualitative studies generally are not well-suited for omnibus tests of many different explanations for some observed association. Qualitative methods *are* well-suited for providing thick description that can help place quantitative results in proper context. Qualitative methods sometimes can also provide precise critical tests—tests that often are difficult with conventional quantitative approaches. Indeed, through strategic data selection, qualitative approaches often extend or correct quantitative studies, as we discover subsequently with examples of rule 3, "Build reality checks into your research."

Is Meaningful Social Research Possible?

October 7, 1903, is famous in aviation history for the test that failed. As news reporters watched expectantly, test pilot Charles Manly assumed his position aboard a curious-looking airship perched on a houseboat in the Potomac River. To avoid fatal landings, the plan was to crash into the water after demonstrating the possibility of human flight in a heavier-than-air machine. As propeller wheels whirred a foot from Manly's head, a mechanic cut the cable holding the catapult, and the airship tumbled ignominiously into the waters of the Potomac.

That spectacular failure, along with a second well-publicized plunge into the icy Potomac two months later, resulted in public ridicule of the airship's designer, the distinguished physicist and astronomer Samuel Pierpont Langley. Armed with a $50,000 grant from the War Department and another $20,000 from the Smithsonian Institution (which combined would be worth over $1.5 million in today's money), Langley had set out to build a heavier-than-air aircraft piloted by humans. His highly visible failures added credibility to Lord Kelvin's famous claim, eight years earlier, that "Heavier-than-air flying machines are impossible."

After Langley's first failed attempt a *New York Times* editorial had this to say about the prospects of human flight ("Flying Machines Which Do Not Fly," *New York Times*, October 9, 1903):

> [It] might be assumed that the flying machine which will really fly might be evolved by the combined and continuous efforts of mathematicians and mechanicians in from one million to ten million years. . . . No doubt the problem has attractions for those it interests, but to the ordinary man it would seem as if effort might be employed more profitably.

In one of the ironies of history, as these words were being penned Wilbur and Orville Wright were preparing their own launch in a remote area on the coast of North Carolina. The first manned flight did not take place a million years later, but just a little more than two months after the *Times* editorial. On December 17, 1903, Orville and Wilbur took turns piloting a flying machine (that cost about $1,000 to build—$22,000 in today's money) over the sand dunes of Kitty Hawk. With no government financial backing and little fanfare, two determined bicycle builders from Ohio had proved Lord Kelvin and the *New York Times* wrong.

In academia there are Lord Kelvins among us today who make similar assertions about the impossibility of meaningful social research. Let me be very clear: I am not talking about those who say that good social research is difficult, or that social research is often badly done, or that some questions about human behavior are inherently unanswerable. (I happen to agree with all those assertions.) Rather, I am talking about those who are skeptical about the possibility of discovering general principles of human behavior. In the view of such skeptics, either such principles don't exist, or the principles are so "contextualized" that we cannot *generalize* from situation to situation. Empirical nihilism of this sort tends to be most prominent in schools of thought containing a "post" prefix: postmodernism, postpositivism, poststructuralism, post-Kuhnian philosophy of science, and so on.

In its most extreme version, empirical nihilism in the social sciences denies the possibility of discovering even regularities in human behavior. That position is obviously silly. Consider the life insurance industry. Actuarial tables presume knowledge about regularities in death rates. Although we cannot predict when specific individuals will die, we do know that women tend to outlive men (in most Western countries anyway), that nonsmokers tend to outlive smokers, and that it's good to exercise and eat your vegetables. Or consider government efforts to monitor economic growth and control inflation. If the discovery of general principles bearing on economic behavior were beyond the ken of humans, the Federal Reserve Board would have no reason to meet to discuss alterations in the prime rate.

Empirical nihilism is not new, nor is it unique to the social sciences. Before attempting to discover principles about the world of nature, physicists and other natural scientists presuppose that observable natural phenomena, such as motion, are real, and that they are amenable to investigation. The ancient Greek philosopher Zeno of Elea believed otherwise. Zeno, like his teacher Parmenides, viewed the world of sense as an illusion. To defend that view, Zeno used paradoxes to demonstrate the impossibility of motion. One paradox can by illustrated by imagining an arrow in flight. At each moment in time, the arrow is located at a specific position. In subsequent moments, the arrow is at rest for the same reason. So the arrow is at rest at all moments. Thus if time is a continuous series of moments there is no time for the arrow to move, and motion is impossible. The paradoxes are challenging—they have engaged philosophers and others since they were introduced by Zeno almost 2,500 years ago— and important, since they undermine the conventional view that the sensory world is real. (The arrow paradox and other paradoxes of motion credited to Zeno are generally thought to have been resolved by calculus and Newtonian physics, although quantum mechanics has complicated that resolution in some instances.)

Is the social world real? Social science would be a strange choice of vocation for someone who answered that question negatively. Yet if we press the social contextualization argument far enough we arrive at an apparent denial of the social world. Substitute the term "context" for the term "moment in time" and you see that the contextualization argument is similar to Zeno's argument about the arrow. In effect Zeno viewed each moment as a separate context and concluded that the physical world is an illusion. If social acts are so radically contextualized that there are no general principles to discover, then one wonders what is the glue that holds human societies together. The existence of routine, predictable human interaction suggests that there is something "there" in the social world, even as the existence of motion suggests that there is something "there" in the physical world.

The best response to empirical nihilism is to ignore it and do the research. The aim of this book is to help both novice and experienced researchers "do the research." I have tried to make the book eminently practical. I provide examples of good social research, as well as examples of the other kind. Obviously I believe that meaningful social research *is* possible—imperfect research, but research that can be valuable nonetheless. (I say "can be valuable" because the findings of social research are subject to misuse. In the worst-case scenario, social science could be used by authoritarian governments for the purpose of large-scale social engineering, which generally has been a miserable failure.) The pitfalls of social research may be many, but so too are the potential benefits. The seven rules are intended to move us closer to that potential in our social research projects.

SUMMARY

There should be the possibility of surprise in social research. Social research requires that researchers remain open to new evidence, whether or not that evidence supports their cherished theories or beliefs. This openness leads to the possibility of surprise. Openness also makes research more exciting. If we know the results beforehand, what is the impetus for the research?

An important first step for effective research is choosing an appropriate research question—one where surprise is possible. Research questions should be both researchable and interesting. Research questions are uninteresting when there is no possibility of learning anything new, when there is no perceived relevance to theory or everyday life, or when the answer is significant only to a very small number of people.

Because important social issues of the day typically have been investigated in one form or another by social scientists, most often research evidence already exists on the question you want to investigate. In that case you need to design your research to ensure that surprise is possible. The first step is to distinguish well-established findings from the other kind. By "the other kind" I mean findings that are mixed or inconclusive, or findings that are new and have not yet been replicated in subsequent studies. Surprise *is* possible in those instances, because in those instances there are lingering questions about earlier results. Hence your research, if properly executed, contributes to knowledge.

By contrast, if prior findings are widely viewed as settled, you contribute little or nothing by merely repeating the analyses of others. Instead you must either challenge the earlier findings or extend/clarify them. If there is a good reason to doubt the results of prior studies, then of course it is worthwhile to challenge them with new research. In that case, though, the burden of proof rests on you to identify the flaws in prior research that are serious enough to cast doubt on their findings (flaws that you will correct in your research). The other strategy—to extend or clarify earlier findings—can be implemented by examining results for a subpopulation or for a different population or time period. New understanding of old findings can also be gained by introducing mediating variables or moderating variables or nonmediating variables (or some combination of all three), or by testing for reverse causation. In some instances a synthesizing study may be possible by bridging prior research in different subfields.

After deciding on a research question, you must decide whom to study. First you decide what population you want to examine. Then you select a sample of that population since generally you will lack resources to collect data on the entire population. The important feature of a sample is not its size (within reason) but its representativeness. When samples are properly selected, it is possible to draw defensible conclusions about large populations (for example, all U.S. citizens) from analyses of only a tiny fraction of the population. These underlying sampling principles are the same for qualitative and quantitative research. Qualitative research, however, usually relies on smaller (sometimes much smaller) samples. Stratified random sampling that purposely oversamples smaller populations might compensate for the limited sample size, particularly if the aim is to test an uncomplicated model. A small sample does, however, limit your ability to make multiple comparisons with different variables. For this reason, qualitative studies generally are ill-suited for providing omnibus tests of multiple explanations for some observed association.

Student Exercises on Rule 1

The exercises for chapter 1 use 1972–2004 data from the General Social Survey (GSS). The GSS is a probability sample of noninstitutionalized English-speaking individuals, age eighteen and older, in the United States. From 1972 to 1994 the GSS was an annual survey (with a few years missed); after 1994 it has been conducted in even-numbered years. The sample sizes of each wave vary from about 1,500 for the annual surveys to about 3,000 for the biennial surveys.

To do the exercises below, go to the web site http://sda.berkeley.edu, click on "SDA archive," and follow the instructions below. The instructions should generate all the statistics you need to answer the questions, so you should not need to do any calculations by hand. Several questions ask about the statistical significance of associations. For these exercises use the .01 significance level as the criterion for statistical significance, that is, when the p-value is .01 or less, we consider the association to be statistically significant. To assist you in completing the assignments, variable names are in **boldface** in the computer assignments in this book. For answers to selected problems, go to http://press.princeton.edu/titles/8593.html.

Note well: (1) The figures given below are for the 1972–2004 GSS, the most recent GSS data available when this book was written. If you are working with more recent data, to replicate exactly the figures given below you will need to use the "selection filter" in the SDA program to remove years after 2004. (2) The instructions below are based on the format used by SDA at the time this chapter was written, in 2006. That format might change slightly in subsequent years, so some of the *specific* directions below might be out of date, but you still should be able to follow the logic of the instructions to obtain the tables you need to answer the questions.

Gender Differences in Abortion Attitudes

The GSS asks the following question, denoted **abany**, about abortion: "Please tell me whether or not *you* think it should be possible for a pregnant woman to obtain a *legal* abortion if the woman wants it for any reason?" [possible answers: yes, no]. This question is asked after a series of questions about particular reasons for abortion (examples: should abortion be permitted if a woman is married and does not want any more children? if there is a strong chance of serious defect in the baby?), so in context the question asks whether a woman should have the legal right to an abortion for any reason at all.

Use the Berkeley SDA web site to cross-tabulate **abany** and **sex** (male, female). Follow these instructions:

- From the SDA homepage, click on "SDA archive," then go to the "GSS cumulative datafile."
- A new screen should appear. On the new screen, type in **abany** for the row variable and type in **sex** for the column variable.
- Ignore the boxes for "control." Use the drop-down box for "Weight" to select "Oversamp—Weight for black oversamples."
- Under "Table options," you want (for now) both column percentages and row percentages, so check those boxes if they are not already checked on your screen.
- Check the box beside "statistics," and use the drop-down menu to indicate that you want 3 decimal points for statistics.
- Check the box beside "Question text." This gives you the wording of questions.
- Remove the check beside "color coding."
- Under "Chart options," use the drop-down menu to indicate that you want "(no chart)."
- Click on "run the table."

"Run the table" should give you a 2×2 table with **abany** as the row variable and **sex** as the column variable. Note the legend for the table under "Frequency Distribution." The numbers in your table should indicate that there are 11,389 male respondents and 14,715 female respondents, for a total N of 26,104 cases. Your table should say that 41.5 percent of male respondents and 39.4 percent of female respondents responded yes, that a woman *should* have the legal right to an abortion for any reason. You should also find that 55.1 percent of those who agree (that abortion should be a legal right for any reason) are women, and 44.9 percent of those who agree are men (second row of table).

Question 1. (a) Which of the two comparisons—41.5 percent versus 39.4 percent, or 55.1 percent versus 44.9 percent—is the relevant comparison here? Explain. [Hint: Percentages should sum to 100 percent within categories of the *explanatory* variable. Does gender affect abortion attitudes, or is it the other way around?]
(b) Summarize your finding in one or two sentences.

Now look at the figures under the heading "Summary statistics." The statistics labeled *eta*, **R,** *Somers' d*, *gamma*, *tau-b*, and *tau-a* refer to measures of association, that is, they refer to how strongly the two variables are related. In this case the figures are close to zero, since the association between **sex** and **abany** is small, as you can tell from the percentages.

Question 2. (a) Is the gender difference in **abany** statistically significant? To determine this, look at the p-values for Chi-square (labeled *Chisq(P)* in the printout). p = .00 in the printout means that the p-value is less than .005—which is highly significant. The smaller the p-value, the more confident we can be that an association we observe in our data is *not* due to sampling error.
(b) Is the gender difference very large? What does that suggest about statistical significance and *substantive* significance (how large an effect is)?
(c) Are you surprised by the *direction* of the gender difference here? Explain.

Question 3. Are women more likely (than men) to approve of abortion for *any* of the specific reasons investigated in the GSS, such as when a woman is pregnant as the result of rape? To find out, return to the cross-tabulation program and replace **abany** with **abrape** as the row variable (dependent variable), then "run tables" again. To avoid confusion, this time suppress the row percentages (that is, ask only for column percentages). Repeat using **abdefect, abnomore, abhlth, abpoor,** and **absingle** as the row variable. What do you find?

Question 4. One thing we learn from these results is that, for Americans, the reason for an abortion matters. While most Americans believe that abortion should be legal for some reasons, such as when a woman's health is endangered, more than half believe that there are conditions under which abortion should not be legal.
(a) Use the appropriate percentages in your seven tables to rank-order the seven conditions here (pregnancy is due to rape, etc.) from "strongest approval for legal abortion" to "least approval for legal abortion."
(b) Is the ranking exactly as you would have predicted, or are you surprised by some of the results?

Question 5. Now cross-tabulate **abany** (row) and **race** (column). The total N should be 26,104 cases.
(a) Are race differences statistically significant? (Again, use p < .01 as the cutoff point.)
(b) Are the differences in the direction you expected? Explain.

MARRIAGE, HUNTING, AND FREQUENCY OF SEX

The GSS variable **sexfreq** asks, "About how often did you have sex during the last 12 months? [not at all, once or twice, once a month, 2–3 times a month, weekly, 2–3 times per week, 4+ times per week]."

In this exercise we use the cross-tabulation program to investigate the association between marriage and frequency of sex, then to investigate the association between hunting and sexual frequency. The first thing you want to do is convert the GSS variable **marital** with five categories (married, divorced, widowed, separated, never married) into a new variable with just two categories, married and not married (which includes separated couples). Let's call that new variable **married**. Return to the original screen where you selected "frequencies or cross-tabulation," but this time select "recode" to create the variable **married**, as follows:

- Under "create variables," click on "recode variables."
- Type in **married** for "name for the new variable to be created."
- For "Replace that variable, if it already exists?" click on "Yes."
- Type in **marital** for "Var 1" under "Name of existing variables to use for the recode."
- For row 1 under "Output variable," type "1" for "value," "married" for "label," and "1" for "Var 1." For the second row, type "0" for "value," "not married" for "label," and "2–5" for "Var 1."
- Click on "start recoding." If you have done this correctly, you should have 20,674 not married cases and 25,828 married cases.

Question 6. Return to the "frequencies or cross-tabulation" screen, and this time cross-tabulate **sexfreq** with **married**. Enter **sexfreq** as the row variable and **married** as the column variable. To make sure you focus on the relevant percentages, select only column percentages. Otherwise, select the same options as in the abortion exercise. Your total N should be 18,594 when you run the table.
(a) Is the association statistically significant? (If you don't see p-values, you must have forgotten to check "statistics.")
(b) What is the association between marriage and sexual frequency—do married people tend to have more sex than others? Is there more variance in **sexfreq** for the married or unmarried?
(c) Summarize your substantive findings in two or three sentences. Is this what you expected?

We can also use the GSS to investigate the association between hunting and frequency of sex. The hunting variable in the GSS is **hunt**: "Do you (or does your [husband/wife]) go hunting? [respondent hunts, spouse hunts, both, neither]." Repeat the procedures you used to recode **marital** into **married** to recode the 4-category variable **hunt** into a 3-category variable, called **whohunts**, coded 0–2 for number of people who hunt: 0 if neither hunts, 1 if respondent or spouse hunts, 2 if both hunt. (Hint: The first row under "Output variable" should be "0, neither hunt, 4"—that is, type in "0" under "Value," "neither hunt" under "label," and "4" under "Var 1." The second row should be "1, one hunts, 1–2" and the third row should be "2, both hunt, 3.") If you have recoded correctly, you should have 18,874 cases of "neither hunts," 4,650 "one hunts," and 576 "both hunt."

Question 7. Cross-tabulate **whohunts** with **sexfreq**, with **sexfreq** again as the row variable and **whohunts** as the column variable. Again, ask for column percentages and statistics. The total N should be 10,894; if your N is somewhat different, make sure you used the proper "Oversamp" weighting.
(a) Is the association statistically significant at $p < .01$?
(b) Summarize your findings in two or three sentences. Is this what you expected?

Question 8. (a) Give two explanations for the association between **whohunts** and **sexfreq**.
(b) Think about the nature of the two explanations you have given. Do your explanations imply that the association is causal—that is, do your explanations imply that **sexfreq** will increase for people who take up hunting?
(c) If you were to test your first explanation, would the test include non-mediating variables? Mediating variables in a causal chain? Moderating variables that condition the effect of **whohunts** on **sexfreq**? Reverse causation? Explain.
(d) What about a test of your second explanation—would that test include nonmediating variables? Mediating variables in a causal chain? Moderating variables that condition the effect of **whohunts** on **sexfreq**? Reverse causation? Explain.

CHAPTER 2

The Second Rule

LOOK FOR DIFFERENCES THAT MAKE A DIFFERENCE, AND REPORT THEM

"How big is big?" is a question that students in introductory statistics courses in the social sciences invariably raise. Students want to know: How should one describe a correlation of $r=.10$ between two variables? Is it large or small? What about a correlation of $r=.20$? Of $r=.30$? At what point does an association go from small to large? In short, what is a "large effect"?

The major point of this chapter is that it is your responsibility, as a researcher, to translate computer printouts into empirical substance using words and visual displays that enable you and your readers to decide whether effects are large or small, important or unimportant. If this is done properly it should be an easy matter to find, and emphasize, differences that make a difference. In the worst case—which occurs more often than we like to admit (McCloskey and Ziliak 1996; Ziliak and McCloskey 2004)—researchers do not even attempt to discriminate results on the basis of the size of coefficients but merely provide a printout dump for readers, with annotation limited to which coefficients are statistically significant and which are not. In the best case, researchers recognize that size matters (and report results accordingly), but other things matter as well. Empirical bigness is not necessarily the same as theoretical importance or importance for policy. Effective social research focuses on differences that make a difference, and it tells readers what those differences are and why they are important.

There are actually two issues involved in the search for differences that make a difference—the issue of size and the issue of importance—and I discuss both of them in this chapter. The issues are related, but they are not the same. Suppose you measured the length of right legs and left legs for a sample of individuals. You would no doubt find a sizable correlation between the two lengths—$r=.99$ or greater. So you would find a very big effect—but one that isn't very interesting or important. Big effects are not necessarily important effects.

Nor are small effects necessarily unimportant. There are instances where small effects matter for theoretical or policy reasons. Yet in those instances it does not suffice to say simply "There is an effect." As a researcher you need to provide criteria for gauging the size of effects, and, if the effects are small, you need to explain why they are nonetheless worth noting.

You Can't Explain a Variable with a Constant

In chapter 1 we looked at the issue of selecting a research project. There I stressed that results from prior studies can be extended and clarified by adding variables—variables that mediate an effect, that moderate (condition) an effect, or that act as a common cause of some observed association. Here I add the point that differences can only be explained by other differences. So if you want to know why an outcome variable Y varies, you need to find explanatory variables (Xs) that also vary.

Social scientists understand that you can't explain a variable with a constant, so I don't know of any research where someone literally tries to do that. But there are instances where theorists and researchers pay too little attention to the amount of variance in their explanatory variables. We know, for example, that demographic changes tend to be slow and continuous, so precipitous change is unlikely to be due to population change. Likewise culture—the beliefs, values, traditions, behaviors, and material objects that collectively form a people's way of life—does not change overnight. The same can be said of a nation's geographic features (distance from the equator, whether it is landlocked, system of navigable rivers, topography, rainfall, etc.), a factor that has received renewed attention in some recent theorizing about why some countries are so rich and others so poor. Of course population, geography, and culture are important. But in general they are unpromising explanations for rapid social change.

Consider the trend in fertility rates in Romania over the second half of the twentieth century (fig. 2.1). The general picture is that of a secular decline in fertility that was interrupted by a stunning increase in fertility in 1967. From 1966 to 1967 fertility in Romania nearly doubled, from an average of about 1.9 children per woman to an average of about 3.7 children per woman (Bradatan and Firebaugh 2007).

How are we to account for the 1967 baby boom in Romania? Cultural explanations aren't promising, since people's views of ideal family size do not change overnight. Nor is it likely that the jump was due to changes in Romania's population composition (for example, an influx of high-fertility immigrants) since a nation's population composition usually does not change suddenly either. In this instance, the most promising route is to examine the historical context. What events were occurring in Romania at this point in time?

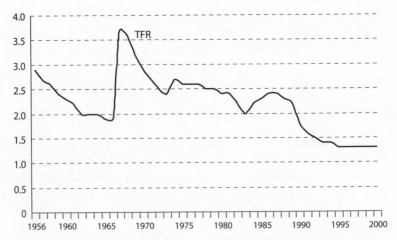

Figure 2.1. Total Fertility Rate in Romania, 1956–2000. *Source*: Romanian Demographic Yearbook, 2001.

From figure 2.1 we note that fertility had declined sharply in the decade before 1967. In 1956 Romanian women were giving birth to almost three babies, on average, over their childbearing years. By the early 1960s fertility had dropped below replacement level, meaning that Romanians were not having enough children to replace themselves. Hence, as Romanian government officials well understood, if that fertility rate continued the population of Romania would be destined to level off and then decline.

It is not surprising, then, that the Communist government took steps to try to boost the fertility rate. First a media campaign was launched in *Scanteia*, the official newspaper of the Romanian Communist Party. Typically the first two pages of *Scanteia* were devoted to political and economic news: foreign dignitaries visiting Romania, new economic successes of the Romanian Communist Party, and so on. That focus changed somewhat in the summer of 1966, however, as articles about maternity as a woman's duty to the nation also began to occupy center stage in the newspaper. On August 4, 1966, Ursula Schiopu, a psychologist, argued that "feminine charm is regenerated by maternity" (*Scanteia*, August 4, 1966, p. 2). Two weeks later there appeared a first-page article on schools and children, and on August 21 another article about "Children's love." In a September 19 article titled "Maternity's Advantages," a physician argued that pregnancy heals acne, eczemas, depression, and melancholy. On September 23, women who ask for abortion were called "superficial" and legislation was blamed for letting them obtain abortions so easily, and the next day Zaharia Stancu, an important Romanian writer and member of the Romanian National Academy, described past times when families had many children and all of them were happy (p. 1). The next day an article titled "Maternity" presented various stories about abortions, concluding that "very few women ask for abortion because of objective reasons" (September 9, 1966, pp. 1–2).

On October 2 the other shoe dropped. Decree 770, called "Measures to regulate pregnancy interruption," was published on the first page of *Scanteia*. The new decree outlawed virtually all abortions (which, until the decree, had been very common in Romania). In addition, the Romanian government ceased to produce or import modern contraceptive methods. Although not prohibited by the new law, modern contraceptive methods became inaccessible—available only on the black market. The effect of these policies was sudden and dramatic, as figure 2.1 shows.[1]

I use this example to show how one might "look for differences that make a difference." Typically the explanation is not as straightforward, of course. But the principles are the same. You need to know something about your subject matter. Learn to think like a detective, using appropriate tools at your disposal, whether qualitative or quantitative or both. And remember that you must have variance to explain variance.

MAXIMIZING VARIANCE TO FIND THE EFFECT OF A CAUSE

In the example we have just considered, our aim was to account for the 1967 baby boom in Romania. In other words, we were trying to find the cause or causes of an effect. Increasingly in social research, however, we want to isolate the *effect of a particular cause*. We start with the cause and try to design an experiment or some other method to determine the magnitude of that effect on some outcome variable.

This strategy is commonplace in medical research. Before a new drug for the treatment of asthma is approved for the general public, experiments are performed to determine how much effect, if any, that drug has on asthma, and what side effects the treatment might have. Or—to use an example that is discussed in detail in chapter 5—we might want to estimate the causal effect of smoking on lung cancer. Smoking is not the only cause of lung cancer, of course. But there is not much we can do to control many of the other causes, and smoking is something we have

---

[1] Over time Romanians figured out ways to circumvent the restrictions—for example, by bribing doctors to say the mother's life was endangered, so a legal abortion could be performed—so fertility began to track back down, as we see in figure 2.1. The abortion law was rescinded in 1990, and since then fertility in Romania has fallen to one of the lowest levels in the world.

some control over, so we are especially interested in the causal effect of smoking.

The same logic applies to much social research. Although it would be nice to understand all the causes of residential segregation, or domestic violence, or the rise in income inequality in the United States, the most interesting causes very often are those that are amenable to public policy (more on this later in the chapter). Thus, instead of trying to understand some phenomenon (such as the rise in income inequality) in its entirety—which might result only in the dim understanding of many causes, or in the understanding of many causes that we can't do much about—effective social research today often focuses on understanding one cause well.

To understand one cause well, we want to maximize the variance of that cause. As discussed in chapter 1, very often we can increase variance through our sample design. We do this by stratifying the target population and oversampling minority groups.

Here we want to maximize the variance of the causal variable, so we oversample the minority groups of the causal variable. To illustrate, think again about cohabitation effects. Suppose we want to determine if there is a link between cohabitation and domestic violence. Although cohabitation is rising in the United States, at any point in time heterosexual married couples still outnumber cohabiting couples by more than ten to one (U.S. Census Bureau 2000). Suppose cohabiting couples make up 9 percent of heterosexual unions in the United States. Then in a simple random sample the expected variance for the variable **cohabit** (coded 1 for cohabiters and 0 for married couples) is $(0.09)(0.91) = 0.082$. By sampling an equal number of cohabiting and married couples, we triple the variance on **cohabit** from 0.082 to 0.25 $[(0.5)(0.5)]$. By tripling its variance, we make **cohabit** a more powerful tool for investigating the consequences of cohabitation.

In short, to "look for differences that make a difference" you need to consider sample design as well as theory and prior research. Because it takes variance to explain variance, you can't evaluate the effect of a particular cause unless the cause varies enough in your sample. To test properly for "differences that make a difference," then, you might need to oversample some categories of the explanatory variables, especially when your sample is small.

Finally, it is important to stress that the purpose of oversampling is to create more variance on X in the sample, without losing sight of the actual distribution of X in the population. Obviously, if there were only one hundred cohabiting couples total in the United States, cohabitation could not be a leading cause of domestic violence in the United States, since domestic violence is much more widespread than that. (In fact, though, cohabiting couples number roughly five million—so cohabitation very well could be a significant factor in domestic violence.) The point of over-sampling is not to magnify a minute effect in the population, but to ensure that there is enough variance *in the sample* to provide a fair test of the effect of a cause.

SIZE VERSUS STATISTICAL SIGNIFICANCE

Before we can talk about the size of an effect, we want to have some sense of how confident we can be that the apparent effect observed in our sample is not due to sampling error. That of course is the purpose of conventional significance tests in the social sciences. In practice, however, social scientists too often conflate statistical significance and substantive significance, resulting in deemphasis on the size of effects. Generally researchers test the null hypothesis that the effect is zero. When the null is rejected, researchers conclude that there is an effect in the population. When the null is not rejected, researchers conclude that there is no effect.

Researchers often appear to forget, however, that statistical significance is a function of sample size as well as size of the actual effect in a population. Thus a sample coefficient can be insignificant for two very different reasons: because there is no effect in the population, or because we have estimated it so imprecisely, due to a small sample. (This problem leads some statisticians to recommend the use of larger p-values with smaller samples.)

Even worse, when findings are statistically significant, significance tests sometimes are misused to blur important differences in the sizes of effects. This blurring occurs when researchers fail to distinguish statistical and substantive significance, resulting in a flattened world where there are only two outcomes, effects and noneffects. The world is flattened because statistically significant effects are all treated the same—stupendous effects, minute effects, and all effects in between are dumped into the same basket. The reader wants commentary on the size of the effect. What she often is given instead is an asterisk indicating how strongly the sample data contradict the null hypothesis that the effect is zero in the population. That practice reduces the effectiveness of social research, as McCloskey and Ziliak (1996) and Ziliak and McCloskey (2004) have forcefully noted.

So the first point I want to make regarding the size of effects is "Talk about the size of effects in your report." In most contexts such advice would be gratuitous, but it seems necessary here, given the apparent trained incapacity for describing effect sizes in some fields of social science.

We return, then, to the question "How big is big?" It is useful to distinguish relative size and absolute size (although the two are related of course). In the case of relative effect size the other causes provide a ready-made reference point. How large is the effect of X on Y relative to the effects of other causes of Y? In the case of absolute effect size, researchers must sometimes search outside their model for an appropriate yardstick or reference point—some sort of benchmark to assist intuition. This is not always easy to do, and perhaps for that reason it is not always done in social research.

COMPARING EFFECTS WHERE THERE IS A COMMON METRIC

In the case of relative size we are interested in which predictors have the strongest effects. What are the most important determinants of one's socioeconomic status (SES) in the United States (Jencks et al. 1972)? Educational attainment? Intelligence? Your parents' SES? Racial or ethnic identity? Ambition? Hard work? Luck?

Determining the relative sizes of effects is particularly important in testing theories since in social science theory very often it is effect size that distinguishes one theory from another. There are, for example, numerous hypotheses and theories in social science that attempt to explain why some countries are so rich and others so poor. Some theories emphasize natural resources or geography, some emphasize culture, some emphasize political systems and the importance of appropriate policies, some emphasize the pattern of technology diffusion, and still others emphasize international relations or colonialism or exploitation. These causes are not mutually exclusive, and cultural theories of development do not say, for example, that political systems don't matter at all—just that culture is primary. Thus tests of theories very often are tests of the relative sizes of effects.

It is not surprising, then, that much of the empirical work in the social sciences turns on the relative importance of causes. What *is* surprising is how frequently one finds a disjuncture between theory and findings in research articles, with the findings section giving equal billing to all statistically significant effects, as if all statistically significant effects are the same. But size matters, and effective research arms readers with the information needed to distinguish bigger effects from smaller ones.

There are two situations to consider: the case where the explanatory variables have a common metric, and the case where they do not. It is easier to compare effects when the explanatory variables have the same metric (dollars, years, etc.). Suppose we want to know, among married couples, whether family size (the number of children a couple has) is linked more closely to the number of siblings the mother has or the number of siblings the father has. We might hypothesize, for example, that individuals who grew up in large families tend to have more children than individuals who grew up in small families, but that the family size experienced by a woman in her youth is more consequential for her fertility than the family size experienced by her husband.

With appropriate data on completed fertility for couples, we could test the hypothesis by regressing number of children for a couple on number of siblings in the wife's family and number of siblings in the husband's family. Because the explanatory variables have the same metric, it is straightforward to compare their effects. If size of the wife's family tends to be more consequential for the number of children a couple has, then the slope for the variable **wifesibs** should be steeper than the slope for the variable **husbandsibs**.

It is useful to think more concretely about how we would graph the results in two-dimensional space. Although generally we need a separate graph for each explanatory variable, the graphs can be superimposed when explanatory variables have a common metric. Here, for example, the graphs for β_{wife} and $\beta_{husband}$ can be placed on the same X–Y plane because the X-axis is the same for both variables. By superimposing graphs and comparing the steepness of the slopes, we can see immediately which variable has the greater effect.

The issue of which graphs can be superimposed and which cannot is central, then, to the comparison of effect sizes. Consider a different sort of comparison, one where we compare the effect of the *same* X across different groups. We might want to know, for example, whether the effect of religiosity on altruistic behavior differs across religious groups (for example, Christians, Jews, Muslims, and Hindus), where religiosity is measured by an index based on frequency of attendance at religious services, participation in other forms of religious activity such as prayer, the intensity of beliefs, and so on. The key here is that X is the same, so the X-axis is the same, so the graphs can be superimposed. It is straightforward to merge the separate X–Y planes (one for each of the religious groups) and compare the size of the slopes, even if the units of measurement have no clear intuitive meaning.

As a third example, suppose we want to know which has the greater effect on a woman's fertility—her religiosity, or the number of siblings she has. In that case we could regress fertility on religiosity and number of siblings, but the slopes would be more difficult to compare. The two X–Y planes could not be merged because religiosity and number of siblings are not measured in the same units.

As these three examples demonstrate, one way to think about the size comparison issue is to think about how to combine separate X–Y planes (one for each of the explanatory variables) into a common plane. Because the outcome variable Y is the same for all Xs, the Y-axis is the same for each of the separate X–Y planes, so the metric for Y doesn't affect combinability. But the metric for X does. Where the metrics differ, we must calibrate the different metrics to compare the effects. That is the subject of the next section.

CALIBRATION: CONVERTING EXPLANATORY VARIABLES TO A COMMON METRIC

Sometimes you find yourself in the happy circumstance that your explanatory variables have the same metric, so you can compare the coefficients directly. In the case of longitudinal studies, for example, the variables might all be expressed as growth rates. Or perhaps all the explanatory variables are expressed in years, or in dollars, or as a simple count, such as number of siblings.

Very often, however, explanatory variables do not come ready-made in the same metric. In that case you must calibrate the various metrics of the explanatory variables to gauge the relative sizes of the effects. In the case of policy analysis, for example, it may be possible to convert variables to a common standard by asking how much it costs to change each of the variables by one unit.

Perhaps the most common practice, though, is to calibrate metrics by converting them either to standard deviation units or to percentage change. The first strategy results in coefficients that are called *standardized coefficients*, and the second results in coefficients that reflect *elasticities*. The approaches are somewhat similar. In the case of standardized variables we ask how many standard deviations we expect an outcome variable Y to change for a one-standard-deviation change in an explanatory variable X. In the case of elasticities we ask what percentage change we expect in Y for a 1 percent change in X.

For the sake of illustration, I will focus on standardization. Because standardized variables have a standard deviation of 1.0, a one-unit change in a standardized variable refers to a one-standard-deviation change in that variable. Thus if all our explanatory variables are standardized, the slope for any given explanatory variable reflects the expected change in the dependent variable given a one-standard-deviation change in that explanatory variable, controlling for the other explanatory variables in the model. In this way we can compare the size of effects directly by comparing the sizes of the slopes—assuming it makes sense to think of standard-deviation changes as having equivalent theoretical meaning for the Xs.

Standardization is common in studies where variables lack a natural metric. Such variables are commonplace in anthropology, education and testing, evaluation studies, psychology, political science, and sociology.

Measures of individual traits such as altruism, intelligence, self-esteem, authoritarianism, prejudice, tolerance, risk-taking, and religiosity, as well as national traits such as degree of political freedom, very often are indexes that are constructed from the results of test items or from the ratings of experts. In such instances the common unit of measurement across the indexes is the standard deviation of the tests or the ratings.

By using standard deviations as the unit, with standardized variables we in essence compare effects on the basis of rankings on different variables. Where distributions are the same for explanatory variables—normal or approximately normal, for example—a one-standard-deviation change in one X is, in terms of change in rank, comparable to a one-standard-deviation change in another X. On the basis of standardized scores, then, we can compare the relative ranking of individuals across variables. We can ask, for example, whether people who score high on a measure of religiosity also tend to score high on a measure of tolerance—which is what we mean when we say that there is an association between religiosity and tolerance.

Introductory statistics textbooks often warn students not to confuse the association of X and Y with the effect of X on Y. That warning bears on the discussion here because the regression of one standardized variable on another yields the measure of association r. That's not what we want when we are comparing effects. As a general rule, then, standardization is not a reliable way to solve the different metrics problem when comparing the size of effects. Other methods should be used where possible.

Consider a simple example. Suppose we collect a large random sample that includes data on individuals' earnings (in thousands of dollars), education (years completed, 0 to 20), and background socioeconomic status (an index of the socioeconomic status of the respondent's family of origin, with values ranging from 0 to 100). Suppose further that the regression of earnings on education and socioeconomic background (SES) yields this equation, where standard errors are in parentheses:

$$Earnings = 2.0 \ Education + 0.4 \ SES + \varepsilon. \qquad (2.1)$$
$$\quad (0.1) \qquad\qquad (0.02)$$

From these findings it isn't obvious whether education or SES background has the greater direct effect on earnings. The issue turns on the calibration of SES units with education units. If we say one SES unit equals one education unit (one year of education), then we conclude that education is five times more important than socioeconomic background since the education coefficient is five times larger. The claim of equivalent units is problematic, though, because SES ranges from 0 to 100 whereas education ranges from 0 to 20. Some might say, then, that we should compare individuals at the highest and lowest levels on the two variables. Using that method, we find that education and socioeconomic status are equally important, since the predicted difference in earnings is $40,000 more for those with 20 years of education as opposed to those with no education (controlling for SES), and $40,000 more for those in the highest SES category as opposed to those in the lowest SES category (controlling for education).

The problem with using the range for comparison is that we don't know how realistic that comparison is. Perhaps most individuals cluster tightly in the middle of the SES distribution, with no one in the highest and lowest categories of SES, whereas individuals are more evenly dispersed across years of education. Standardization takes into account this difference in dispersion. In other words, by standardizing variables we obtain summary coefficients that take into account both the steepness of the original slope and the dispersion of explanatory variables in the particular sample that we have. The dependence of standardized coefficients on sample variances is important to note, since that dependence can affect the generalizability or *external validity* (Campbell and Stanley 1966) of your results using standardized coefficients. The issue arises when variances in the sample deviate from variances in the population to which you want to generalize.

Of the three bad options above—compare the unstandardized coefficients for education and income, compare predicted Y-values using the high and low values of education and income, and compare coefficients for education and income as standardized variables—the comparison of standardized coefficients is the least likely to mislead. Generally, though, there are better options, and you should work hard to find them. Where a common metric is not readily available, you should attempt to supplement your discussion of coefficient size with a more targeted discussion that employs concrete comparisons. That is the topic of the next section.

SUBSTANTIVE PROFILING: THE USE OF TELLING COMPARISONS

In some instances the calibration of variables' metrics is informal or implicit. For example, a researcher might dichotomize a continuous variable to enable comparisons with a true dichotomy, such as marriage. We might want to know, for example, whether money or marriage has a greater effect on one's happiness. As a first stab at the answer, we might first create a dummy variable for income coded "1" for those with above-average income and "0" for those with below-average income, and regress happiness on the income dummy and a dummy for marital status. (A dummy variable is a variable with two values, 0 and 1.) In comparing the coefficients for the income and marital status dummy variables, we compare the difference in the expected values (means) of Y for the statuses "married" and "not married" with the difference in the expected values of Y for the statuses "above-average income" and "below-average income."

Dichotomizing a continuous variable to compare its effect with that of a true dichotomy is a simple example of a more general strategy that could be called *substantive profiling*: the translation of model coefficients into substantively meaningful results by reporting predicted Y-values across a range of strategic X-values. Effects of two variables are compared by noting the size of the differences in the predicted values for Y at the values selected for each of the Xs. Profiling in this way gives substantive flesh to the coefficients whether or not the variables have a common metric.

The use of substantive profiling for determining the relative sizes of effects is most effective when you can defend your choice of values for the Xs as representing comparable differences on the Xs. Most often the comparison is somewhat loose, since it is difficult to determine precisely what differences are comparable when variables are measured in difficult-to-calibrate metrics (for example, years and dollars). An inexact comparison generally is better than no comparison at all, however, since the aim of the exercise is to assist the reader's intuition in gauging which effects are the larger ones.

Probably the most common example of substantive profiling is the simple comparison of differences in means (for categorical Xs) or expected values of Y for strategic values of X (for continuous Xs). Imagine a regression analysis of annual salaries for university faculty where we find that the coefficient for gender (a dummy variable coded female = 1) is $b = -1.0$ with a standard error $\sigma = 0.1$. If salary is coded in thousands of dollars, and we have controlled for other determinants of faculty salary such as academic field, research productivity, success in obtaining research funding, teaching evaluations, experience, and so on, then we can say that "Other things equal, faculty salaries are on average $1,000 less for women than for men."[2]

It is hard to evaluate whether a gender gap of $1,000 is big or small in the absence of context: $1,000 *compared to what?* If the issue is the size

---

[2] In many instances a great deal of information can be imparted very simply by translating results from statistical language into substantive language, as in the previous sentence. This translation is easy when the dependent variable is already measured in some readily understandable metric, such as dollars or percentages. Some researchers may hesitate to include such translations in their report for fear of insulting the intelligence of their audience. That point may be valid when the audience is statistically sophisticated and gender is not a focus of the analysis. If gender is a focus of the study, however, it is important to state the effect in plain English, if only as a starting point for a discussion of whether the gender effect is large or small.

of the gender effect compared to the effect of the other determinants of faculty salary, the reference points are obvious: other effects in the study. Is the $1,000 gender difference about the same as, say, the effect of publishing one more article in a peer-reviewed journal? Is it larger or smaller than the effect of obtaining one more research grant? How large is it compared to the effect of publishing a book? How large is it compared to the effect of being in an engineering department as opposed to a humanities department? And so on.

To assist readers' intuition about the magnitude of the $1,000 gender gap in faculty salaries, we might compare that gap to gaps for other dichotomies of interest, such as the difference between associate professors and full professors, or between faculty in humanities departments and faculty in engineering departments. Let's say full professors on average make $40,000 more than associate professors, but this difference shrinks to $2,000 when we control for cumulative research productivity, teaching evaluations, and so on. We can say, then, that the unaccounted-for gender gap in faculty salaries is one-half as large as the unaccounted-for gap in salary between associate and full professors, and let the reader decide whether that is large or small. Or we might find that, even with all our control variables, market forces not captured in our model dictate that average salaries for engineering faculty exceed those for humanities faculty by $25,000, so the unaccounted-for gender gap is 4 percent as large as the unaccounted-for gap between salaries for engineering versus humanities faculty.

In short, to gain a better sense of the size of the gender gap, we compare *differences in the differences* in predicted values of Y for selected values of X. The income difference (as predicted by the regression model) for men versus women is compared with the income difference for engineering professors versus humanities professors, with the income difference for an additional journal publication, and so on. We can benchmark using results from other studies as well. We might ask, for example, how the gender gap in faculty salaries compares to the gender gap in related fields, such as the gender gap in salaries for public high school teachers. Or we might ask how the gender gap in faculty salaries today compares to the gender gap ten years ago or forty years ago.

Well-chosen comparisons, then, provide context for readers to determine the magnitude of the effects of interest (see examples in box 2.1). Although that seems to be common sense, many researchers appear to give the matter little thought. It is surprising how often meaningful comparisons are missing in research articles. The issue is not just that researchers miss an opportunity for a clear story that will leave a lasting impression. Equally serious is the danger that—absent the discipline imposed by well-chosen comparisons—articles become fixated on small effects while missing the five-hundred-pound gorilla in their midst. Even seasoned researchers sometimes make that mistake. In fact, "missing the five-hundred-pound gorilla" was a complaint I received fairly often from reviewers during my stint as a journal editor.

A final point: It is possible to miss the interesting story by focusing just on means or on predicted Ys more generally. Sometimes the "difference that makes a difference" lies in dispersion rather than in averages. Consider the question of whether working women are happier than housewives in

---

Box 2.1
Examples of Telling Verbal Comparisons in Gauging Effect Sizes

The following claims—accurate or not—provide good examples of comparisons that are memorable because they help readers gauge the size of observed effects.

- *On the effect of religious attendance on life expectancy.* On the basis of longitudinal data from a national sample of the U.S. population, Hummer et al. (1999, p. 277) find substantial differences in life expectancy by religious attendance: "For the overall population, the life expectancy gap [at age 20] between those who attend more than once a week (62.9) and those who never attend (55.3) is over seven years, similar to the female-male and white-black gaps in U.S. life expectancy."
- *On gender differences in the effect of marriage on life expectancy.* "Other factors constant, nine out of ten married women alive today at age 48 would still be alive at age 65; by contrast, eight out of 10 never-married women would survive to age 65. The corresponding comparison for men reveals a more pronounced difference: nine out of ten for the married group versus six out of ten for those who were never married" (Waite and Lehrer 2003, p. 256).
- *On the effect of race on employment.* Using an employment audit where job applicants were similar on other background characteristics, Devah Pager (2002) found that callbacks were much higher for applicants without felony convictions. Among both white and black applicants, a felony conviction reduced one's chances of a callback by one-half or more (from 34 percent down to 17 percent for white applicants and from 14 percent down to 5 percent for black applicants). As expected,

(continued on next page)

the United States. The General Social Survey (GSS), a biennial survey of U.S. adults, includes this question: "Taken all together, how would you say things are these days—would you say that you are very happy, pretty happy, or not too happy?" Coding "very happy" as 3, "pretty happy" as 2, and "not too happy" as 1, the average happiness of American adults is 2.203—between pretty happy and very happy, but closer to the former. Making this comparison for housewives versus women who work full-time or part-time, we find no meaningful difference in average happiness: The mean is 2.222 for working women and 2.219 for housewives (see the exercises at the end of this chapter).

(continued from previous page)

then, a felony conviction hurts one's employment prospects. The telling comparison, though, is the 17 percent callback rate of white applicants *with* a conviction versus the 14 percent callback rate of black applicants *without* a conviction. In this study, being black hurts one's prospects of a callback more than being an ex-felon.

- *On the political impact of felon disenfranchisement in the United States*: The issue of whether felons and ex-felons should have the right to vote is usually framed in terms of civil rights for individuals. In the United States, however, the issue has profound political implications for the nation as a whole. On the basis of their demographic characteristics, disenfranchised felons and ex-felons would tend to vote heavily for Democratic candidates if they were allowed to vote (Uggen and Manza 2002). Because disenfranchised felons and ex-felons currently make up about 2.3 percent of the voting age population, and the margin of victory in three of the last ten presidential elections has been 1.1 percent or less of the voting-age population, the rising population of felons likely has been a decisive factor in recent U.S. political history: As shown by the projections of Uggen and Manza, in 2000 Republican George W. Bush would certainly have lost the Florida vote, and thus the election, if disenfranchised felons had been allowed to vote in Florida; and the results of the 1960 and 1976 elections (won by Democrats John F. Kennedy and Jimmy Carter, respectively) might have been reversed had current (higher) levels of felon disenfranchisement prevailed in those elections.

Yet that comparison masks a telling difference in happiness between housewives and working women. Compared to women who are in the paid labor force, housewives are significantly more likely to report being either very happy *or* not too happy: 3.1 percent more housewives report being very happy (35.3% versus 32.2%) *and* 3.4 percent more housewives report being not too happy (13.4% versus 10.0%). As a result, the cross-tabulation of happiness by housewife status yields a Chi-square value (a test of statistical independence) that is highly significant, indicating that happiness for American women is *not* independent of their location in the workplace versus the home. Here, however, the difference that makes a difference is not the average level of happiness, but the *variance* on happiness in the two groups.

The moral is that good social research looks at variances as well as at means. And in presenting findings—whether based on variances or means—good research most often relies on pictures as well as on words. That is the topic of the next section.

VISUAL PRESENTATION OF RESULTS

A good graph is often worth a thousand words of text in a research article. Graphic displays are pictures of numbers. The aim is to make large data sets coherent by revealing the data without distorting what the data have to say. Edward Tufte's *The Visual Display of Quantitative Information* (1983) is a landmark work for presenting data graphically, and it is worth quoting from the book's introduction (p. 8):

> Data graphics visually display measured quantities by means of the combined use of points, lines, a coordinate system, numbers, symbols, words, shading, and color. The use of abstract, non-representational pictures to show numbers is a surprisingly recent invention. . . . It was not until 1750–1800 that statistical graphics—length and area to show quantity, time-series, scatterplots, and multivariate displays—were invented, long after such triumphs of mathematical ingenuity as logarithms, Cartesian coordinates, the calculus, and the basics of probability theory.

"Excellence in statistical graphics," Tufte writes (p. 13), "consists of complex ideas communicated with clarity, precision, and efficiency." The best way to make the point is through examples. Box 2.2 provides two examples focusing on displays depicting trends in American society (see Tufte for other examples).

Box 2.2
Visual Presentations of Trends

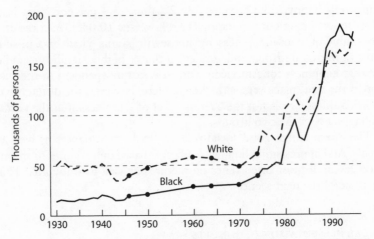

Example 1. Prison Admissions by Race in the United States, 1930–1995. *Source*: http://purl.access.gpo.gov/GPO/LPS20268.

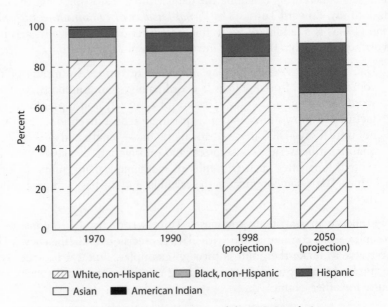

Example 2. Racial/Ethnic Composition of the U.S. Population, 1970–2050. *Source*: http://purl.access.gpo.gov/GPO/LPS20268.

POLICY IMPORTANCE

Size matters, but it is not the only thing that matters. Sometimes a small effect can have big implications for a large population. Clearly this is true in a simple numerical sense: Small effects in terms of rates or percentages imply big numbers for big populations. For example, the U.S. Census Bureau estimates that the U.S. population surpassed three hundred million sometime in 2006. If the percentage of Americans who are obese increases by just one percentage point, that's three million more obese people—a population about the size of the city of Chicago. In China, the effect of a one percentage point increase would be even greater—thirteen million more obese people, more than the number of people in New York City and Los Angeles combined.

We might call this the *market share principle*—in a large market, a small change in market share makes a big difference in total sales. Companies understand the principle well, and that's why the fight for market share is so intense. If just one American in fifty buys a Ford this year, that's about six million Fords sold. If Pepsi can convince just 1 percent of the people in China to buy one can of Pepsi each week, that's about 675 million cans of Pepsi sold in China per year.

The market share principle very often drives public policy in the United States and elsewhere. Small effects—"small" in the sense that they affect a minuscule portion of the population—can carry enormous policy implications, particularly in the realm of public health and safety, where consequences for the affected population can be enormous (for example, death). As I write, the U.S. Congress is considering new regulations mandating stronger roofs for sport utility vehicles (SUVs) and light trucks to reduce the number of deaths from vehicle rollover. The new standards are estimated to cost $88–95 million per year, and to prevent 13 to 44 deaths each year in the United States (Reuters, "U.S. Proposes Plan to Strengthen Automobile Roofs," August 19, 2005). If we use the higher estimate of 44 lives saved, that would have reduced the number of U.S. highway deaths in 2004 from 42,636 down to 42,592. In terms of risk, for the average American the annual probability of death from a highway accident will be reduced from about 1/6,919 or .0001445 to about 1/6,926 or .0001444. In terms of money, the new standards will cost $2 million per life saved. Calculations such as this indicate that Americans indeed place a high value on preventing deaths on U.S. highways, though the value is not infinite, since we could prevent vehicular highway deaths altogether by banning vehicular traffic. Congress does not appear to be considering that option at the moment, however.[3]

---

[3] To be sure, a ban on vehicular travel would not save 42,000 lives, since Americans would find alternative means of transportation that also carry the risk of death. The ban

There is another reason why small effects can be important for policy: Sometimes major determinants cannot be manipulated, or they are unknown, so we focus policies on the small effects that are within the reach of policy and that we know something about. Examples are commonplace. We know, for example, that many diseases have a genetic component that we cannot do much about. Hence policies focus on what we can more readily control, such as the promotion of health practices that are known to foster good health and reduce the risk of disease (exercise, eat your vegetables, don't smoke). We promote these practices even though in some instances their effects are relatively small compared to one's genetic endowment. Consider physical exercise. There is some debate over just how much one's life expectancy is increased by regular exercise—the answer might be "not much." Yet the effect, even if small, is important, since people desire long and healthy lives, and amount of physical exercise is something we can control.

IMPORTANCE FOR THEORY

Relatively small effects sometimes can have big implications for theory as well. The effect of income on happiness, for example, is fairly modest in rich countries. The issue of income's effect on happiness is nonetheless theoretically loaded. Economic theory has long assumed that income has positive utility—the more money, the more satisfaction or happiness one has. Studies show that richer people are somewhat happier than poorer people, at least on average. However, in a classic article three decades ago, economist Richard Easterlin asks "Does economic growth improve the human lot?" In that article, and in a body of work since, Easterlin (1974, 1996, 2001) answers, "No, it does not—at least not in rich countries." In his view the rising material well-being in the West is not being translated into increased subjective well-being or happiness, as demonstrated, for example, by the lack of growth in the general level of happiness in Japan and the United States, rich countries where incomes have grown substantially over the past half century.

Robert Frank reaches the same conclusion in his book *Luxury Fever: Money and Happiness in an Era of Excess* (1999). There *is* an income effect on happiness, he says, but it is a relative income effect: Happiness is

---

would no doubt dramatically reduce the number of miles Americans travel, however, and that alone should reduce the number of deaths. In any case, the point is that there are limits to the price Americans will pay to reduce deaths. We are not willing to ban cigarette smoking, for example, even though we know that a smoking ban would improve the overall health of Americans and save thousands of lives each year.

affected by how much money you make *relative to your peers.* In other words, income gains produce no gains in overall happiness in a society because our standards keep rising as we try to "keep up with the Joneses."

This argument has profound implications. In a rich country that is growing richer, individuals become engaged in what Frank (1997) calls a "consumption arms race" akin to a military arms race. That is, if your consumption lowers my happiness, and incomes are rising, then I must consume more just to keep up, resulting in a never-ending "hedonic treadmill" for individuals (Layard 2005, chap. 4). This treadmill could have perverse effects for society in general as well as for individuals, since we could end up consuming more than is socially optimal.

To test the hedonic treadmill theory with data at the individual level, Laura Tach and I analyzed survey data for over sixteen thousand respondents in the 1972–2002 General Social Surveys (Firebaugh and Tach 2005). We examined responses to the general happiness question in the GSS ("Taken all together, how would you say things are these days. . . ."). Note that the preliminary statement "Taken all together" invites respondents to think of happiness in terms of a durable trait rather than a temporary emotion or mood—which is what we wanted, since our focus was on happiness as an enduring individual trait rather than a temporary state or mood. Of course, it might be argued that individuals don't really know whether they are happy or not—is self-reported happiness a valid indicator of one's true feelings? A number of studies have addressed the issue, with the weight of the evidence indicating that a respondent is very often in the best position to judge his or her own happiness (Konow and Earley 2003).

Because the hedonic treadmill requires a specific type of relative income effect—one where keeping up with the Joneses means continually increasing one's own income, because we can be sure that the Joneses are increasing theirs—we used age as the basis for our peer groups. Age is strategic for testing the hedonic treadmill hypothesis, since average incomes in the United States rise over most of the working lifespan. So as Americans we must continually increase our income to keep up with the Joneses who are our age peers.

Do, then, Americans compare themselves to other Americans the same age, resulting in a hedonic treadmill as individuals try to keep up economically with their same-age peers? In line with the treadmill hypothesis, we found that the higher the income of others in one's age group, the lower one's happiness, other things equal (we controlled for the individual's own income, age, physical health, education, marital status, and so on). The relative income effect we detected was modest, however. Health and marital status have much stronger effects on happiness than relative income does (at least as we were able to measure relative income).

The important finding here is that age-based relative income effects apparently do exist. Regardless of their size, they are important theoretically for two reasons. First, age-based relative income effects (or relative income effects in general, whether or not age-based) suggest that individuals' utilities are interdependent. My happiness is affected by the income of my peers. I tend to be less happy, for example, when my peers receive raises and I do not. Second, age-based relative income effects raise difficult questions about the value of continued income growth in rich countries. Rather than promoting overall happiness, continued income growth in rich countries could promote an ongoing consumption race where individuals consume more and more just to maintain a constant level of happiness (for further discussion, see Frank 1997; Layard 2005). At the extreme, if peer incomes matter as much to us, dollar for dollar, as our own income does, then relative income is the entire income-happiness story (not the entire *happiness* story, since income is not the only determinant of happiness). And if relative income is the entire income-happiness story—that is, if there is no absolute income effect at all—then overall happiness in a society does not increase as individuals in the society become richer.

In short: Even modest effects can have immodest implications for theory. Very often modest effects are just that—modest, with limited implications. Readers need to know which is which. It is up to you, the researcher, to make that distinction.

CONCLUSION

This chapter can be summarized in a single sentence: Look for differences that make a difference—and tell us about them. Be sure to report the differences in such a way that your readers can gauge the sizes of the effects.

Reporting differences in such a way that readers can gauge the sizes of the effects implies well-chosen comparisons. An apt comparison can be worth a thousand asterisked coefficients. Consider Devah Pager's (2002) dissertation research on the effect of imprisonment on job prospects (box 2.1, above). To isolate the effect of a criminal record on employment chances, Pager conducted an audit study of employers, sending two pairs of well-groomed, well-spoken college men (one white team and one black team) to apply for 350 advertised entry-level jobs in Milwaukee. Their résumés were identical, except that one member of each team said he had served an eighteen-month prison sentence for cocaine possession. Within each team, one member was randomly assigned the "criminal record" for the first week; then they took turns playing the ex-offender role each week. Pager found, unsurprisingly, that job prospects are poorer for those with a prison record. Surprisingly, though, the imprisonment effect was trumped by a race effect, resulting in the comparison widely reported in the media: "it is easier for a White with a felony conviction to get a job than it is for a Black with a clean record" (*New York Times*, Arts & Ideas, March 20, 2004). The point to emphasize is that it is the *comparison* that makes Pager's results compelling. Pager did not merely report that race has an effect on employment prospects—she gave us a well-chosen comparison to help us gauge the magnitude of that effect.

Instead of comparisons such as this, what we find too often in the social sciences is the findings dump—authors present a laundry list of effects ("X_1, X_2, and X_3 affect Y") with little or no commentary on the relative or absolute sizes of the effects. There are probably two reasons why findings dumps are so common. The first is that variables in social research very often are measured in different units (dollars, years, points on a test) that are hard to calibrate. Second, emphasis on significance tests has had the unintended consequence, perhaps, of devaluing calibration work. To put it more bluntly, the inability or unwillingness to distinguish big effects from small effects may be a learned incapacity stemming from a preoccupation with statistical significance. Although we all know better, too often social scientists confuse statistical significance with substantive significance—a problem that is exacerbated by the convention in some journals of replacing standard errors with asterisks to indicate statistical significance at some arbitrary cutoff point (one asterisk means $p < .05$, two asterisks means $p < .01$, etc.). The net result too often is a two-step degradation of information, first compressing information on sampling errors into two or three categories, then confusing those categories with substantive significance.

This rampant imprecision in reporting the sizes of effects stands in stark contrast to the careful attention usually paid to using estimation methods that will yield the most precise estimates possible. Given the effort required to collect and analyze data in social research, it is amazing how often researchers quit just before the finish line.

Student Exercises on Rule 2

The exercises below use 1972–2004 data from the General Social Survey. The GSS is a probability sample of noninstitutionalized English-speaking individuals, age eighteen and older, in the United States. From 1972 to 1994 the GSS was an annual survey (with a few years missed); after 1994 it has been conducted in even-numbered years. The sample sizes of each wave vary from about 1,500 for the annual surveys to about 3,000 for the biennial surveys.

To do the exercises below, go to the web site http://sda.berkeley.edu. The instructions below should generate all the statistics you need to answer the questions, so you should not need to do any calculations by hand. Use the .01 significance level for questions about statistical significance. Again, variable names are in **boldface** in the computer assignments in this book, and answers to selected problems are provided at http://press.prince ton.edu/titles/8593.html.

Note: The student exercises on rule 1 (at the end of chapter 1) use the same data and web site. The site is user-friendly, so if you did the chapter 1 exercises you should have no trouble doing the exercises here. To avoid redundancy, the instructions below include only the key commands; I do not give step-by-step instructions as I did in the exercises for rule 1. Recall that the figures given below are for the 1972–2004 GSS, the most recent GSS data available when this book was written. *So if you are working with more recent data, to replicate the figures exactly you will need to use the "selection filter" in the SDA program to remove years after 2004.* Also recall that the format in the SDA web site might have changed somewhat since these directions were written, so some of the specific directions below might be out of date, but you still should be able to follow the logic below to obtain the tables you need to answer the questions.

Assignment 1. What Determines Happiness?

The GSS asks the following question, denoted **happy**: "Taken all together, how would you say things are these days—would you say that you are very happy, pretty happy, or not too happy?" Note that the question asks about happiness in general, not about happiness in a specific domain, such as happiness with one's job or marriage or financial situation.

You have probably heard someone such as your grandmother say that if you have your health, you have it all—you should be happy. Let's see if there is empirical evidence for the proposition that health is linked to happiness. From the Berkeley SDA homepage, click on "SDA archive," then go to the GSS cumulative data file and follow these instructions:

- Recode **happy** so high values denote greater happiness, as follows: From the recode screen, type in **happy_re** for "name for the new variable to be created." Type in **happy** for "Var 1" under "Name of existing variables to use for the recode." For row 1 under "Output variable," type "1" for "value," "not too happy" for "label," and "3" for "Var 1." For the second row, type "2" for "value," "pretty happy" for "label," and "2" for "Var 1." For the third row, type "3" for "value," "very happy" for "label," and "1" for "Var 1." Then click on "start recoding" to convert **happy** to **happy_re**, a variable that ranges from 1 for "not too happy" to 3 for "very happy." You should have 43,317 valid cases.
- Recode **health** the same way, by reversing the coding so that it ranges from 1=poor health to 4=excellent health. Call your new variable **health_re** (for "health recoded").
- Cross-tabulate **happy_re** with **health_re**. Insert **happy_re** as the row variable and **health_re** as the column variable (explanatory variable). Use the options that you used for the exercises at the end of chapter 1. Ask for column percentages, not row percentages (1 decimal point is fine for the percentages, except where I note otherwise). Check the box beside "statistics," and use the drop-down menu to indicate that you want 3 decimal points for statistics. Remove the check beside "color coding" and use the drop-down menu to indicate that you want "(no chart)" under "Chart options."
- If you have followed the instructions properly, using "Wt for black oversample," you should have 4,124 respondents who are "not too happy," 18,476 who are "pretty happy," and 10,808 who are "very happy."

Question 1. (a) Is the association between health and happiness positive and statistically significant?
(b) On the basis of your examination of the cell percentages, how would you characterize the size of the association?
(c) Observe that percent "very happy" increases *without exception* as you move from the poor health category to the excellent health category. This is called a "monotonic increase." Is the change also linear—that is, are the changes in the percentages roughly the same between each category, or is the jump noticeably larger between some categories of health than others?

(d) What about "not too happy"—does the percent "not too happy" decline monotonically as you move from poor to excellent health? Does the change appear to be linear?

Next let's cross-tabulate **happy_re** with **housekeep** to test the claim in this chapter that housewives and working women have the same average level of happiness, but the variance on happiness is greater for housewives.

- Create a new variable **housekeep** by collapsing **wrkstat**—an eight-category measure of work status (e.g., full-time worker, part-time worker, retired, keeping house)—down to two categories, "keeping house" versus "working full-time or part-time." Use the recode command to collapse **wrkstat** as follows: **housekeep** is the new variable to be created. Insert **wrkstat** for "Var 1" under "Name of existing variables to use for the recode." For row 1 under "Output variable," type "0" for "value," "working" for "label," and "1, 2" for "Var 1." For the second row, type "1" for "value," "housekeeper" for "label," and "7" for "Var 1." The remaining categories of **wrkstat** are automatically coded as missing. The new variable **housekeep** has 27,784 workers (this includes men and women) and 8,219 housekeepers (this also includes men as well as women).
- Cross-tabulate **happy_re** (row variable) with **housekeep** (column variable). Remember to select "Oversamp—Weight for black oversamples" as before. In this case, however, we want to restrict the sample to women, so insert **sex(2)** for the "selection filter" box, and indicate 3 decimal points for statistics. (**Sex** is coded 1 for men and 2 for women.)

Question 2. (a) Did you reproduce the percentages "very happy" and "not too happy" cited earlier in the chapter? (very happy: 35.3% for housewives, 32.2% for working women; not too happy: 13.4% for housewives, 10.0% for working women). These percentages suggest that housewives are more likely to be "very happy" *and* they are more likely to be "not too happy."
(b) Give a plausible explanation for the greater variance in happiness among housewives.

Question 3. Do the cross-tabulation necessary to examine the difference in happiness *for men* who are keeping house versus men who are in the paid labor force. [Hint: cross-tabulate **housekeep** with **happy_re** as before, but this time insert something else as "selection filter" to restrict the analysis to men.] Your total sample size should be 13,781, of whom 199 keep house.
(a) Compare your results for men with your results for women.

(b) Give a plausible explanation for why the association differs for men and women.

Now use the Berkeley SDA web site to determine whether men or women tend to be happier in the United States.

- Cross-tabulate **happy_re** (row) with **sex** (column). If you select "Oversamp—Weight for black oversamples" along with the other options chosen above, you should get 43,326 cases. Select 3 decimal points for statistics.

Question 4. On the basis of the 3-point happiness scale—coded 1 for not too happy, 2 for pretty happy, and 3 for very happy—for the 1972–2004 GSS the average (mean) happiness for men is 2.198 and the average happiness for women is 2.207. (This result is found in the row just below the column total row.)

(a) Explain this difference as clearly as you can in ordinary English. How happy are men on average and women on average? How large is .009 *points* on this scale of happiness?

(b) Is this gender difference statistically significant? (In other words, is there an association between gender and happiness?)

(c) With regard to happiness, do you see any differences of consequence between men and women?

Question 5. (a) Compare the magnitude of the gender difference on happiness with the magnitude of the differences in means across the health categories.

(b) In comparing averages on this 3-point scale of happiness, what assumptions are we making about the differences between the three response categories (very happy vs. pretty happy vs. not too happy)?

Question 6. (a) Rank the following variables in terms of their association with happiness, from strongest association to weakest association: college degree, gender, health (4 categories), and married (dichotomize **marital** into "married" and "not married" as in the exercises for chapter 1). Use the recode command to create a new variable **college** (college degree = 1, otherwise 0) by collapsing the GSS variable **degree**. Here is the information you need to know to create **college: degree** is 0 for no high school degree, 1 for high school degree only, 2 for junior college degree, 3 for bachelor's degree, 4 for graduate degree. **College** should have 46,349 valid cases, of whom 19.4 percent have four-year college degrees.

(b) Defend your ranking of the four variables.

(c) Consider the size of the associations in an absolute sense. On the basis of your examination of differences in the cell percentages, which associations are large, which are medium, which are small, and which are trivial?

Question 7. Is there an association between age and happiness in the United States? Before looking at the data, write down which one of the following you expect to find: a positive association between age and happiness (older people tend to be happier), no association, or a negative association. To see if you are right, recode **age** into 20s, 30s, 40s, 50s, 60s, 70s (or older). (There are some respondents in the GSS who are 18 or 19—code them with the 20s.) Then cross-tabulate **age_re** and **happy_re**. What do you find?

Assignment 2. Visual Representations

The aim in this assignment is to create pie graphs to visually represent Americans' changing sexual attitudes over the past quarter century. We will examine attitudes about homosexuality, premarital sex, sex among unmarried teenagers, and extramarital sex.

Question 8. Before doing the analysis, make your best guess about what percentage of American adults (1980-2004) think that:

- homosexuality is always wrong
- premarital sex is always wrong
- sex between unmarried teens is always wrong
- extramarital sex is always wrong

(a) Write down your ranking, from type of sex you think is most frowned upon to type of sex that is most tolerated.
(b) Then, for each of the above, write down whether you think the percentage of Americans saying "always wrong" has increased, declined, or stayed about the same since 1980.

Now go to the homepage for the GSS cumulative file on the Berkeley web site. The relevant GSS variables are **homosex**, **xmarsex**, **teensex**, and **premarsx**. To find out how **homosex** is coded, enter **homosex** in the box beside "view" (unless the SDA format has changed, you will find it in the upper left of the page), and click on "view." Use the recode command to create four new variables that are coded 1 for "always wrong" and 0 for the other three categories ("almost always wrong," "sometimes wrong," and "not wrong at all"). You have had enough experience with the recode function that you should be able to do this by yourself. Call those variables **homosexwrong**, **xmarsexwrong**, **teensexwrong**, and **premarsxwrong**.

The next step is to use the recode command to create a variable called **decade** from the GSS variable **year**. You want to enter three values under "Value" for the output variable: 1980, 1990, and 2000. For 1980, enter "1980s" under "Label" and "1980–1989" under "Var 1." For 1990, enter "1990s" under "Label" and "1990–1999" under "Var 1." For 2000, enter "2000s" under "Label" and "2000–2004" under "Var 1." Click "start recoding." You should have 14,241 cases for the 1980s, 13,223 cases for the 1990s, 8,394 cases for 2000–2004, and 10,652 cases of "no data" (these are the respondents in the earlier surveys).

The final step is to cross-tabulate each of the sex variables with **decade** (column variable). Select "Wt for black oversamples" from the Weight dropdown menu, and remove the check beside "color coding." Select "Pie Chart(s)" under "chart options" and then run the table.

Question 9. (a) Compare the percentages with your guesses in question 8. (b) Then summarize the results in one or two paragraphs. There are two big issues to discuss: first, the level of Americans' approval or disapproval of premarital sex, teenage sex, homosexuality, and extramarital sex; second, the *trends* in these attitudes. The pie charts should be especially helpful in seeing the trends.
(c) Which results surprised you the most?

CHAPTER 3

The Third Rule

BUILD REALITY CHECKS INTO YOUR RESEARCH

To determine the height of a tree or the distance of a ship from the shore, we can use a method known as *triangulation*. Triangulation is based on the principle that if we know the length of the base of a triangle along with the two angles at either end of the base, then we can calculate the height of the triangle. In other words, we use elementary geometry and trigonometry to calculate an unknown distance from a known distance.

The term triangulation has been embraced by social scientists, who use it to refer to the practice of using more than one method in a study as a way of double-checking results. The idea is that we can be more confident of our results if different routes lead to the same conclusion.

This chapter presents rule 3, the *reality check rule*. In the chapter I discuss the importance of building reality checks more routinely into social research. Triangulation using alternative methods is one approach, but it is not the only approach. Some of the reality checks apply to data preparation, some apply to data analysis, and some apply to checks on conclusions after the analysis. In many instances the word "check" would probably suffice, but I use the term "reality check" deliberately, to emphasize the importance of stepping back from our analysis occasionally to see if what we are doing is sensible. In many instances the reality checks are commonsensical or pedestrian, yet even experienced researchers sometimes go astray by failing to build checks into their studies. Indeed, some of this chapter consists of case studies of research that has gone astray (research illustrating how *not* to do it) in the hope that as social scientists we can learn as much from our mistakes as from our successes. I have taken most of the examples from research in sociology, since that is the field I know best. Because they provide the most arresting and memorable examples, I tried to select lines of research involving influential studies of important issues. In instances where it was appropriate to focus on a specific study to illustrate a point, I hope authors understand that it is the importance and clarity of their work that compels the close scrutiny of it.

INTERNAL REALITY CHECKS

Reality Checks on Data—Dubious Values and Incomplete Data

The first step in any analysis of quantitative data is to check means, variances, and correlations for plausibility. Experienced researchers know to do this but are often eager to "run some models" before carefully checking the data. Researchers are especially likely to skip this step when using secondary survey data from large survey firms, where the data presumably are already clean. It is nonetheless a good idea routinely to look at the means, variances, and ranges for each of the variables in our analysis. Are the means and variances reasonable? Do all the values fall within a plausible range?

You should examine scatterplots for outliers and nonlinearities in the early stages of your analysis. For surprising correlations—ones that are smaller or larger than expected, or not in the predicted direction—scatterplots can reveal if there are single cases or clusters of cases that might account for the unexpected result.

It is especially important throughout the analysis to keep track of the item nonresponses, that is, missing entries because a respondent failed to answer a question. How are those missing values coded? How do you want to code the response category "not sure"—is it coded as missing, or as neutral? Item nonresponses are a potential pitfall in any analysis, and inattention to missing values can lead to serious blunders. (It is also important to pay attention to missing data due to *nonrespondents*—individuals who were chosen for the sample but who fail to participate. This issue is discussed in the next chapter.)

TRADITIONAL METHODS FOR DEALING WITH MISSING DATA

If you encounter missing entries in your study—as you will sooner or later—the first question to ask is how much missing data there is. That question is first because, as Paul Allison (2002) observes, a standard old method called *listwise deletion* is an attractive option for dealing with incomplete data, so long as the amount of missing data is not intolerable. Listwise deletion (also known as *casewise deletion* or *complete case analysis*) removes individuals with incomplete information. Although that appears to be very wasteful, listwise deletion has several important advantages. First, it can be used for any kind of statistical analysis, from ordinary regression to the most sophisticated methods, with no special software required. You use the methods that you had planned to use, with off-the-shelf software, but you include only the cases with complete data. Second, although your standard errors will tend to be larger because you are using less information, you will obtain appropriate estimates of those standard errors. As a result, "you do not have to worry about making inferential errors because of missing data—a big problem with most of the other commonly used methods" (Allison 2002, p. 6).

Third, if all the standard assumptions of regression are met, listwise deletion provides unbiased estimates of the regression slopes when "missingness" is caused by independent variables but not by the dependent variable (Little 1992). Imagine, for example, that we are studying the effect of income on happiness, and that some respondents have missing data on income or happiness or both. We might suspect that the missingness is causally related to income, the independent variable, since those with more income are less likely to answer the income question. That sort of missingness would not bias our estimate of the effect of income on happiness (see box 4.1 in the next chapter). However, if missingness is also affected by *happiness* (the dependent variable)—that is, independent of income level, if happy people are more likely (or less likely) to answer the questions about income and happiness—then our estimates of the effect of income on happiness are biased when we use listwise deletion.

Other traditional methods for handling missing data are less attractive. Researchers sometimes have filled in missing data by inserting the average X for cases where X is missing. To avoid discarding cases with missing data on income, for example, you might simply insert the mean income. This method is called *mean substitution* or *mean imputation*. Mean imputation is not to be confused with *multiple imputation*, a method discussed subsequently. Mean imputation understates uncertainty and thus understates standard errors; multiple imputation introduces randomness in order to provide better estimates of the standard errors (below).[1]

Another traditional method for handling missing data is *pairwise deletion*, or *available case analysis*. Pairwise deletion takes advantage of the well-known fact that regression slopes can be estimated from sample means and the covariance matrix. In other words, you can do linear regression without knowing values on the variables for the individual cases, as long as you know the means, variances, and correlations of the variables. This suggests the following strategy: On the assumption that some information is better than no information, use all the cases available to estimate the covariance matrix, and estimate the regression slopes from that matrix. Because all available cases are used, the correlation of X_1 and Y may be based on 300 cases, while the correlation of X_2 and Y is based (say) on 250 cases. Despite the apparent advantages of pairwise deletion—

---

[1] In a more sophisticated version of the mean substitution strategy, researchers insert a conditional mean (from a regression equation) instead of the overall mean. This strategy is superior to substituting the simple mean, but it still produces understated estimates of standard errors. Multiple imputation methods were developed in large part to overcome such problems.

no information is discarded, and no values are imputed—pairwise deletion generally should be avoided because the standard errors given by standard software will be biased.

Allison (2002, p. 12) sums up the situation as follows: "All the common [traditional] methods for salvaging information from cases with missing data typically make things worse. . . . In light of these shortcomings, listwise deletion does not look so bad."

In some instances, however, listwise deletion is unattractive because it discards too much data. How much data discarding is "too much"? Unfortunately, there are no hard and fast rules. Discarding 50 cases is problematic if you have 100 cases but barely matters if you have 100,000 cases. One point is clear: Other things equal, the more variables you have in your model, the more likely you are to face missing data problems. Suppose you have twenty variables in your regression model. Then, as Allison (p. 2) points out, even if you have only 5 percent missing data for each of the twenty variables, you can expect only 36 percent of the cases to have complete data on every variable under the assumption that the chance of missing data on one variable is independent of the chance of missing data on any other variable. In other words, by using listwise deletion you would expect to discard nearly two-thirds of your cases, even though each variable has data for 95 percent of respondents!

In short, listwise deletion is not always a viable option. What do you do when you cannot use listwise deletion? That is the topic of the next section.

NEWER METHODS FOR DEALING WITH MISSING DATA

In instances where listwise deletion is not viable, you should consider recent data augmentation methods that have been developed to fill in missing entries in data sets. Modern methods of data augmentation use what is called multiple imputation to impute values for individual units. The logic is to use information we know (information already in the data) to impute values we don't know. In effect, then, we insert values where none existed before in the data.

Before describing the multiple imputation method, it is important to clarify two points. First, imputation is not fudging the data. At first blush it might appear unseemly or even unethical to impute values for individuals—when you impute values, are you not "making up data"? In point of fact, however, you are imputing on the basis of information that is already there, in the data. The aim of social research is to determine how X is related to Y, and that is done on the basis of information that is in the data. Because imputation, done properly, does not distort or add to information that is already in the data, imputation is not fudging. (If you are uncomfortable with multiple imputation, then you should also be uncomfortable with mean substitution, since that also "makes up data." The difference is that mean substitution makes up worse data.)

The second point is that there are proper and improper ways to impute missing values from the data. We already noted that the old strategy of mean substitution is a bad idea. It's a bad idea because we end up turning a variable into a constant for respondents with missing values on that variable. As a result, we fail to control for the variable over that portion of the sample where the data are missing. Mean imputation produces biased estimates of regression coefficients, variances, and standard errors.

Newer imputation methods differ from earlier ones by deliberately introducing random variation as part of the imputation procedure (Rubin 1987; Schafer 1997). Multiple imputation (MI) uses Monte Carlo techniques to replace the missing values with $m > 1$ simulated versions. There are three steps: imputation, analysis, and pooling.

- *Imputation.* Random draws from some distribution are used to fill in the missing entries. (The distribution is selected to inject the right amount of uncertainty to produce unbiased estimates of variances and standard errors: see Allison 2002, chap. 5.) The missing entries are filled in m times, resulting in m complete data sets, where m typically is small (say 3–10).
- *Analysis.* Each of the m data sets is analyzed, resulting in m analyses.
- *Pooling.* The m analyses are combined into a final result.

The method is called multiple imputation because multiple complete data sets are produced and analyzed. Single imputation sometimes is adequate if the proportion of missing values is small. However, single imputation requires almost as much set-up as multiple implication does (though less computer time), and single imputation tends to understate standard errors because it omits the between-imputation component of variability (Allison 2002, p. 29).

Specialized software programs have been developed for multiple imputation, and more are on the way. The key assumption of these programs is the so-called missing at random (MAR) assumption: Data on Y are said to be missing at random when the probability that Y is missing for the ith unit is unrelated to the value of Y for the ith unit, after controlling for the other variables in the analysis.

Because multiple imputation is computationally demanding, even fast computers may require several hours of number crunching to obtain estimates for very large data sets. Other than its demands on computer time, the downside of multiple imputation is that it yields somewhat different results each time you do it, so there is no "right answer" that others can duplicate exactly when applying the same method to the same data.

Reality Checks on Measures—Aim for Consistency in Conceptualization and Measurement

Inconsistency in the conceptualization and measurement of key concepts can lead to problems that range from confusing presentations to fatal errors in the conclusions. I begin with the problem of opaque prose resulting from fuzzy conceptualization and measurement.

While dense prose sometimes may be a sign of deep thinking on difficult issues, more often it is merely a sign of muddled thinking. The point that I want to stress here is that clear writing begins with clear thinking, and clear thinking includes transparency and consistency in the measurement of key concepts.

CONSISTENCY BETWEEN CONCEPT AND MEASUREMENT

Social scientists sometimes introduce needless complexity, as if to keep readers off balance and guessing. Let me provide a simple illustration. As a journal editor I often received papers where one of the critical variables was coded in a direction opposite to the concept (for example, a paper on poverty that uses income as the dependent variable; or the title of the paper uses the term *equality* but the study uses the Gini coefficient or some other measure of *inequality*). This might not seem like a big deal, since the reader can just remember to reverse the signs of the coefficients, but why should the reader need to do this? Placing the onus on readers to reverse the signs is an unnecessary burden, particularly in studies where some of the variables are coded in a direction consistent with the concept and some are not. It is hard for readers to keep this straight—as witness, for example, instances where a double-reversal is called for (both variables are coded opposite to the concept), so the original sign is correct. Sometimes authors stumble over their own coding, and in the worst cases readers can't even interpret the reported coefficients because it isn't clear whether the reported coefficients are intended to correspond to the concept as stated or to the concept as actually measured!

The simplicity of this illustration should not detract from the importance of the issue. The purpose of a research report is to communicate research findings, and the stage for clear communication of findings is set well before the first word of text is written. If you have trouble keeping everything straight as a researcher, you can be sure that readers, who are not as familiar with your research as you are, will be even more befuddled. Where there is fog in the pulpit, there will be dense fog in the congregation.

CONSISTENCY IN THE MEASUREMENT OF SIMILAR CONCEPTS

Sometimes researchers become so involved in the nuts and bolts of their project that they lose sight of the big picture. One of the big-picture issues is consistency in measuring variables. Variables that measure the same essence should be measured in the same way. In comparing the effects of financial investment in different regions of the world, for example, we would want to use a consistent measure of investment. Otherwise, if we found regional differences in the effect of investment, we would not know whether those differences reflected real differences in investment effects, or merely differences in the way investment was measured.

Lest this example seem far-fetched, it is instructive to consider a booming line of research in the 1970s and 1980s on the determinants of economic growth in poor countries. At that time a number of sociologists and political scientists advanced an unorthodox idea: Poor countries would be better off with less, not more, economic contact with the richer nations of the West. The prediction was that poor countries engaging heavily in economic exchange with rich countries would, due to exploitation by the rich countries, tend to experience slower economic growth than poor countries not so heavily engaged. Contrary to the prediction, however, empirical studies found beneficial trade effects: Other things equal, poor countries that traded more with rich countries generally experienced faster, not slower, growth.

So the focus on this line of research shifted from the effects of trade to the effects of foreign investment on economic growth in poor countries. Here the findings seemed to support the prediction. Literally dozens of studies concluded that foreign investment from rich countries has short-term positive effects—so-called investment *flow effects*—but harmful long-term effects (*stock effects*) on income growth in poor countries. Because the negative stock effect was judged to overshadow the positive flow effect, some scholars believed that social research had discovered an important principle for economic growth in poor countries: Do not permit foreign investment from rich countries.

It turns out, however, that this conclusion was based on inconsistent measures of investment. Foreign investment and domestic investment are similar concepts—they differ only in the *source* of the funds—yet they were measured in very different ways in this body of research. When foreign investment and domestic investment are measured the same way, we find that both types of investment tend to boost income growth in poor countries (case study, box 3.1). The error was not discovered until studies applied the reality check suggested here: Use consistent measures of the same concept. In other words, a misguided line of research could have been avoided if researchers had done a simple reality check by asking the question: What do we find when we measure foreign and domestic investment the same way?

Reality Checks on Models—The Formal Equivalence Check

Sometimes—as in the example of the effects of foreign and domestic investment—social scientists use aggregates instead of individuals as their unit of analysis. The aggregates could be precincts, as in studies of voting; census tracts, as in studies of residential segregation; classrooms, as in studies of teacher effectiveness; school districts, as in studies of educational funding and equity; cities, as in studies of crime rate, employment rate, and suicide rate, to name a few; states or provinces, for any number of investigations; countries, as in studies of the causes of economic growth; and so on.

Box 3.1
Case Study: The Effect of Foreign Investment on Economic
Growth in Poor Countries

Dozens of cross-country regression studies in the 1970s and 1980s concluded that foreign investment from rich countries reduces economic growth in poor countries. However, when we replicate the studies applying the same measures and the same logic to domestic investment as to foreign investment, we conclude that *domestic investment also harms economic growth in the long run* (Firebaugh 1992).

Because no one believes that countries fare better in the long run economically by lowering their domestic investment, there is a serious problem here. To identify that problem, let's look at the cross-country model used in this line of research. The outcome variable is rate of growth of income per capita for some sample of poor countries over some time period. The control variables vary somewhat from study to study, but the investment measures always consist of these three: (1) *stock* of foreign investment as of the first year of the study, measured as the cumulated foreign investment in a country divided by the size of the country's economy; (2) *flow* of foreign investment over the period of the study, measured as change in foreign investment stock over that period, divided by the size of the country's economy; and (3) domestic investment *rate*, measured as the rate of growth of domestic investment over the period of the study.

In short, the dependent variable is measured as a rate and domestic investment is measured as a rate, but foreign investment is

---

(continued on next page)

Most often the variables that are employed in aggregate analyses are composites of some kind—per capita measures, growth rates, ratios, and so on. By *composite measures* I am referring to variables that are composed of two or more separable variables. Per student expenditure, for example, is total expenditure divided by number of students. Crime rate is number of crimes divided by population size. Percent Latino in a census tract is number of Latinos divided by total population in the tract. Composite measures such as these are standard fare in aggregate-level social research.

(continued from previous page)

---

measured in a very different way. To appreciate the problem caused by this measurement inconsistency, suppose we measure growth rate as proportional change, that is, as $(Y_2 - Y_1)/Y_1$, where the subscripts 1 and 2 denote the initial and final years of the study. (I use proportional change for convenience; alternative ways of measuring growth rate yield the same result.) Then the foreign investment model used by researchers in the 1970s and 1980s is as follows, where I denotes per capita income, F denotes foreign investment, and D denotes domestic investment:

$$(I_2 - I_1)/I_1 = \alpha + \delta(F_2 - F_1) + \gamma F_1 + \beta[(D_2 - D_1) / D_1] + controls + \varepsilon \tag{3.1}$$

This model states that a country's rate of growth of per capita income from time 1 to time 2 is determined by foreign investment inflow $(F_2 - F_1)$ over the period, by level of foreign investment at time 1 (F_1), by rate of domestic investment, and by other factors captured in the control variables and in ε.

The dozens of studies using this model report these findings and conclusions:

- $\delta > 0$. Conclusion: In the short run, foreign investment boosts economic growth in poor countries.
- $\gamma < 0$. Conclusion: In the long run, poor countries are better off economically without foreign investment.
- $\beta > 0$. Conclusion: Domestic investment boosts economic growth in poor countries.

Note that these conclusions are based on a model that measures domestic investment as the single variable $(D_2 - D_1) / D_1$ and foreign

---

(continued on next page)

As a general rule there is no special difficulty in interpreting the results of studies with composite measures when the composites are all formed the same way (Kuh and Meyer 1955; Firebaugh and Gibbs 1985). An example would be studies where all the variables are expressed as percentages, such as percent single-parent households and percent poor in a neighborhood, or as per capita measures, such as income per capita and nurses per capita in a country. The denominator, population size, is the same for all variables. Because a researcher uses per capita measures to adjust for the fact that the units (census tracts, schools, countries, and so on) vary in size, there would be no need for such a denominator if all units

(continued from previous page)

investment as two variables, $F_2 - F_1$ and F_1. To make the measures consistent, suppose we split the numerator and denominator of the domestic investment measure, entering $D_2 - D_1$ and D_1 as separate variables for domestic investment, just like they are for foreign investment. It follows logically that, since $\beta > 0$, the effect of the numerator will be positive and the effect of the denominator will be negative when entered as separate variables (see Firebaugh 1992 for empirical verification). To be consistent with the conclusions above, then, we have this new set of conclusions:

- $\delta > 0$. Conclusion: In the short run, foreign investment boosts economic growth in poor countries.
- $\gamma < 0$. Conclusion: In the long run, poor countries are better off economically without foreign investment.
- $\beta_{numerator} > 0$. Conclusion: In the short run, domestic investment boosts economic growth in poor countries.
- $\beta_{denominator} < 0$. Conclusion: In the long run, poor countries are better off economically without domestic investment.

The conclusion that poor countries would have higher incomes if they had lower levels of domestic capital investment is ludicrous, of course, and it points out the danger of measuring an outcome variable as a growth rate and explanatory variables in terms of components of growth rate. When foreign investment and domestic investment are both measured as rates (consistent with the outcome variable), cross-country regressions indicate that *both types of investment are associated with faster income growth* in poor countries (Firebaugh 1992).

were the same size. In effect, by using per capita measures, a researcher uses a mathematical operation (division) to control for differences in the populations of units. Alternatively, a researcher could use raw totals rather than per capita measures, and control for population by adding population size as a control variable in a regression model. Whichever method is used—controlling for population by division (per capita method) or by residualization[2] (regression method)—there should be no special difficulty in interpreting the results.[3]

Sometimes researchers perform analyses where the numerator of one variable is the denominator of another variable. In that case, you are not using division in a consistent fashion to control for population size, so results are not always easy to interpret. The general point is that the use of *dissimilar* composite variables (where, for example, some variables are per capita measures and others are raw counts, or where the numerator of one variable is the denominator of another) in some instances can produce results that are tricky to interpret.

Reality checks are particularly important when you estimate models containing dissimilar composite variables. In the case of dissimilar composites, it is often useful to try to express the model in alternative forms. The aim is to see if there are different ways to express the same model that will aid your intuition in interpreting the model's coefficients.

Consider this example, again from the cross-country regression literature. On the basis of an analysis of income growth for about five dozen poor non-Western countries from 1960 to 1998, Giovanni Arrighi, Beverly Silver, and Benjamin Brewer (2003, hereafter ASB) claim that industrialization does not promote economic advancement in poor countries. "For most [poor] countries," they write (p. 18), "industrialization [has] turned out to be an ineffectual means of economic advancement." This claim is questioned by Alice Amsden (2003), who notes the contradiction between the ASB claim and the strong association between industrialization and income growth in poor countries in recent decades.

---

[2] By "residualization" I refer to the fact that the effect (slope) of X on Y controlling for population can be obtained by regressing the residual $(Y-\hat{Y})$ on the residual $(X-\hat{X})$, where $\hat{Y}$ is from the regression of Y on population and $\hat{X}$ is from the regression of X on population.

[3] That is, there is no special difficulty arising from the use of composite measures per se. With aggregate data there *is*, however, the very real danger of committing the "ecological fallacy" of drawing conclusions about individual relationships from aggregate-level relationships. That practice is called a fallacy because it makes the problematic assumption that relationships at the aggregate level mirror relationships at the individual level (see the section "Context Effects as Nuisance" in chapter 7).

Amsden appears to be correct: Using the same countries as ASB, and weighting by population size, I found a whopping correlation of $r = 0.98$ between industrial growth and income growth over the period 1960 to 1998. How do we account, then, for the ASB claim that industrialization has not benefited poor countries economically? Amsden suggests that the ASB finding must be due to a "bug in their program" (2003, p. 34). In their reply, however, ASB state that they double-checked their computer program and are satisfied that their finding is not due to a programming error.

It turns out that ASB appear to be correct on this point: The problem is not their computer program. The problem lies in their model. To understand where the confusion comes from, begin with the essential model that ASB estimate:

$$(Y/P)_i' = \beta_0 + \beta_1 (M/Y)_i' + \varepsilon_i \qquad (3.2)$$

where Y denotes income (total national output), P denotes population, M denotes manufacturing output, prime denotes growth rate, and the subscript i identifies the individual case (here, the country). Hence $(Y/P)_i'$ is rate of growth of per capita income in the ith poor country and $(M/Y)_i'$ is rate of growth of manufacturing output as a fraction of total output in the ith poor country. For this model, ASB report a slope of zero for fifty-eight poor countries, 1960–1980, as well as a slope of zero for fifty-nine poor countries, 1980–1998.

Now let's rewrite the ASB model. Because rate of growth of a ratio A/B is the rate of growth of A minus the rate of growth of B, we can write $(Y/P)_i'$ as $Y_i' - P_i'$ and $(M/Y)_i'$ as $M_i' - Y_i'$. Thus we can rewrite equation 3.2 as:

$$(Y_i' - P_i') = \beta_0 + \beta_1 (M_i' - Y_i') + \varepsilon_i. \qquad (3.3)$$

When expressed this way, it is clear that this model does not actually estimate the economic effect of industrialization in poor countries. In plain English, the ASB model states that the extent to which income growth exceeds (or lags behind) population growth is a function of the extent to which manufacturing growth exceeds (or lags behind) income growth. Thus the coefficient β_1 reflects the effect of *segregated* manufacturing growth on economic growth in poor countries. Because β_1 is zero, we conclude that the difference between income growth rate and population growth rate is uncorrelated with the difference between manufacturing growth rate and income growth rate (growth rate of total output)—precisely as we would expect if industrialization boosts economic performance. Successful industrialization means that manufacturing growth boosts not just manufacturing but other economic sectors as well, so that manufacturing growth rate does not greatly outrun rate of growth for *total* output.

In short, Amsden and ASB are talking about different things. For the countries that ASB analyzed, the correlation between industrial growth and income growth is close to $r = 1.0$ for the 1965–1998 period, so Amsden is correct in her claim that industrialization benefits poor countries. Poor countries that are industrializing clearly tend to grow faster economically than poor countries that are not. Yet it is also true, as the ASB results indicate, that successful industrialization means manufacturing growth that links to growth in the rest of the economy.

The bigger lesson here is that reality checks are important for models, especially in the case of models with dissimilar composite variables. Social science researchers should try to express models formally, and to search for alternative expressions that facilitate interpretation of empirical results.

EXTERNAL REALITY CHECKS: VALIDATION WITH OTHER DATA AND METHODS

The reality checks described to this point are internal, in the sense that they can be done by researchers without reference to other data sets or results from other studies. Thus we can check our data for dubious values, we can check our measures for consistency with each other and with the concepts they are intended to capture, and (sometimes) we can express our models in alternative forms to check the interpretation of our results.

In this part of the chapter I turn to methods for evaluating the sensibility of social science results by comparing them with results drawn from other types of data and methods. I have in mind *purposive* checks for the sensibility of our results. The checks might involve thought experiments, simulations, or the direct comparison of quantitative and qualitative research. I give several examples below from the research of others. These examples do not exhaust the possibilities but are intended instead to stimulate thinking in this area.

In describing these methods I do not mean to suggest that current research practice ignores external reality checks. The most obvious reality check is the comparison of one's results with the results of prior research, and that is done routinely. Journal articles in the social sciences typically include a discussion-of-results section, for example, and the comparison of one's results with the results of other studies is standard fare in that section. But we can do better. We need to devote greater attention to the development of cleverer and more direct reality checks for our conclusions.

Using Causal-Process Observations to Test Plausibility of Results

Henry Brady (2004) uses a causal-process observations approach (his terms) to provide an example of what I mean by an external reality check. A causal-process observation is defined as "an insight or piece of data that provides information about context, process, or mechanism, and that contributes distinctive leverage in causal inference. A causal-process observation . . . is frequently viewed as an indispensable supplement to correlation-based inference in quantitative research" (Seawright and Collier 2004, pp. 277–78).

In Brady's example a causal-process observations analysis serves to provide evidence against a claim that was made on the basis of a regression analysis of election data. The election in question is the 2000 U.S. presidential election in Florida. On the basis of his analysis of turnout data for all sixty-seven Florida counties in 1988, 1992, 1996, and 2000, John Lott (2000) concluded that the networks' premature projection of Al Gore as the winner in Florida cost George W. Bush at least 10,000 votes in ten predominantly Republican counties in the panhandle of Florida. (The ten panhandle counties are in the central time zone, and the projection was made when the polls were still open in those counties but closed in the rest of the state.) The votes were lost, then, by dampening vote turnout in counties where Bush was popular. As Lott explains (quoted in Brady 2004, p. 268):

> By prematurely declaring Gore the winner shortly before polls had closed in Florida's conservative western Panhandle, the media ended up suppressing the Republican vote. . . . An examination of past Republican presidential votes by county in Florida from 1988 to 2000 shows that while total votes declined, the Republican voting rate in the western Panhandle was significantly suppressed relative to the non-Republican vote. The 4 percent greater reduction in Republican votes averages about 1,000 votes per county, [yielding] 10,000 Republican votes for all 10 counties in the western Panhandle.

Lott bases his conclusion on a difference-of-difference analysis of turnout data for the four presidential elections. The networks' premature projection of Gore as the winner is perceived as a kind of natural experiment where ten counties received the "treatment" and the other fifty-seven counties did not. The basic logic for the analysis is this: Since the "experiment" occurred only in the 2000 election, compare county turnout differences in the 2000 election with county differences in the three earlier elections to estimate the effect of the networks' projection. In effect, data on past turnout is used to project the number of additional votes Bush would have received in the panhandle counties under the counterfactual condition that the networks had not projected Gore as the winner. Lott's answer: 10,000.

There is nothing wrong with Lott's method per se; difference-of-difference models are standard in many social science applications. But the 10,000 figure invites a reality check. As Brady (2004, p. 269) explains, there are ways to test the plausibility of the 10,000 figure: "Is Lott's estimate reasonable, given the numbers of voters who had not yet voted when the media called the election for Gore? How many of these voters heard the call? Of these, how many decided not to vote? And of these who decided not to vote, how many would have voted for Bush?"

To address these questions, Brady first determined the precise time the media declared Gore the winner: 6:50 pm central time, ten minutes before the polls closed in the panhandle. Data from 1996 on time of voting indicate that no more than 1/12 of the voting in Florida occurs during the last hour, and interviews with election officials indicated that there was no last-minute rush to the polls in 2000. The assumption that voters go to the poll at an even rate during the last hour implies 1/6 of the 1/12 total voters went to the polls in the last ten minutes. This figure is about 4,200 voters for the panhandle (1/72 of the approximately 300,000 panhandle voters that day). If *all* of those voters were Bush voters and they *all* gave up and returned home when the media called the election for Gore, that would imply 4,200 lost votes for Bush. As Brady goes on to observe, however, even the 4,200 figure is implausible since only a fraction of the 4,200 would-be voters were likely to have heard about the projection, and not all of them were Bush voters in any case. On the basis of plausible assumptions about what fraction of the 4,200 voters heard the announcement and, of that group, what fraction were Bush voters who would have been dissuaded from voting, Brady (p. 270) concludes that the upper bound for Bush's vote loss was 224—a far cry from 10,000.

As Brady (p. 270) observes, although his detective work uses quantitative data, it uses methods typically more characteristic of qualitative research. "It tries to approach the problem in several different ways, cross-checking information at every turn, and asking if the posited causal effect is probable, or even possible, given what we know from many different sources." The lesson for quantitative researchers, Brady (p. 271) writes, "is the necessity of paying attention to the causal processes underlying behavior. Otherwise, regression analysis is likely to go off the rails."

Using Ethnographic Data to Help Interpret Survey Results

Social scientists often specialize either as quantitative researchers or as qualitative researchers. (There are further specialties within each, but the quantitative/qualitative distinction is the major divide: See Brady and Collier 2004, and King, Keohane, and Verba 1994 for recent discussion.) As a result, studies in sociology and the other social sciences tend to be either quantitative *or* qualitative. Although mixed qualitative-quantitative studies are becoming more common, they remain the exception in the social sciences.

Very often, however, a full understanding of some phenomenon of interest to social scientists requires both types of data. To advance knowledge significantly, we might need fieldwork as well as survey data, ethnographies and case studies as well as census data. In that regard, there are large-scale projects under way in the social sciences that involve teams of specialists collecting both qualitative and quantitative data. One example is an intensive study of the effects of welfare reform on the well-being of children and families in Boston, Chicago, and San Antonio—called "Welfare, Children, and Families: A Three-City Study" (http://www.jhu.edu/~welfare)—which features an ethnographic component (in-depth interviews and participant observation) as well as a longitudinal survey.

These big studies aside, the typically more modest social science study involving a single researcher or a small team of researchers could also benefit from the juxtaposition of quantitative and qualitative evidence. In this section I provide an example of how census and survey data, the staples for nonexperimental quantitative research in the social sciences, can benefit from the insights of ethnographic fieldwork. Of the many examples that could be given, I focus on the important and timely issue of racial and ethnic self-identity in the United States.

Race and ethnicity continue to serve as important sources of economic and social cleavage in the United States and elsewhere. Consider again the hotly contested 2000 presidential election in the United States. Although George W. Bush and Al Gore each received 48 percent of the total vote nationwide, that overall equality masks sharp differences across racial and ethnic groups. White voters, for example, favored Bush by 54 percent to 42 percent for Gore. By contrast, Asian American, Hispanic, and African American voters all favored Gore: Gore received 54 percent of the Asian American vote, 67 percent of the Hispanic vote, and 90 percent of the African American vote (cited in Luhman 2002, p. v).

While scholars have long recognized the presence and importance of racial and ethnic divisions in the United States, recent research underscores just how difficult it is to capture the complexity of race and ethnicity in a census or survey. Individuals' racial and ethnic identities can be very fluid. Multiracial individuals might view themselves as white in some contexts and as nonwhite in other contexts, for example. Mary Waters (2002) cites the example of one of her undergraduate students at Harvard who had been told by her mother that she is an American Indian with Irish, Scottish, and African American ancestry also in the mix. In filling out applications for college admission she had routinely checked all the boxes that applied. Upon her arrival at Harvard she began to receive mail from the African American Association. By contrast her identical twin sister, who had checked the same boxes she had, was being lobbied by the Native American Students Association to join their group. How could she and her twin sister, she asked, have different racial identities?

How indeed? Yet that is precisely the sort of situation many Americans face. The situation has important implications for census and survey data on race and ethnicity. Consider the case where adolescents report their racial identities differently at home and at school (Harris and Sim 2002). In survey analysis this type of inconsistency might be viewed as misclassification—that is, as *error* in the data. In the case of racial and ethnic identities, however, it is more fruitful to view such inconsistencies not as error but as raising issues to be probed further.

The issues to be probed involve the rules governing racial self-identities. What rules do multiracial individuals use to choose their racial identities? Why do children's racial self-identities sometimes vary from context to context, and why do they sometimes differ from the racial self-identities of their biological parents? And what does this tell us about race and ethnicity in the United States? Both quantitative and qualitative evidence is critical in our attempt to understand these vexed issues.

"Currently the social rule in the United States governing racial and ethnic identity is self-identification," writes Waters (1998, p. 29), and "For a large portion of the population, this involves some degree of choice." How large is this portion? For that question it is useful to turn first to survey data. David Harris and Jeremiah Sim (2002) analyze data from the first wave of the National Longitudinal Study of Adolescent Health (Add Health) for their study "Who Is Multiracial? Assessing the Complexity of Lived Race." The Add Health data set is ideal for such a study because it provides self-reported race data for parents, for adolescents at school, and for adolescents at home. By comparing parent-based race, school race, and home race, Harris and Sim find considerable fluidity in racial identity. For example, on the basis of responses adolescents give at school, 6.8 percent of them are multiracial. On the basis of responses they give at home, only 3.6 percent of youth are multiracial.

Overall, while 8.6 percent of adolescents gave a multiracial response either in the home survey *or* in the school survey, only 1.6 percent gave a multiracial response in *both* contexts (and, of the 1.6 percent who identified themselves as multiracial in both contexts, only 1.1 percent selected the same combination of two or more races at home and at school).

Ethnographic evidence is often vital for understanding patterns such as these. Consider, for example, Waters's (1999) ethnographic study of the racial and ethnic identities of immigrants from the West Indies (mainly Jamaica, Guyana, Trinidad, and Haiti). Her study is strategic in understanding racial self-identities since West Indians, though generally viewed as blacks by most whites in the United States, do not necessarily think of themselves as black Americans. In the early 1990s Waters began a study of West Indian immigrants and their teenage children in New York City. She was particularly interested in how these immigrants would balance their identities as West Indians and as Americans, and in tracing intergenerational changes in racial and ethnic identities for the immigrants and their children. From in-depth interviews with second-generation adolescents from various West Indian groups, Waters (2004) identified three broad "paths of identity development" that underlie West Indians' responses to questions of racial identity: some identified themselves primarily as black Americans, some as ethnic Americans (with some distancing from black Americans), and some as foreign-born individuals not beholden to American racial and ethnic categories. In her interviews of West Indians she also found, however, that "The situation determines the identity chosen by most people, and there is a great deal of ease in moving back and forth between different identities" (1999, p. 62). She found, for example, that most West Indians think of themselves as black when they feel threatened by whites, or find themselves in the minority. Or West Indians might adopt a black identity to conform to the majority, as in the case of the woman who recalled "being black by day and being West Indian by night" (Butterfield 2004, p. 298). This sort of detail is not easily obtained from standard survey data.

Other Examples of Multiple-Method Research

Multiple-method studies employ more than one type of analysis. Often these studies draw on data from more than one source as well. The key is that the multiple data sets and methods are used in a *single study*. Multiple-method studies differ from what I call *replication studies* in rule 4. Replication studies apply the *same methods* to *different samples*. In replication studies the aim is to see if identical analyses yield similar results for different samples of people. In multiple-method research the aim is to see if different methods lead to the same conclusions.

Multiple-method research has become more common recently in the social sciences. This trend likely has been encouraged by the migration of social science research funding from projects done by single investigators to projects involving multidisciplinary research teams. Whatever the reasons for its growing popularity, multiple-method research promises to be better research, if only because it permits more reality checks throughout the research process.

Many combinations of methods are possible, as illustrated by research appearing in recent issues of the *American Sociological Review* (Jacobs 2005). A study of Americans' changing perceptions of President Abraham Lincoln as a leader, for example, draws on data from diverse sources—surveys, the writings of leading historians, treatments of Lincoln in history textbooks, and even statues and memorials (Schwartz and Schuman 2005). The researchers conclude that, while Lincoln's reputation as a great leader has remained intact, the popular basis for that reputation changed with the civil rights movement, from "Lincoln as savior of the Union" to "Lincoln as the great emancipator."

In other studies qualitative and quantitative methods are employed in sequence, with one method building on the results of the other. Thus, for example, Brian Uzzi and Ryon Lancaster (2004) interviewed a small group of lawyers and clients before beginning their study of social ties and pricing in U.S. law firms, and Rodney Benson and Abigail Saguy (2005) interviewed journalists and others before conducting a statistical analysis of media coverage of social problems in the United States and France. Sometimes the quantitative analysis comes first. In a recent study of physical and sexual abuse (Cherlin et al. 2004), for example, researchers followed up a survey of over 2,000 families with a series of repeated open-ended interviews with 256 of the families over a period of twelve to eighteen months. Reports of abuse surfaced increasingly in the subsequent interviews. In this case, then, the follow-up qualitative component was key to obtaining accurate information on the phenomenon of interest.

Concluding Remark

In his critique of current methods in the social sciences, David Freedman (1991, p. 358) concludes that what we need is "reality tests instead of *t* tests." I agree, and in this chapter I described some possibilities. I do not have all the answers, and the examples I gave are intended to suggest and to provoke, not to be exhaustive. I do know this: We need to think seriously and creatively about how to incorporate reality checks more routinely into our research. I want this chapter to serve as a push in that direction. The next chapter pushes even further, by suggesting that we should strive to make replication—the identical analysis of parallel data sets—the rule rather than the exception in social research.

Student Exercises on Rule 3

This chapter has stressed the importance of checking and double-checking your data, measures, and results. You should look for ways to cross-check your results both internally—using other information in your data set—and externally—against other data sets. You should check for consistency between concept and measurement, and for consistency in the measurement of similar concepts. Most basic of all, you must be sure that your data are appropriate for the question you are asking or the theory you are testing. In this assignment we rework data from an earlier study where there is an apparent disjuncture between theory and data. The study involves differences in nations' income inequality.[4]

NATIONAL DIFFERENCES IN INCOME INEQUALITY

There are several well-established facts about the degree of income inequality within nations. One is that income inequality within nations generally does not change precipitously. Income inequality might rise or fall, but change tends to be glacial and may take several years to be noticed. (Exceptions occur in the wake of radical economic transformation, as we saw with the sharp rise in inequality in the 1990s following the fall of communism in East Europe and the former Soviet Union.) Second, differences in income inequality from nation to nation are, by contrast, quite noticeable. Some nations, such as Brazil and South Africa, have stubbornly high levels of income inequality, whereas other nations such as Sweden are characterized by much lower levels of inequality. Third, the causes and consequences of national differences in income inequality are hard to pin down. Economists, for example, have long debated whether income inequality tends to have a positive effect, a negative effect, or no effect on economic growth (Kaldor [1956] argued that inequality boosts growth, but later evidence suggests the opposite: Aghion, Caroli, and García-Peñalosa 1999; Benabou 1996), and political scientists and sociologists continue to argue about the nature of the association between democracy and income inequality (Bollen and Jackman 1995; Muller

---

[4] I thank Shawn Dorius for assistance in designing this exercise.

1995). One of the few associations that virtually everyone agrees about is that income inequality tends to be lower in communist countries than in capitalist countries. Apparently communist societies are successful in reducing economic inequality.

These facts provide the background for a reality check on the findings reported by Steven Stack (1978) for a cross-section of thirty-two nations circa 1960. The aim of his paper is to test "the Keynesian notion that the degree of direct government involvement in the economy should reduce income inequality" (abstract). Stack's central finding is a correlation of $r = -.74$ between level of income inequality in a nation and the nation's level of "direct government involvement" (DGI) in the economy. In other words, Stack reports that more than one-half ($r^2 = .55$) of the variance in income inequality from nation to nation is associated with variance in the level of government involvement in the economy, where government involvement in the economy is measured by expenditures of the central government as a proportion of total gross national product. The startling size of this association suggests the need for a reality check, since it is difficult to find anything that accounts for more than one-fourth, much less more than half, of the nation-to-nation variance in income inequality.

Note that what we are interested in here is national differences in income inequality among nations with market economies, not nations with centrally planned economies, since Keynesian theory bears on how government spending and manipulation of the money supply affects economic performance in *capitalist systems*. Quoting Robert Jackman (1980, p. 132): "If it is possible not to overstate the obvious, the Keynesian perspective addresses government intervention in market economies, as opposed to the central planning that is typical of the Soviet and East European economies." If this is a test of Keynesian theory, then, the $r = -.74$ correlation between DGI and income inequality reported by Stack (1978, table 1) ostensibly applies to market economies. The text of Stack's article reinforces that impression by emphasizing, for example, that the impact of government spending on income inequality should be felt through "the multiple reinvestment of money obtained from higher levels of consumption in job creative ventures in the *private sector*" (p. 883, italics added).

In fact, however, eight of the thirty-two countries used in the study had centrally planned economies in 1960: Bulgaria, Czechoslovakia, East Germany, Hungary, Poland, Romania, the Soviet Union, and Yugoslavia (Stack 1978, appendix). This is an instance, then, where the data do not match the theory because we have cases in the data that do not belong (Jackman 1980).

What we want to know is whether the results Stack reports were biased by including eight cases that do not belong in a test of Keynesian theory. Perform this thought experiment. Imagine there is little or no association between *DGI* and income inequality among market economies, so in a scatterplot relating income inequality (Y-axis) to *DGI* (X-axis) the regression line would be horizontal, or nearly so. Now add the eight non-market economies. We would expect now to see a negative association between *DGI* and inequality, since the nonmarket economies all fall in the southeast quadrant of the scatterplot (high *DGI* and low inequality).

It is quite possible, then, that the strong negative association between *DGI* and inequality would disappear, or nearly so, if we removed those eight nonmarket countries in the southeast quadrant of the scatterplot.

Your assignment is to find out if removing the nonmarket countries indeed removes the negative association between *DGI* and income inequality. Table 3.1 gives the data you need to complete the assignment (*N*=24 market economies). They are the data Stack used in his study.

Assignment 1 (for everyone)

Use your favorite package program (SPSS, SAS, Minitab, Stata, etc.) to do the analysis required to answer these questions. Recall that variable names are in **boldface** in the computer assignments in this book.

Question 1. What is the correlation between *DGI* and **Gini** for these twenty-four market economies? [Answer: *r*=−.16.] Does that correlation provide strong support for the argument that government intervention in the economy is associated with lower levels of income inequality in capitalist countries? Defend your answer.

Question 2. For the eight centrally planned economies included by Stack (1978), **Gini** for 1960 is estimated to be 0.17 for Poland, 0.20 for Czechoslovakia and East Germany, 0.21 for Bulgaria, 0.23 for Hungary and Romania, 0.26 for Yugoslavia, and 0.28 for the Soviet Union (Paukert 1973). The mean for these eight countries is 0.2225. On average, then, is income inequality larger or smaller in these nonmarket economies than it is in the twenty-four market economies? What is the difference in the average **Ginis** for the two types of economies?

Question 3. Use your program to produce a scatterplot *for the twenty-four market economies*, where the Y-axis is **Gini** and the X-axis is *DGI*. If possible, use your computer program to add the regression line to the scatterplot. Either way—with or without the regression line—print the scatterplot. (There should be twenty-four dots, one for each country; and the regression line should have a downward slope, since the association of *DGI* and **Gini** is slightly negative.)

TABLE 3.1
Data on Income Inequality and DGI for
Twenty-four Market Economies, circa 1960

	1960 Gini[a]	1959 DGI[b]
Argentina	0.42	0.170
Australia	0.30	0.180
Bolivia	0.53	0.161
Brazil	0.54	0.137
Burma	0.35	0.291
Denmark	0.37	0.214
Finland	0.46	0.301
France	0.50	0.400
Greece	0.38	0.236
India	0.33	0.139
Iraq	0.60	0.325
Israel	0.30	0.382
Italy	0.40	0.342
Japan	0.39	0.345
Netherlands	0.42	0.370
Norway	0.35	0.286
Peru	0.61	0.131
Philippines	0.48	0.092
South Africa	0.58	0.311
Sweden	0.39	0.391
United Kingdom	0.38	0.388
United States	0.34	0.210
Venezuela	0.42	0.272
West Germany	0.45	0.306

[a] The Gini is an index of inequality that ranges from zero for complete equality to 1.0 for maximum inequality. *Data source*: Paukert (1973).

[b] Direct government involvement in the economy, measured as proportion of total GNP. *Data source*: Russett et al. (1964).

Now place a "C" on the Y-axis where **Gini**$=0.2225$ (the average degree of inequality for the eight nonmarket or communist countries). Similarly, place an "M" at the proper location on the Y-axis to indicate the average **Gini** for the twenty-four market countries.

(a) On the basis of the relative locations of C and M on the scatterplot, and on what you see in the rest of the scatterplot, approximately how large would you guess **DGI** needs to be for the eight nonmarket countries to reproduce the $r = -.74$ correlation obtained by Stack (1978)? (Don't try to do any calculations—just make a reasonable guess, based on what you see in the scatterplot.)

(b) To determine the accuracy of your guess, add the eight nonmarket countries to the twenty-four market countries above, and calculate the correlation between *DGI* and income inequality for the thirty-two countries together. For the eight nonmarket countries, insert the **Gini** figures given in part 2 above, and the *DGI* figures that you guessed. How close did you come to reproducing the $r=-.74$ correlation when you insert the new data? Stop, if your correlation was between $r=-.72$ and $-.76$; otherwise, insert another value for *DGI* for all eight nonmarket countries and keep trying until you produce a correlation between $-.72$ and $-.76$.

(c) Do your findings cast doubt on the conclusions of the original 1978 study? Explain.

ASSIGNMENT 2 (FOR STUDENTS WITH A STRONGER BACKGROUND
    IN STATISTICS)

While it is clear that income inequality was (and is) higher in Latin American countries such as Bolivia, Brazil, and Peru than in Scandinavian countries such as Norway and Sweden, estimates of income inequality for 1960 are far from perfect. To gauge the consequences of this unreliability for correlations involving *Gini*, use the random number generator in your computer program to create a standard normal deviate R (that is, a normally distributed random variable that has a mean of zero and a standard deviation of 1.0). For the twenty-four market economies, use R to simulate the effect of measurement error on the *Gini* by creating three new variables, as follows:

- $Newgini01 = Gini(1+.01R)$
- $Newgini25 = Gini(1+.25R)$
- $Newgini50 = Gini(1+.50R)$

Note that each of the *Newgini* variables adds random error to *Gini* by multiplying *Gini* by $1+kR$, where k is a constant and R is a random variable with a mean of zero and a standard deviation of 1.0. You are adding error randomly to each of the twenty-four countries individually. Consider Argentina, for example. You are multiplying the stated *Gini* value for Argentina (0.42) by $(1+kR)$, where R is a normally distributed random variable whose average value is zero. Hence you expect the *Newgini* value for Argentina to be larger than *Gini* half the time and smaller than *Gini* half the time. The same logic holds for the values of *Newgini* versus *Gini* for the remaining twenty-three countries.

Because R is distributed symmetrically around zero, **Newgini** should be greater than **Gini** for about half the countries, and smaller than **Gini** for about half the countries. For all twenty-four countries, then, we expect the *mean* for **Newgini** to be approximately the same as the mean for **Gini**, though the two means could diverge quite a bit *due to chance*. The more measurement error, the greater the possibility that the two means will differ substantially.

The size of k determines the degree of measurement error. Thus **Newgini01** adds a trivial amount of measurement error to **Gini**, **Newgini25** adds moderate to large measurement error, and **Newgini50** adds quite large measurement error.

With these observations in mind, complete the following exercises, and answer the following questions, involving correlations (not just means):

Question 4. (a) Correlate **Newgini01** with **DGI** for the twenty-four market economies. Is the correlation larger or smaller than it was using **Gini**? (b) Repeat nineteen more times, using a new R for each trial. Calculate the mean of the twenty correlations of **Newgini01** with **DGI**. Is the mean of the **Newgini01-DGI** correlations similar to the original correlation of **Gini** with **DGI**?

Question 5. Now introduce greater measurement error on the income inequality measure by using **Newgini25**. Repeat the procedures you used for **Newgini01** to generate twenty correlations of **Newgini25** with **DGI**. (a) Is the *mean* of the **Newgini25-DGI** correlations similar to the original correlation of **Gini** with **DGI**? (b) What about the *variance* of the correlations: Do the correlations with **DGI** vary more with greater measurement error (**Newgini25**) or less measurement error (**Newgini01**)?

Question 6. Generate twenty new correlations, this time using **Newgini50**. (a) Is the *mean* of the **Newgini50-DGI** correlations similar to the original correlation of **Gini** with **DGI**? (b) What about the *variance* of the correlations: Do the correlations with **DGI** vary more using **Newgini50** than they did using **Newgini25** and **Newgini01**?

Question 7. (a) Random measurement error tends to reduce correlations in the bivariate case. We expect that, the greater the error, the greater the bias toward zero. Is that what you found in your simulations? (b) We also expect that random measurement error will increase the variance in our estimates. Is that what you found in your simulations?

CHAPTER 4

The Fourth Rule

REPLICATE WHERE POSSIBLE

Rule 4 is the *replication rule*. The replication rule is a natural follow-up to rule 3, "Build reality checks into your research." Rule 3 advises you to look for ways to cross-check your results both internally—using other information in your data set—and externally—using different methods and data sets. In multiple-method research, as described in the previous chapter, your aim is to see if different methods and different sorts of data lead to the same conclusions.

Rule 4 advises replication—the identical analysis (same measures, models, and estimation methods) of parallel data sets (different samples of the same population)—to see if you obtain similar results. In replication studies your aim is to see if identical analyses yield similar results for different samples of people. Hence rule 4 can be thought of as a special type of reality check, one that involves the parallel analysis of multiple data sets.

Note the qualifier "where possible" in rule 4. Often it is difficult to find one data set that meets your needs, much less several. For that reason it is still relatively rare in the social sciences to find single studies that report analyses of multiple data sets. Hopefully there will be more examples to cite in subsequent editions of this book.

Hence the chapter is forward-looking, focusing more on what can be done than on what is being done. The issues discussed should become more relevant in the future as the stock of good data sets increases in the social sciences. There is reason for optimism. Just a few decades ago cross-sectional analyses prevailed in political science and sociology, and time-series analyses of small samples were standard fare in economics, even though everyone knew that large longitudinal data sets generally are better suited for answering the sorts of questions that we ask as social scientists. Today cross-sectional and small-N time-series studies have been largely replaced by studies using larger samples and better longitudinal designs, such as the panel and repeated cross-section designs described in chapter 6. In the future we might expect the analysis of parallel data sets to become more routine as large representative data sets cumulate.

This chapter also serves to reinforce one of the major themes of the book—that progress in social research will come mainly from better research design, not from statistical wizardry (see rule 7). The parallel analysis of multiple data sets opens new possibilities, and we should be thinking now about how best to exploit those possibilities in social research.

Sources of Uncertainty in Social Research

It is easy to be lulled into a false sense of security about uncertainty in social research. We are very conscious of the possibility of sampling error and generally devote a great deal of attention to it in our research. Standard statistical packages all report standard errors, and we dutifully gather that information and report it in tables in our research reports.

The false sense of security arises when we forget about the other sources of uncertainty and assume that by ruling out sampling error we have ruled out all uncertainty. In many instances sampling error is not even the most important source of uncertainty in social research. Indeed, for very large data sets—which are becoming more common in the social sciences—sampling error becomes relatively less important as a source of uncertainty. Nonsampling error, by contrast, generally is not relieved by larger samples.

I want to make two main points in this chapter. The first is that we should take a holistic approach to uncertainty in social research. Robert Groves et al. (2004) describe the move toward a *total survey error paradigm* in survey methodology. The virtues of such a paradigm are apparent for all types of observational studies in the social sciences, not just survey analyses. We should aim to develop and refine a total uncertainty perspective that is based on all sources of error, not just sampling error. To be sure, sampling error receives a lot of attention in social research. We give it a lot of attention in part because we can: We have methods for estimating the uncertainty arising from the use of a probability sample. Other sources of uncertainty are harder to quantify, but they are often no less important than sampling error. We need to find better ways to gauge the effects of these other sources of uncertainty as well.

The second big point in this chapter is that *replication provides a means for gauging total uncertainty*. This is the triangulation point again, except that here the triangulation involves the same methods applied to different data sets. The juxtaposition of results from identical analyses of parallel data sets in a single study should provide more realistic appraisals of the uncertainty in our conclusions than do significance tests alone. If so, then comparison of results across data sets might become a standard feature of articles in social science journals in the future, just as significance tests are today.

It is useful to begin with an inventory of the sources of uncertainty in observational studies in the social sciences. Clifford Clogg and Aref Dajani (1991) identify six separate sources of uncertainty in the modeling of social statistics. "Our main point," they write (pp. 12–13, italics added), "is that we must seriously consider the uncertainty in inferences created along the way *by the data collection processes* so common in social research." Their thesis, and mine, is that uncertainty "crops up all along the way" (p. 16) in data collection due to numerous problems that are encountered, and decisions that must be made, in the process of collecting data. Thus even if there were no sampling error, the use of the same models and estimation methods across different data sets most likely would deliver somewhat different results. Any given data set, then, is subject to uncertainty about how much (if at all) the conclusions were affected by the data collection methods.

Where possible, then, it is important to compare results across data sets. Of course, we hope to find consistency in our results, since similar results across data sets increases confidence in our conclusions. Where we find inconsistent results, we must temper our conclusions accordingly, or find reasons for the divergence. In some instances we might be successful in pinpointing the major sources, and in other instances we might not be able to do so.

What are the sources of uncertainty associated with data collection?[1] For convenience I focus on survey data, but the general principles apply to other types of social science data as well. My accounting scheme relies heavily on discussions in Kish (1987), Clogg and Dajani (1991), and Groves et al. (2004). We want to focus on sources of uncertainty other than sampling error since methods for estimating and evaluating sampling error are already well known. In typical studies we know much less about the nature of the other sources of uncertainty arising from the data collection process.

Let me make the point as clearly as I can. Imagine we have two large probability samples (say of 100,000 cases each) of the same population. The samples are collected by two first-rate survey firms. Due to the size of each sample, sampling error should be minimal in either case. Yet the two data sets could yield different results even if they used exactly the same questionnaire. What might account for the differences?

[1] The problem of uncertainty due to data collection is independent of other major problems we face in social research, such as the problem of omitted variables bias (discussed in chapter 5). So error-free data would not solve all the problems we face in social research. Even with error-free data, for example, we would still need to find ways to compare like with like when making causal inferences (rule 5).

Overview: From Population to Sample and Back to Population

Consider two simultaneous surveys of the same population. An example would be a Harris poll and a Gallup poll just before an election in the United States. Even if both polls used the same questions and procedures, they might yield somewhat different percentages. We want to locate the sources of that divergence. By thinking through the process by which data are obtained in this simple example, we can better understand the sources of uncertainty in social research more generally.

The Harris and Gallup results differ, obviously, because they collect different samples. (For now we assume no measurement error. Measurement error is addressed later in the chapter.) So let's look more closely at the process by which a sample is extracted from a population. The extraction of a sample can be thought of as a successive process of exclusion, or winnowing. The population is winnowed in three steps (fig. 4.1). As figure 4.1 indicates, error can be introduced in each step. I will refer to the sum total of this error as *exclusion error*, since it results from the exclusion of individuals as you move from the target population down to the collected sample.

The target population is the universe you want to study, such as all U.S. adults. The frame population is "the set of target population members that has a chance to be selected into the survey sample" (Groves et al. 2004, p. 45). In the case of U.S. adults, for example, a sample collected by telephone excludes some members of the target population because they don't have a telephone. Likewise, a survey conducted only in English excludes Spanish speakers; a survey of citizens residing within the country excludes military personnel and others living overseas; and so on.

The next step, the selection of the sample from the frame population, is by far the most dramatic of the winnowing processes. In the case of the General Social Survey and similar surveys of the U.S. adult population, for example, millions of cases are reduced to a sample that typically numbers in the thousands. Because most of the exclusion takes place in this step, you might suppose that most of the exclusion error also is introduced in this step. As noted in chapter 1, however, *how* individuals are selected is more critical than *how many* individuals are selected. With the use of probability sampling methods, exclusion error actually can be less problematic for this step than for the other two.

Finally, there is the sample that is actually collected. Because some individuals in the selected sample may not respond—perhaps they cannot be located, or they decline to participate if they are located—the collected sample differs from the selected sample. (Even the U.S. Census Bureau is unable to elicit 100 percent cooperation.)

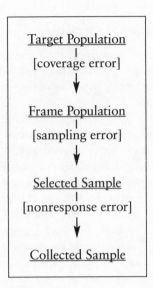

Figure 4.1. Sources of
Exclusion Error in Data
Collection

There is the possibility of error at each step, so each step adds uncertainty about your results. We examine this uncertainty for each of the steps in turn. It is convenient to consider the steps in reverse order, beginning with selected sample → collected sample, since as analysts our inferences move in opposition to the direction of the arrows. In other words, as analysts, we move in reverse order to the winnowing process, using observations based on the collected sample to draw conclusions about the target population.

SELECTED SAMPLE → COLLECTED SAMPLE: ERROR DUE TO UNIT NONRESPONSE

Typically the sample you obtain differs from the sample you selected because some individuals who are selected are never contacted (they might be difficult to locate, for example), and some of those contacted decline to participate. The failure of some selected units to respond (for whatever reason) is called *unit nonresponse* (Groves et al. 2004, p. 45) or *total nonresponse* (Kish 1987, fig. 2.1.1). It is important to distinguish unit nonresponse from *item nonresponse*—the failure of participants to answer particular questions—a subject addressed in the discussion of missing values in chapter 3. Although both involve missing data, item nonresponse is often addressed using data imputation methods, as described in chapter 3. In the case of unit nonresponse, however, there is no information about the person (with the possible exception of some basic information such as the person's gender and address) from which to impute values.

The most obvious problem with unit nonresponse is reduction in the size of the sample. This problem is easily remedied, though, by selecting someone else. In the case of limited funds, replacement may not be possible, so the final sample is smaller. If that is all there is to it—that is, if unit nonresponse results merely in a smaller sample—then the problem is fairly minor for studies with good response rates: At worst, unit nonresponse inflates standard errors somewhat due to a smaller N.

But that is not all there is to it. Unless unit nonresponse is random—which is unlikely—the collected sample will fail to constitute a random sample of the selected sample. As a result, unit nonresponse will introduce an unknown amount of bias in the collected sample. This bias can affect means, variances, and associations among variables (box 4.1).

The most serious problem with unit nonresponse, then, is that it tends to change the *composition*, and not just the size, of the sample. Change in the sample composition due to unit nonresponse results in what is called *nonresponse error* (Groves et al. 2004). Because nonresponse error is the result of bias in the sample—the collected sample is not a random subset of the selected sample—the solution is not a larger sample. Unlike sampling error, nonresponse error does not diminish with sample size.

The solution lies instead in reducing the rate of nonresponse. The lower the response rate, the greater the potential for nonresponse error, whatever the sample size. That is why survey research firms try so hard to raise response rates, and why prudent researchers try to gauge the representativeness of samples by comparing sample data with census data on basic demographic characteristics (age, gender, level of education, etc.) of the target population.

In sum: Unit nonresponse contributes to uncertainty in the results of social research. Because people can decline to participate, the problem is inherent in the collection of data on human subjects. Because nonresponse error exists independent of sampling error, it is neither reflected in significance tests nor remedied by larger samples.

FRAME POPULATION → SELECTED SAMPLE: SAMPLING ERROR

As noted earlier, the selection of the sample would appear to provide the greatest opportunity for exclusion error, since most of the members of the frame population are excluded from the sample selected. So long as exclusions are determined probabilistically, however, statistical significance tests apply. In this case, then, we at least have direct methods for estimating the amount of uncertainty introduced at this stage in the exclusion process.

Indeed, it is fair to say that error linked to sample size (sampling error) tends to be less formidable than error linked to response rate (nonresponse error). As a practical matter, sampling error becomes less worrisome in the social sciences as we accumulate larger data sets. Nonresponse error is a different matter. Response rates appear to be declining in the United States and elsewhere (Groves et al. 2004, chap. 6). Large samples or not, nonresponse error is likely to become more problematic if, as seems plausible,

---

Box 4.1
When Does Unit Nonresponse Produce Bias?

Unit nonresponse can affect estimates of descriptive statistics, such as means, as well as analytic statistics, such as regression coefficients. The conditions are different for means and regression coefficients, so I consider them separately.

- *Means.* The mean of some variable X is understated when those with above-average X values are underrepresented and the mean of X is overstated when those with below-average values of X are underrepresented. So estimates of the mean of X are biased when unit nonresponse is related to X. If, for example, the rich are less likely to participate in a study, then income estimates are biased in a downward direction; on the other hand, if the poor are less likely to participate, then income estimates are upwardly biased.

  If unit nonresponse is random, then we expect respondents and nonrespondents to be the same, on average, for all the variables. In that happy case we do not expect the means to be biased by unit nonresponse for *any* of the variables. Typically, though, nonresponse is not random. In the case where unit nonresponse is not random, the estimates of means and percentages could be either unbiased or biased for a particular variable, depending on whether those who participate, and those who do not, differ for the variable in question. Suppose, for example, that married people are more likely to participate in a study, but that political party identification is unrelated to response rate. In that study, then, estimates of percentage married will be biased by unit nonresponse, but estimates of political party identification will not be biased by unit nonresponse.

(continued on next page)

response rates continue to decline. In the foreseeable future, then, we anticipate that sampling error will become less problematic due to larger data sets, but also that the problem of nonresponse error will become more severe, due to declining response rates. That is not a good tradeoff for social research.

(continued from previous page)

- *Linear regression coefficients.* Unit nonresponse leads to biased estimates of regression coefficients when nonresponse is causally related to the *dependent* variable. Nonresponse that is related only to independent variables does not result in biased estimates of regression coefficients.

  To assist our intuition on these points, it is helpful to visualize how a scatterplot is "thinned" by nonresponse. Imagine a scatterplot of the X-Y relationship for a target population. To make this concrete, suppose income is the X-axis and happiness is the Y-axis. We want to estimate β_{YX}, the effect of income on happiness. To isolate the effect of unit nonresponse, assume the selected sample is a random sample of the target population (so any bias in our estimate of β_{YX} is due to unit nonresponse). Under what conditions will unit nonresponse bias our estimate of β_{YX}?

  To answer, consider how unit nonresponse thins the scatterplot. Suppose first that unit nonresponse is independent of income and of happiness. In that case unit nonresponse thins the scatterplot uniformly from left to right and from top to bottom, so the regression line is unaffected. In other words, unit nonresponse does not affect the estimate of the regression coefficient in this case.

  Now imagine that nonresponse *is* related to income, so the thinning is no longer uniform from left to right (for example, if the rich are less likely to participate in surveys, then the thinning of the scatterplot increases as you move from left to right). Does that affect our estimate of the regression slope? The answer depends on whether, at a given income level, happy and unhappy people are equally likely to participate. In other words, the answer depends on whether unit nonresponse is causally related to happiness, the dependent variable. If happiness does not causally affect response—so happy people and

(continued on next page)

(continued from previous page)

unhappy people are equally likely to respond at each income level—then the greater thinning of the right side of the scatterplot does not affect the slope: Nonrespondents (the missing points in the scatterplot) are equally likely to have come from above or below the regression line. Although our estimate of the overall mean of Y is biased, *at every income level* our estimate of the mean of Y is unbiased.

Suppose, on the other hand, that happiness *is causally related to unit nonresponse*—happiness independently affects participation. Perhaps happy people are more cooperative regardless of their income, for example. If so, we will tend to overestimate the mean of Y (happiness) *at every income level*. Moreover, unless $\beta_{YX}=0$, overestimation of the Y-mean will be related to X; that is, the bias will be more severe at higher (or lower) income levels. Hence the slope of the regression line is affected.

The same principles hold for bias due to coverage error. Coverage error leads to biased estimates of the mean of a variable X when noncoverage is related to X, and noncoverage leads to biased estimates of nonzero regression coefficients when noncoverage is causally related to the *dependent* variable.

TARGET POPULATION → FRAME POPULATION: COVERAGE ERROR

The frame population is only as good as the list from which it is derived. If we used a phone book to select our sample, for example, we would miss those who do not own phones as well as owners whose numbers are not listed. This would not pose a problem if our research was on behalf of the phone company, and they were interested only in the characteristics of customers with listed numbers. As social researchers, though, we typically are interested in a more general population, such as all adults in some region, not just people with listed phone numbers.

Exclusion error due to incomplete sampling frames is called *coverage error* (Groves et al. 2004). Lists are never complete, and even fairly complete lists are soon out of date, particularly in geographically mobile societies. Sometimes exclusions are dictated by the nature of the population. Consider, for example, the U.S. adult population (age eighteen and older). At first blush U.S. adults might appear to be an easy population to demarcate and sample. But some adult U.S. citizens are in relatively inaccessible places, such as in prison, or serving in the military overseas. Some do not speak English. Some are homeless and have no postal address. Hence obtaining a perfectly representative sample of the U.S. adult population is more complicated than it might at first appear. Survey firms have limited budgets. To get the most for the dollar, compromises must be made. The frame population for the U.S. General Social Survey, for example, consists of the noninstitutionalized English-speaking adult population. (Spanish interviews were added in 2006.)

In some instances, then, the exclusion is purposive, arising from budgetary limits, as in the case of the absence of institutionalized adults in the GSS frame population. In other instances exclusions occur because of difficulty in identifying the target population very precisely. Consider polls before elections, for example. The target population here is voters, since it is voters who will determine the outcome of the election. But voting has not yet taken place, so it is impossible to identify the members of the target population with complete precision. For our frame population, then, we want to use those who are most likely to vote. How do we determine that? One possibility is to use voter registration lists. But even if we had access to up-to-date lists, the lists are rarely complete, and some registered voters don't vote while others who aren't registered do.

In short, each of the steps from target population to frame population to selected sample to collected sample excludes people, and exclusion adds uncertainty. Some individuals are excluded because of incomplete lists for the frame population (coverage error), some are excluded because they weren't selected for the sample, and some exclude themselves (unit nonresponse).

While all exclusions add uncertainty, some exclusions are more problematic than others. The key is whether the consequences of the exclusion can be modeled, as in the case of random exclusion or some other kind of exclusion that relies on the laws of probability. Probabilistic exclusion results in uncertainty, but a type of uncertainty that can be estimated— that's what significance tests are all about. We could say, then, that probabilistic exclusion results in "manageable uncertainty" in the sense that we can at least quantify our level of uncertainty. Coverage errors and unit nonresponse errors, by contrast, are likely to be nonprobabilistic and thus more elusive. With nonprobabilistic exclusion it is more difficult to bound our uncertainty: We are less certain about the level of uncertainty.

Because conventional standard errors do not reflect nonprobabilistic exclusion error, conventional confidence intervals understate the uncertainty in our inferences (Clogg and Dajani 1991), sometimes dramatically so. From a total error perspective, it is important to go beyond sampling error to try to gauge the level of uncertainty. That is why replication is valuable. It is perhaps the best tool we have for providing a sober assessment of the total level of uncertainty in our inferences.

Measurement Error as a Source of Uncertainty

In addition to exclusion error, there are other sources of uncertainty that can arise in the process of data collection. Within surveys themselves, the greatest source of uncertainty involves question wording. An apparently innocent change in wording sometimes prompts a notable change in responses, so survey researchers are loathe to modernize the wording of a question that has a long tradition in prior surveys. When new wording is introduced (for example, changing the word "blacks" to "African Americans") the time-series is usually spliced by using two forms of the survey in the transition survey, with respondents randomly assigned to one of the two forms. In that way it is possible to determine if the wording change itself has affected responses.

The concern about precise wording is fueled by a number of famous examples in the history of surveys. In 1992, for example, a stir was created when a Roper poll commissioned by the American Jewish Committee was said to have found that 22 percent of Americans thought the 1939–1945 Holocaust never happened. Here is the question: "Does it seem possible or does it seem impossible to you that the Nazi extermination of the Jews never happened?" A subsequent poll, using clearer language, found that fewer than one American in 200 said the Holocaust "definitely" did not happen, and about one in 50 said it "probably" did not happen— presenting a far different picture from the earlier 22 percent figure.

Another potential source of uncertainty involves the general content and ordering of questions in the survey. For example, a question about tolerance toward atheists might elicit somewhat different responses if embedded in a general survey on tolerance than in a survey on religious beliefs. Moreover, respondents' answers to a question might be influenced by the immediately preceding questions. In the 1972 and 1985 General Social Surveys, for example, a question about general happiness was preceded by a similar question about the respondent's marital happiness, and Smith (1990) found that this ordering may have influenced responses to the general happiness question—a survey-context effect. In some instances, then, two surveys with the same question may elicit somewhat different results because *other* questions in the survey are different.

Responses for some questions might be particularly sensitive to world events at the time of the survey, resulting in another source of uncertainty. Responses to questions about suicide, for example, might be sensitive in the short term to highly publicized suicides, such as Marilyn Monroe's suicide in August 1962. This is also a type of context effect, but the context here is time, not the other items in the questionnaire.

In short, there are many sources of uncertainty in social research other than sampling error. Thus a preoccupation with sampling error alone is short-sighted; a greater premium should be placed on research that attempts to capture the total uncertainty arising from multiple sources of error.

It is time now for an example.

Illustration: Two Methods for Estimating Global Poverty

To illustrate the sorts of exclusion errors and measurements errors just discussed, I describe a current example from economics. The example involves the pressing question of how quickly the world's poverty rate is declining. It turns out that the answer depends on how income is measured. The decline in the world poverty rate (the percentage of the world's citizens who are poor) is steeper when you measure income using production data than it is when you measure income using consumption data from household surveys.

In this case, then, measurement matters a lot. Recent work in economics seeks to understand why (Deaton 2005; Milanovic 2005; Ravallion 2003; Triplett 1997). The issue is more than academic. Measuring the change in world poverty is an urgent task for the social sciences. Even casual observation reveals that many millions of the world's citizens live in abject conditions. The poorest poor in the world are immeasurably worse off materially than the richest rich. Yet comparing living standards across countries is a vexed issue (see Firebaugh 2003, chap. 3). Rich countries are those that have an abundance of valuable material commodities to consume. Poor countries by contrast are those that have a scarcity of valuable commodities to consume.

How do we measure material differences across countries? To simplify, let's suppose we can establish standard international prices for all goods and services.[2] That takes care of the problem of how to value or weight different goods and services differently. What remains then is to estimate the total *quantity* of goods and services available for consumption in a society. One approach is to focus on the production side or retail side, either by surveying producers to determine how much they have produced, or by surveying retailers to determine how much they have sold. Alternatively, you could focus on the consumption side. In

---

[2] Of course, setting a standard international price that fits all countries is a heroic undertaking. First, quality might vary across countries. Not all watches or shoes or radios are the same quality. It is hard to take quality into account when attempting to arrive at an international price for some good. Differences in relative prices are not a reliable guide, since differences in relative prices across countries might reflect differences in preferences, not differences in quality. Moreover, climate, location, and natural resources can affect relative prices. We expect bananas to be cheap in countries where bananas are grown and coal to be cheap in countries where coal is abundant.

this case you would survey consumers to determine how much they have consumed.

Using either approach, we find that living standards are improving for the world as a whole, as well as in most regions of the world (sub-Saharan Africa is the notable exception in recent decades). Typically, however, the production-based estimates are higher than the consumption-based estimates: Production data generally suggest somewhat higher levels of welfare *and* somewhat more rapid growth in welfare than do the consumption data. To shed light on the possible sources of these discrepancies, let us consider the consumption and production data in light of the exclusion errors and measurement errors described above. We begin with the consumption data.

NATIONAL EXPENDITURE (CONSUMPTION) SURVEYS

One way to estimate consumption is to ask people about their expenditures. The number of such surveys available to the research community has mushroomed in recent years. For example, Angus Deaton (2005, table 1) locates 557 surveys from 127 different countries that can be used to estimate average consumption or average income per person. There were only three such surveys collected in 1979, representing 9 percent of the world's population; in 1998 there were 57 surveys, covering 53 countries that are home to 70 percent of the world's population.

One source of uncertainty is measurement error in the household surveys. In contrast to the highly scripted surveys of national *production*, there is no strict protocol for data collection for national expenditure surveys. Hence discrepancies can arise due to measurement differences. In some surveys respondents keep a diary of their expenditures. In other surveys respondents are asked to recall expenditures. The length of the recall period might matter since respondents are more likely to remember

---

In addition—and most important—a country's price structure for goods and services is related to the country's level of economic development itself. Labor is abundant and cheap in poor countries, so labor-intensive goods and services (e.g., haircuts) are cheaper in poor countries than in rich countries. Capital, on the other hand, is scarce in poor countries, so goods that require more capital than labor tend to be relatively expensive in poor countries. Because foreign exchange rates are based largely on the trade of capital-intensive goods that disfavor poorer countries, exchange rates cannot be relied upon for setting international prices to compare living standards across countries. As a result, scholars have developed special currency indexes, called purchasing power parity (PPP) measures, based on prices from an extensive market basket of goods and services, not just on prices of goods that nations trade (Nuxoll 1994; Summers and Heston 1991). Almost all studies now use PPP measures for comparing material well-being across countries, in line with instructions in the United Nations *System of National Accounts* (1993, para. 1.38): "When the objective is to compare the volumes of goods and services produced or consumed per head, data in national currencies must be converted into a common currency by means of purchasing power parities."

more recent purchases. In India, for example, a split-sample experiment found that a recall period of seven days as opposed to thirty days increased reported expenditures by about 30 percent for food and about 17 percent for all purchases (Deaton 2005, p. 16). Surveys of household consumption sometimes differ on the number of separate items that are distinguished. In other words, there is no uniform list of items used in every survey. Surveys of household consumption might also differ on whether household members are questioned individually, or whether one person is permitted to speak for everyone. These are design differences that could affect results, especially in richer and more diverse households.

Even with perfect measurement, we would still face the problem of exclusion error, which in many studies is just as great a threat. Some national expenditure surveys avoid remote or dangerous regions of the country, and some exclude rural households altogether (Deaton 2005). Hence there is the possibility of substantial coverage error. Incomplete household lists exacerbate the coverage problem. Probably the most serious exclusion problem, however, is unit nonresponse. Unit nonresponse is especially problematic since those who consume the most (the rich) are the least likely to participate in an expenditure survey (Deaton 2005; Ravallion 2003); and among the rich who do participate we expect greater item nonresponse as well. Thus there is good reason to believe that most household expenditure surveys understate actual consumption.

In short, most experts believe that there is nontrivial bias in income estimates based on household expenditure surveys. Because people are more likely to forget items they purchased (or were given) than they are to claim items that they do not possess, expenditure surveys tend to understate income and thus overstate poverty. It is important, then, to find alternative estimates of income and poverty.

National production data can be used for alternative estimates. The two data sets provide the basis for just the sort of comparison we need to isolate the effect of data collection methods. The target population is the same in each case (all the world's citizens). The objective is the same (to measure the material well-being of the world's citizens). The key concepts coincide. Yet the data collection procedures are quite different; as Martin Ravallion (2003, p. 646) observes, data on national production and data on household expenditures "could hardly be more different in the way they are obtained." These data present, then, a strategic opportunity to illustrate in concrete ways how measurement errors and exclusion errors can result in discrepant findings across data sets.

NATIONAL PRODUCTION DATA

In the title of an article about measuring welfare in developing countries, Ravallion (2003) asks "How well do national accounts and surveys agree?" The term "national accounts" here refers to production data and the term "surveys" refers to consumption data from household surveys. Consumption data are collected from consumers. Production data are collected from producers, or from retailers. There is no standard consumption survey used by all countries, nor do all countries field consumption surveys on a regular basis. By contrast, virtually all countries attempt to estimate their total annual economic output using highly scripted methods developed by the United Nations. National accounts are compiled following the protocols spelled out in the 1993 version of the *Systems of National Accounts* or SNA93 (United Nations 1993). To the extent that national accounting practices differ across countries, then, the fault lies with uneven implementation, not with uneven standards, since the standards are set internationally.

Household or private consumption is estimated from national account data as a residual (Deaton 2005; Triplett 1997). Total domestic production is estimated for each commodity, then government consumption, investment, intermediate consumption, and net exports are subtracted out to estimate private consumption. Domestic food production is estimated by weighting the acreage of land under cultivation (from agricultural censuses) by an estimate of average yield per acre (from crop-cutting surveys). This figure is important because the food that is produced for home use constitutes a large portion of the total consumption in poor countries.

The key point to note here is that there are ample opportunities for error in each step of the estimation process (Deaton 2005). Let's begin with the estimation of total production. As defined by SNA93, production includes all goods whether they are exchanged or not, so food produced for your own consumption counts. In the case of services, however, exchange or work within the household, such as care of children, typically does not count. As societies become richer, within-household exchanges that didn't count before might be replaced by market exchanges that now count (for example, someone is paid to care for children), so the rate of welfare growth is likely to be exaggerated by national account estimates.

There are other issues that make it difficult to estimate national production, even for statisticians who are highly trained in following the U.N. protocols. One is the problem of economic activity that is concealed from authorities to avoid taxation or regulation (or prosecution, if the activity is illegal). Because producers typically have greater incentive than consumers to conceal such activity, concealed economic activity is expected to bias production estimates of income downwardly more than it does expenditure survey estimates of income. This difference between national account (production) and household survey (consumption) estimates of income is likely to be more than offset, though, by the failure of household surveys to include the imputed rent of homeowners. Homeowners of course avoid rent, and this important dimension of consumption is captured by production data but generally not by household survey data.

The take-home point of this example is that the national account and household survey methods—imperfect as they are individually—provide strategic independent estimates of economic well-being in the world. If the data yield consistent findings, that consistency cannot be easily dismissed as an artifact of correlated errors linked to the way the data were collected. Given the differences in the data collection procedures, the results on world trends are somewhat reassuring, since both methods point to rising incomes, and declining poverty rates, in most regions of the world. As noted earlier, however, production-based estimates generally (but not always) indicate faster rates of income growth than do household-survey-based estimates. The actual rate of growth in economic well-being is probably somewhere between the two (Deaton 2005). For such an important question, it is useful to have independent estimates, if only to give us some sense of the degree of uncertainty surrounding the estimates.

Toward a Solution: Identical Analyses of Parallel Data Sets

In this chapter I have argued that social scientists should place a greater premium on research that attempts to capture the total uncertainty arising from multiple sources of error. That is not an easy task. The most promising long-run strategy appears to be identical analyses of parallel data sets.

Imagine we had 1,000 data sets drawn from the same target population. (Usually we are fortunate to have two data sets, much less 1,000, but the thought experiment here is useful for clarifying key concepts.) We analyze all 1,000 data sets in exactly the same way—same variables, same models, same estimation methods, and so on. So we have 1,000 replications—1,000 estimates of the same parameters. If all 1,000 data sets are randomly drawn from the same frame population with 100 percent response rates and perfectly reliable measures for each sample, then our results will differ only because of sampling error. From the Central Limit Theorem for means we know that the mean of the sample means provides an unbiased estimate of the population mean. In other words the samples themselves are unbiased (in the sense that they provide unbiased estimates of the mean), so differences in sample estimates of the mean reflect only sampling error. The same principles hold for other population parameters such as regression slopes.

Now consider the more realistic case where response rates are less than perfect, frame populations vary across data sets, and there are survey context effects and other types of measurement error. In the (unlikely) event that these exclusion errors and measurement errors are random, sample estimates will provide unbiased estimates of population parameters but the variance of the sample estimates will increase. Even in the best of circumstances, then, we expect exclusion errors and measurement errors across data sets to add uncertainty to our results—uncertainty that is not captured by the usual estimates of standard errors (Clogg and Dajani 1991).

This is the sort of uncertainty that we want to gauge by replication across data sets within a given study. The explicit purpose of such internal replication is to provide a method for gauging total uncertainty arising from the data collection process itself. We want to compare results from the identical analysis of different data sets. We want the replications to be done in parallel, by the same researchers, to make the analyses as similar as possible.

Internal replication is especially useful in the case of large data sets where sampling error is not a major problem but other types of exclusion error could be. Examples of internal replication are nonetheless hard to find. Replication across data sets requires data sets with overlapping content. Understandably, funding agencies want to support new and unique data, not repetitive data sets. As a result the overlap of content across major social science data sets is often less than ideal for extensive replication work.

One solution might be to piggyback on surveys done by independent polling organizations such as Gallup and Harris. Ideally this would be done when different polling agencies are in head-to-head competition to make accurate predictions about a common target population, as occurs, for example, in the polls leading up to an election. By enabling identical analyses of parallel data sets, the addition of economic and social indicators to these simultaneous polls should provide leverage for investigating the effects of the nonprobabilistic exclusion errors discussed in this chapter.

As it stands now, however, it is hard to find studies that perform parallel analyses of different data sets as described here. Hopefully this mode of research will become more common in the future. In the meantime, it is instructive to consider a more common mode of research, called *meta-analysis*, which also uses multiple data sets in a single study. The aim in meta-analysis, however, is not the parallel analyses of a limited number of data sets but the averaging of effects across many data sets to obtain more dependable estimates of effect sizes.

META-ANALYSIS: SYNTHESIZING RESULTS FORMALLY ACROSS STUDIES

To gauge uncertainty, ideally we want to analyze different data sets in a single study because in a single study we can make every effort to run identical analyses across the data sets. Our goal then is identical analytic procedures, so that any differences in results can be attributed to differences in the data, not to differences in the way the data are analyzed. Of course, exactly identical analyses might not be possible across data sets. Hence compromises may be inevitable. Importantly, though, the researcher has control over those compromises.

As noted above, however, this sort of internal replication is rare; single studies typically analyze only one data set. Very often, then, to compare results across data sets we must compare results across studies—an *external replication* strategy.

In the case of external replication we might think of each study as a data point and use conventional methods for summarizing the central tendency and dispersion of the *effects* of interest. External replication has been formalized using a method (or a family of methods) known as meta-analysis. Modern meta-analysis was developed by educational researchers such as Gene Glass (1976, 1977) as a method for combining the results of multiple studies to arrive at a more accurate estimate of effect sizes. We might want to know, for example, the effect of class size on student achievement, and whether the effect varies across contexts.

The literature review—a longstanding tradition in research articles— can seen as a kind of precursor to meta-analysis. Meta-analysis involves much more standardized and rigorous procedures than found in standard literature reviews, however (see Cooper and Hedges 1994 for a handbook on meta-analytic methods). Whereas literature reviews generally present a narrative look at some subset of prior studies as a context for viewing results from a new study, in meta-analysis the prior studies themselves constitute the data. Thus the studies are codified according to categories such as size of the sample, the use of randomization, whether control variables are used, quality of the study, whether the study appeared in a peer-reviewed journal, whether the dependent variable came from the same source as the independent variables, and year of data collection. Because the studies themselves are the data, data collection involves locating all relevant prior studies, or at least the high-quality studies. Hence meta-analyses tend to rest on much more comprehensive reviews of the literature than one finds in most other research studies.

Meta-analysis is best understood by looking at an example. Consider the issue of nonresident fathers and children's well-being. There is some evidence that a father's payment of child support has a positive effect on his children's academic and social well-being, but that the frequency of his visits with his children has little or no effect. To address these and related issues, Paul Amato and Joan Gilbreth (1999) performed a meta-analysis of 63 studies. The first step is to demarcate the studies that qualify: "To be included, studies had to (a) include a sample of children in father-absent households, (b) present quantitative data on a measure of paternal involvement and a measure of child well-being, and (c) present enough information to allow the calculation of an effect size summarizing the strength of the association between the two variables" (p. 561). The next step is to determine a search procedure to locate the studies that qualify. Amato and Gilbreth used three computerized data bases (Sociofile, Psychlit, and Family Studies Database), and they supplemented the computer search with the literature review sections of the articles uncovered by the computer search. They excluded conference papers and dissertations, as well as studies published in non-English publications.

Because some studies reported data separately for boys and girls, the 63 studies included data from 100 independent samples. Measures of the dependent variable, children's well-being, were categorized as school achievement (for example, grades), externalizing problems (for example, misbehavior at school), and internalizing problems (for example, low self-esteem). Measures of nonresident father involvement were categorized as payment of child support, frequency of contact, feelings of closeness, and authoritative parenting (for example, listening to children's problems, monitoring school performance, helping with homework, providing explanations for rules).

Amato and Gilbreth used the product-moment correlation coefficient r as their measure of effect size (partial r for the studies that used control variables). Some studies reported effect sizes in terms of other statistics, such as regression coefficients or logits. In those instances Amato and Gilbreth used formulas from Hedges and Olkin (1985) and Rosenthal (1994) to translate the reported statistics into rs and partial rs. It is a simple matter then to calculate the mean and variance of the associations of each of the three dependent variables with each of the four independent variables. The associations show that three of the dimensions of father involvement—payment of child support, feelings of closeness, and authoritative parenting—are associated with positive child outcomes, with authoritative parenting having the most consistent positive effect. Frequency of visitation, by contrast, had little or no association with child outcomes.

Amato and Gilbreth employ several tests to gauge the robustness of their results. One concern is publication bias, or the "file drawer problem" (Rosenthal 1979)—the problem that occurs when researchers put their negative results in a file drawer rather than submitting them for publication. In the case of father involvement and child outcomes, one might expect that researchers are less likely to submit their findings when there is no association, and editors in turn might be less likely to accept a paper with null findings. The result then is publication bias favoring studies that find correlations between involvement and child well-being.

If only the largest associations end up being published, then meta-analyses of published studies will overstate effect sizes. To address the issue, Amato and Gilbreth report "fail safe N values" using procedures suggested by Rosenthal (1979). This statistic refers to the number of new studies that would be required to reduce a significant mean effect size to nonsignificance if all the new studies had null results. Amato and Gilbreth also compare the effect sizes for large and small samples. This serves as another check for publication bias, as follows: Suppose authors are reluctant to submit (and editors are reluctant to accept) articles in which results are not statistically significant. If so, it follows that published correlations should tend to be larger in small samples than in larger samples, since a larger correlation is required to attain statistical significance in a small sample. Thus larger effect sizes in published studies with smaller samples may indicate the existence of publication bias.

Quality of the study might matter, of course, and we would want to give more weight to the findings of the better studies. Amato and Gilbreth test for the effect of study quality by coding each study as 0 (no) or 1 (yes) on the following characteristics: whether families were selected randomly, whether the sample size is at least 100, whether the dependent variable had a reliability coefficient of 0.8 or greater, whether the study employed control variables, and whether the study used different informants for the independent and dependent variables. By codifying the studies in this way they were able to assess whether the quality of the study moderated the strength of the association between paternal involvement and offspring outcome. Our confidence that the effects are real is enhanced if we find that the better studies find the stronger results.

Finally, it should be noted that meta-analysis is not useful where a literature has gone off the rails. Recall, for example, the fatally flawed cross-country studies of foreign investment effects described in chapter 3 (where foreign investment and domestic investment were measured very differently). Meta-analysis would not have helped in that case, since conclusions were based on a fundamental misinterpretation of the model being estimated. A meta-analysis would simply have averaged the erroneous interpretations.

SUMMARY: YOUR CONFIDENCE INTERVALS ARE TOO NARROW

One key to the scientific method is the validation of one's results with repeated trials. In the case of nonexperimental social research, "repeated trials" often means different samples. Yet it is rare to see that type of validation in sociological research articles (though the findings might be replicated in subsequent research), and in my reading in the other social sciences it appears to be relatively uncommon in those other disciplines as well. I am hard-pressed to find examples of substantial literatures where parallel analyses in a single study have become an integral part of the research process. If my observations are correct, we will know that social researchers are coming to grips with the uncertainty issue when the reporting of identical analyses of parallel data sets becomes as commonplace in research articles as the reporting of significance tests is today.

Identical analyses (same measures, models, and estimation methods) of parallel data sets (different samples of the same target population) can yield divergent results due to exclusion error and measurement error. Of the "big three" exclusion errors—coverage error, sampling error, and nonresponse error (error due to unit nonresponse)—only sampling error is reflected in conventional standard errors. And measurement error is not reflected at all in conventional standard errors. As a result, confidence intervals understate the true level of uncertainty.

Unlike sampling error and measurement error, which often can be modeled using probability theory, coverage error and nonresponse error generally cannot be modeled or are very difficult to model. To gauge total uncertainty, then, we must often proceed inductively, that is, by examining more data. That's where internal replication—the identical analysis of parallel data sets by the same research team—comes in. Realistically, replication may not be possible for most social research today. But that should not prevent us from being alert to the possibility. Rule 4 is a call for social scientists to become more opportunistic regarding replication. Perhaps internal replication will become a hallmark of social research later in the twenty-first century, replacing today's norm of relegating replication to follow-up studies.

Student Exercises on Rule 4

The exercises below use data from the American National Election Study (ANES). ANES data are collected every two years around both presidential and midterm elections. Each survey is carried out in two waves, one wave before the election and one after the election. Much like the GSS, the ANES contains a multistage probability sample of noninstitutionalized individuals in the United States, age eighteen or older on Election Day of each national election year.

To do the exercises below,[3] go to the web site http://sda.berkeley.edu. As with previous exercises, the instructions below should generate all the statistics you need to answer the questions, making hand calculations unnecessary. Again, remember that variable names are in **boldface**. Note well: The student exercises at the end of chapters 1 and 2 use the same web site. The instructions below include only the key commands; I do not give step-by-step instructions. The format in the SDA web site might have changed somewhat since these directions were written, but you still should be able to follow the logic below to obtain the tables you need to answer the questions.

ASSIGNMENT 1: SHIFTING SUPPORT FOR THE EQUAL RIGHTS AMENDMENT (ERA)?

In 1972 Congress submitted the Equal Rights Amendment to the state legislatures for ratification. It read, in part, "Equality of rights under the law shall not be denied or abridged by the United States or by any State on account of sex." Approved quickly by several state legislatures, the amendment seemed headed for certain ratification. But in the mid-1970s conservative activists capitalized on growing opposition to federal governmental action and concern with the health of the traditional family to prevent ratification by the requisite 37 state legislatures. They did so by stoking fears that "equal rights" would further erode traditional gender roles, subject women to Selective Service registration and higher insurance premiums, and outlaw sex-segregated restrooms and organizations.

---

[3] I thank Matt Schroeder for assistance in designing the exercises.

One might think, therefore, that public support for the ERA declined as well in the face of these arguments. But the data are less than definitive on that issue, as we see from these trends in Gallup and Roper polls spanning the period March 1976 to June 1982.

According to the Gallup polls, the percentage in favor declined from 70 percent in 1976 to 62 percent six years later. On the basis of the Gallup series, then, it appears that support for the ERA in fact eroded over the late 1970s. But the Roper polls indicate no such erosion of support for the amendment (and perhaps even a slight increase in support).

Question 1. The question wording differs for the Gallup and Roper polls. Observe that the Gallup poll says that the Equal Rights Amendment "would give women equal rights *and responsibilities.*" The Roper question says nothing of equal responsibilities for women. Do you think the addition of "and responsibilities" in the Gallup question is the decisive difference that explains the divergence in the Gallup and Roper trends, or are there other differences in the polls that you think are more important? Defend your answer.

Public Opinion Surveys on the ERA, 1976–1982

Gallup Polls
Have you heard or read about the Equal Rights Amendment to the Constitution which would give women equal rights and responsibilities? Do you favor or oppose this amendment?

	3/1976	6/1978*	7/1980*	7/1981*	12/1981	6/1982*
Favor	70%	65%	65%	66%	63%	62%
Oppose	30%	35%	35%	34%	37%	38%

*Question asked only of those who had heard or read about the ERA.

Roper Polls
The various State Legislatures are now voting on an amendment to the United States Constitution which would assure women equal rights under the law. As I'm sure you know, there is a lot of controversy for and against this amendment. How do you personally feel about it—are you in favor of the Equal Rights Amendment or opposed to it?

	12/1977	7/1978	10/1979	12/1981
In Favor	67%	69%	69%	71%
Opposed	33%	31%	31%	29%

Note: Only valid responses are shown. Data provided by the iPoll Databank of the Roper Center for Public Opinion Research.

We find similar inconsistencies when we compare the ANES and GSS trends. Let's begin with the ANES. In 1976, 1978, and 1980 the ANES queried respondents on their support for the ERA (the variable label is **v833**): "An effort is being made to pass an amendment to the U.S. Constitution which would guarantee equal rights for all citizens regardless of sex. Do you approve or disapprove of the Equal Rights Amendment to the Constitution?"

- From the SDA homepage (http://sda.berkeley.edu), select "SDA archive" and then "ANES Cumulative Datafile 1948–2000."
- You will need to recode **v833** to exclude the "Don't Know" responses from your analysis. The ANES has included the "Don't Know" responses among the valid response categories, and researchers usually treat those who decline to give a firm answer to the question as missing.
- From the recode screen (found under "Create variables"), type in **era** for "Name for the new variable to be created." Type in **v833** under "Name(s) of existing variables to use for the recode." Be sure to select "yes" for the "Replace that variable, if it already exists?" option. For row 1 under "Output variable," type "1" for "value," "approve" for "label," and "1" for "Var 1." For the second row, type "2" for "value," "disapprove" for "label," and "5" for "Var 1." Under "What to do with unspecified combinations of input variables (if any)," make sure "Convert them to MD code" is selected. (This will automatically code the "Don't Know" responses as missing.) Then click on "Start recoding" to convert **v833** to **era**. You should have 4,589 valid cases.
- To cross-tabulate the recoded variable with survey year, return to the menu at the top of the home page. Select "Analysis," then "frequencies or crosstabulations." Because **era** is the outcome or dependent variable of interest here, enter **era** as the row variable and **v4** (year of study) as the column variable, and be sure to ask for the column percentages. Select "No weight" under the "Weight" drop-down menu. Under "Chart options" use the drop-down menu to indicate "no chart" (unless you want a chart). Leave the other options in "default" mode, as you have done in previous assignments. Click "Run the table" to obtain the cross-tabulation. You should have 4,589 valid cases, of whom 3,215 are in support of the ERA and 1,374 are in opposition.[4] Print out your results.

[4] Some readers might wonder why they are instructed to choose the "no weight" option for ANES. As discussed in the section on sampling in chapter 1, reweighting of the data is necessary to reconstruct the overall means and variances where minority populations were oversampled. (Recall that the GSS oversamples blacks in some surveys, for example.) In the

GSS Results

Next let's see what the trend looks like using the General Social Survey. In 1977 and 1982 respondents were asked "Have you heard or read about the Equal Rights Amendment?" For those who answered yes, the GSS variable **era** asks simply, "Do you strongly favor, somewhat favor, somewhat oppose, or strongly oppose this amendment?"

- You will notice that there are four response categories. To allow for an easier comparison with the ANES, collapse the **era** variable into a dichotomy scored 1 for "Strongly favor / Somewhat favor" and 2 for "Somewhat oppose / Strongly oppose."
- From the recode screen, type in **era2** for "Name for the new variable to be created." Type in **era** under "Name(s) of existing variables to use for the recode." For row 1 under "Output variable," type "1" for "value," "favor" for "label," and "1–2" for "Var 1." For the second row, type "2" for "value," "oppose" for "label," and "3–4" for "Var 1." Make sure to select "yes" for the "Replace that variable, if it already exists?" option. Then click on "Start recoding" to convert **era** to **era2**. You should have 2,765 valid cases.
- From the "frequencies or cross-tabulations" screen, enter **era2** as the row variable (dependent variable) and **year** as the column variable (independent variable). Select "oversamp—weight for black oversamples" in the "Weight" menu and retain the same options as in previous examples. Then click "Run the table" to obtain the cross-tabulation. You should have a total of 2,025 respondents who favor the ERA and 749 who oppose it. (If your numbers differ, you probably selected a different weighting option.)

Your results should show different trends for the ANES and GSS data. On the basis of the ANES data you would conclude that support for the Equal Rights Amendment declined sharply after 1976, from 80.8 percent approval in 1976 down to 61.3 percent approval in 1980. On the basis of the GSS data, by contrast, you would conclude that support for the ERA did not change from 1977 to 1982. (Note that the Chi-square value indicates no association between **year** and **era2** in the GSS data—in other words, there was no statistically significant change in **era2** from 1977 to 1982.)

---

case of the ANES data examined here, there are no oversamples, and the weighting scheme is intended instead to weight respondents as necessary to obtain a sample that looks *in the aggregate* like the U.S. population with respect to age, educational attainment, and geographical location. Because the provided weights adjust for nonresponse, using them would take away some of the heuristic value of this exercise.

What accounts for the large discrepancy between the GSS and ANES results? Two possibilities can be ruled out at the beginning. First, *sampling error* is highly unlikely. For samples this large, it is extremely unlikely that differences this big are due entirely to sampling error. Second, *year of measurement* is also unlikely. Consider the differences in the approval rates based on the ANES in 1980 and the GSS in 1982: 61.3 percent versus 72.8 percent. Although historical events could account for a shift of this magnitude over a two-year period, that appears unlikely here, since the Gallup results (above) show no evidence of radical swings in public opinion on the ERA from 1980 to 1982.

Question 2. (a) Describe the critical differences in the wording of the questions in the ANES and GSS.
(b) Describe the differences in the population actually surveyed. (Recall that the GSS question uses the filter, "Have you heard or read about the Equal Rights Amendment?" whereas the ANES does not.)
(c) Either difference—the difference in wording, or the difference in the population surveyed—could plausibly account for some or all of the discrepancy in the two trends. Which difference do you think is more critical here? Defend your answer.

ASSIGNMENT 2: ESTIMATED VOTE TURNOUT USING DIFFERENT
SAMPLING FRAMES

In 2000 the ANES experimented with drawing respondents from two different sampling frames. In the first method (referred to here as the FTF frame, for "face-to-face"), a traditional multistage probability sample design was used to select respondents for home interviews. In this design, large regions are selected probabilistically, then subregions are selected within the chosen larger regions, and so on, down to the household level. In the final step, a single respondent (an adult) is randomly selected from the chosen housing units. The FTF sample includes 1,001 respondents in the preelection wave. All FTF interviews were conducted in respondents' homes in face-to-face interviews.

In the second method, random-digit-dialing (RDD) was used to select respondents, and all interviews were conducted over the telephone. In the case of RDD, then, the frame population excludes individuals who do not have telephones. The 2000 RDD sample includes 806 respondents in the preelection wave of the survey.[5]

[5] For further explanation of the RDD and FTF designs used in the 2000 ANES, go to ANES 2000, click on "codebook" at the top of the SDA analysis page, then click "Introductions" in the left frame. Finally, click "Sample Design" from the introduction menu.

You will be investigating the consequences of the different sampling techniques for estimates of voting turnout. We want to see if sampling method and mode of interview (face-to-face versus over the telephone) matter. That is:

- If the same question is asked at the same historical time point to different samples of individuals, to what degree do the results differ if the respondents are selected using RDD and interviewed over the telephone as opposed to being selected using a multistage area sample design and interviewed in person?

The ANES asks the following question, denoted **v1241**: "In talking to people about elections, we often find that a lot of people were not able to vote because they weren't registered, they were sick, or they just didn't have time. Which of the following statements best describes you:

One, I did not vote (in the election this November);
Two, I thought about voting this time—but didn't;
Three, I usually vote, but didn't this time; or
Four, I am sure I voted?[6]

Use the Berkeley SDA web site to examine the differences in voting turnout between the two sampling frames described above. From the SDA homepage, click on "SDA archive," then go to the American National Election Study (ANES) 2000 data and follow these instructions:

- Recode **v1241** into a dichotomous variable, coded 1 for respondents who voted and 2 for respondents who did not vote, as follows: From the recode screen, type in **vote2000** for "name for the new variable to be created." Type in **v1241** under "Name(s) of existing variables to use for the recode." For row 1 under "Output variable," type "1" for "value," "voted" for "label," and "4" for "Var 1." For the second row, type "2" for "value," "did not vote" for "label," and "1–3" for "Var 1." Then click on "Start recoding" to convert **v1241** to **vote2000**. You should have 1,554 valid cases.
- Cross-tabulate **vote2000** with the sampling frame variable, denoted **v4**. Insert **vote2000** as the row variable (dependent variable) and **v4** as the column variable (explanatory variable). In the "Weight" drop-down menu, select "No weight." Use the options for previous

---

[6] The wording may seem a bit lengthy, but this is designed to avoid what survey researchers call "social desirability effects." Because people often feel ashamed to admit that they failed to vote, this wording aims to avoid falsely affirmative answers from these non-voting respondents by giving them other, less stigmatizing reasons that they might not have voted. And by calling attention to a specific election, they attempt to avoid memory recall errors by forcing respondents to think carefully.

exercises. Ask for column percentages and not row percentages (one decimal point will suffice unless otherwise noted). Check the box beside "statistics," and use the drop-down menu to indicate that you want three decimal points for them. Remove the check beside "color coding" and use the drop-down menu to indicate that you want "(no chart)" under "Chart options." Finally, click "Run the table."

• If you have followed the instructions properly, you should have 1,554 valid cases, of whom 1,182 voted in the 2000 election and 372 did not vote.

Question 3. (a) Suppose you want to use the ANES to determine voting rates in America—the proportion of adults who voted. What do you discover in the cross-tabulation of voting rate by method that complicates your task? In a paragraph, describe how the two samples differ in their *reported* rates of voting. In your description, be sure to note both the substantive and the statistical significance of the difference.
(b) Which method—FTF or RDD—would you suspect gives the more accurate estimate? Explain.

Question 4. Observe that the target population is the same for both FTF and RDD—voting rates for Americans—so we can rule out differences in the target population as an explanation for the observed difference in the FTF and RDD results. What, then, does account for the higher reported rate of voting among those interviewed by telephone? Let's proceed systematically by considering differences between the FTF method and the RDD method with regard to the frame population, the representativeness of the collected sample, and the likely measurement error. Consider each in turn:

Coverage error (differences in frame populations)
The RDD sample excludes those without telephones, who are probably poorer, less educated, and more transient than people with telephones. They would be included in the FTF sample.
(a) Is this type of exclusion likely to bias the RDD sample results on reported voting in a positive direction (over-reporting on voting) or in a negative direction (under-reporting of voting)? Explain.

Unit nonresponse (representativeness of collected sample)
The RDD sample has higher nonresponse—it's easier to refuse a phone call than someone at your door. (The FTF sample had a response rate of 64.8 percent in the preelection wave, while the RDD sample had a 57.2 percent response rate.) Suppose this excludes the poor and less educated (those who are less likely to vote) more than the FTF sample does.

(b) Is this type of exclusion likely to bias the RDD versus FTF results on reported voting in a positive direction for RDD (higher reported rates of voting in RDD) or in a negative direction for RDD (lower reported voting in RDD)? Explain.

(c) Additionally, the FTF sample may find it harder to reach the relatively well-off and older people who live in gated communities, further differentiating the composition of the two samples. This type of exclusion is likely to exacerbate the difference in the RDD and FTF reported rates of voting. Explain why this is the case.

Measurement error

(d) People interviewed over the telephone may give less thought to the question, or it might be easier to lie over the telephone. Is this type of measurement error likely to bias the RDD versus FTF results on reported voting in a positive direction for RDD (higher reported rates of voting in RDD) or in a negative direction for RDD (lower reported voting in RDD)? Explain.

ASSIGNMENT 3: COMPARING RDD AND FTF SAMPLES TO CENSUS DATA

In assignment 2 we hypothesized that a sample based on random digit dialing is likely to over-represent the more educated. If so, our estimate of vote turnout is likely to be inflated or "upwardly biased" in the RDD sample, since there is a strong positive association between education and voting in the United States. The FTF estimate of voting rate may well be upwardly biased as well, since Americans are reluctant to admit that they did not vote. But we expect the upward bias to be greater in the RDD sample than in the FTF sample.

Now we test those hypotheses. Let's begin by comparing the proportion of college graduates in the FTF and RDD samples. If both samples are representative, then of course the proportions should be roughly the same. Are they?

- Using the ANES data file for 2000, first recode **v913** (the ANES variable for highest degree earned) into a dichotomous variable coded 1 for respondents with a college degree and 2 for respondents without a college degree. From the recode screen, type in **college** for "name for the new variable to be created." Type in **v913** under "Name(s) of existing variables to use for the recode." For row 1 under "Output variable," type "1" for "value," "college degree" for "label," and "6–7" for "Var 1." For the second row, type "2" for "value," "no college degree" for "label," and "1–5" for "Var 1." Then click on

"Start recoding" to convert **v913** to **college**. You should have 1,800 valid cases, of whom 556 have college degrees.
- Cross-tabulate **college** with **v4** (sampling frame). Enter **college** as the row variable and **v4** as the column variable (explanatory variable). Use the same options as above. Be sure to specify "No weight."

Question 5. (a) A higher proportion of respondents in the telephone sample are college graduates. Is that likely to be due to sampling error? (Use the .05 level of significance.)

(b) Give at least two reasons why the reported education level is higher in the RDD sample than in the FTF sample. Remember that discrepancies can be due to differences in the frame population, differences in response rates, and/or measurement error. Make sure that the reasons you give for the higher reported education in the telephone sample are consistent with the arguments you made in assignment 2.

Question 6. As noted in this chapter, you can assess the representativeness of a sample by comparing your sample data with census data (or other high-quality data) on key variables. According to the U.S. Census Bureau, about 22.3 percent of the U.S. population eighteen years of age or older possessed college degrees in 2000, while about 67.4 percent of eligible Americans voted in the 2000 presidential election.

(a) In one paragraph, compare the FTF and RDD results to the census figures for education and voting.

(b) Were you surprised that the RDD estimates are farther off than the FTF estimates? Did you expect the FTF and RDD estimates to be closer to the census estimates than they were, or did you expect them to be even farther off the mark?

CHAPTER 5

The Fifth Rule

COMPARE LIKE WITH LIKE

This chapter examines causal inference, an issue of rekindled interest lately in the social sciences. The relevant literature on causal analysis in nonexperimental social research spans statistics, economics, political science, and sociology. This literature is far too extensive to cover completely in a single chapter, and the flowering of recent work in this area makes it hard to keep up (see "selected further reading" at the end of this chapter for a few useful references). It is possible, however, to spell out the fundamental logic and principles of causal inference. That is my goal in this chapter.[1]

I want to stress four points at the outset. First, the term *cause* is used in a probabilistic sense when applied to human outcomes. In this chapter I use the example of smoking and lung cancer: When we say that smoking causes cancer, we mean that smoking *increases the risk* of contracting lung cancer. We do not mean that all smokers contract lung cancer, nor do we mean that smokers are the only ones who are susceptible to lung cancer.

Second, the search for causal relationships is not the only reason for doing social research. The objective of social research may be descriptive—to get the facts right. Even if our ultimate objective is to estimate causal effects, accurate description is vital, since questions of *what* come before questions of *why* or *how*. Often half the battle involves determining precisely what it is to be explained. With regard to rising income inequality in the United States, for example, is the dilation of incomes occurring primarily at the top, at the middle, or at the bottom of the income distribution? Policymakers want to know the answers to these and other questions, if only to fashion policies to ameliorate the consequences of the trends. If incomes are skyrocketing for the rich and stagnating for everyone else, that knowledge can be useful for fashioning tax policies, even if we do not fully understand the reasons for the rising inequality.

---

[1] To simplify the discussion in this chapter, I assume that causal effects are the same for everyone. See Winship and Morgan (1999) and Moffitt (2005) for good overviews of literature that relaxes the constant-effects assumption.

Third, the search for causal relationships is a reasonable enterprise in the social sciences. As social scientists we would like to understand what is causing the rise in inequality, for example. Causes are important for policymakers as well; otherwise, policies are restricted to addressing the consequences rather than addressing the causes. And social scientists do have tools that can be effective in investigating causal relationships.

Fourth, I agree with those who argue that it is time to consider alternatives to the standard regression approach to causal inference. The methods I describe in this chapter are widely applicable. They may require particular types of data, but generally they do not require sophisticated statistical techniques to execute. Their practical simplicity suggests that as social scientists we can strive to do better than business-as-usual analysis in which we measure all the variables we can, put them in a regression equation, and hope that we haven't omitted anything important.

We can do better, and we should do better. *Although there are no magic bullets for estimating causal effects in observational data, there is a cardinal rule: Compare like with like.* It is time to employ alternatives to the standard regression approach to causal inference precisely because standard regression is a relatively blunt tool for comparing like with like. The next section explains the logic behind the compare-like-with-like rule for causal inference.

CORRELATION AND CAUSALITY

The first law of causality that students are taught in introductory statistic classes is "No causation without correlation." Causality, then, implies correlation. But the reverse is not true, as students learn from the second law—"Correlation does not prove causation." Thus students are sternly warned: "Thou shalt not infer causation from correlation."

Many homespun examples can be given of the second law. There is, for example, a nearly perfect correlation between length of individuals' right and left legs. Yet we would not conclude that the length of the right leg causes the length of the left leg, or vice versa. Nor would we infer that the absence of gray hair is causally related to having babies, even though we observe that women without gray hair are more likely to have babies than women with gray hair.

The classic textbook example of a noncausal correlation is a reported positive association between presence of storks and presence of babies. In one version there is said to be a significant positive relationship between the prevalence of nesting storks and the prevalence of human births in villages in southern Germany (the explanation being that houses with a newborn are preferred by nesting storks because they tend to be warmer). It is hard to know whether or not such accounts are apoc-ryphal, since they very often are inadequately documented (an exception is Matthews [2000], who finds a highly significant correlation between stork populations and human birth rates across Europe). Apocryphal or not, the accounts illustrate the point that two variables could be corre-lated because they share a cause rather than because one variable causes the other.

Many other examples could be given as well, such as the positive sta-tistical correlation between number of churches and number of bars in a city. Before trying to determine whether it is bars that cause churches or churches that cause bars, it is important to note that larger cities naturally have both more bars and more churches. The point is that the correlation between number of bars and number of churches in a city reflects a com-mon cause, population of the city. Figure 5.1 represents this situation, where $P \to Y$ means P causes Y, $P \to X$ means P causes X, and the εs are error terms reflecting the other causes of X and Y. The absence of an ar-row from X to Y indicates that X does not cause Y (nor does Y cause X)—bars do not cause churches, nor do churches cause bars.

By the phrase "X causes Y" I mean that individuals (or firms or nations or whatever you are studying) with higher levels of X have different levels of Y than they would have had otherwise (with lower levels of X). This is known as the *counterfactual approach to causal inference* (Morgan 2001; Morgan and Winship 2007; Winship and Morgan 1999) because it concep-tualizes causality in terms of a counterfactual situation: Would Y differ for individuals with $X=1$ if they instead had value $X=0$? In the language of experiments, the question is whether Y would differ for the treatment group ($X=1$) had individuals in the treatment group been in the control group instead ($X = 0$).

Consider the issue of whether cigarette smoking causes lung cancer. When we say that smoking causes cancer, we mean that smokers have higher rates of lung cancer than if they had not smoked. Evidence dating

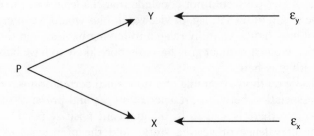

Figure 5.1. Correlation of X and Y Is Due to Common Cause P

from nearly a century ago finds a *correlation* between smoking and cancer. In the *New England Journal of Medicine* in 1928, Drs. Herbert Lombard and Carl Doering report results from a comparison of 217 cancer patients with a matched control group of 217 individuals without cancer, where individuals in the control group were matched to individuals in the cancer group on the basis of age and sex. No differences were found between the cancer and control groups with regard to their contact with other people who have cancer (to test the contagion theory of cancer), their housing conditions (to test whether cancer is spread by creatures such as rats—the vermin theory of cancer), their use of laxatives (to test the constipation theory of cancer), their diet, alcohol use, height, or even the history of cancer in their families (a family history of cancer was somewhat more common in the cancer group, but the difference was not statistically significant). The two groups differed significantly only in terms of smoking behavior, leading Lombard and Doering (p. 486) to conclude that "heavy smoking has some relation to cancer in general."

A second landmark study on the possible danger of smoking appeared a decade later in *Science*. Raymond Pearl, a medical statistician at Johns Hopkins, had carefully maintained health records of hundreds of families in the Baltimore area. Unlike the retrospective Lombard-Doering study, the Pearl study was prospective, following 6,813 subjects over time (Pearl 1938). Thus Pearl was able to construct life tables, which he did separately for heavy smokers, moderate smokers, and nonsmokers. The results were unequivocal: At every age from thirty to ninety, heavy smokers had lower survival rates than moderate smokers, who in turn had lower survival rates than nonsmokers (for example, only 46 percent of heavy smokers lived past age sixty, compared to 67 percent of nonsmokers).

The Pearl study was followed by two much larger prospective studies of smoking and lung cancer, one in England and one in the United States. In England, Richard Doll and Bradford Hill sent questionnaires about smoking habits to all 60,000 members of the medical profession, receiving replies from about 40,000. Then, using data from the British registration system, they calculated death rates from lung cancer for smokers and nonsmokers over ensuing years. The results were astounding: For men, the death rate from lung cancer was 24 times higher for heavy smokers than for nonsmokers (Brown 1972). In the United States, Cuyler Hammond and Daniel Horn collected smoking data on 200,000 men ages 50–69. On the basis of data from death certificates, Hammond and Horn reported results very similar to the Doll-Hill findings: Over the next four years, the death rate from lung cancer was 23.4 times higher for heavy smokers than for nonsmokers.

With the mounting evidence of a large and robust statistical correlation between smoking and cancer, in 1952 the *Reader's Digest* published "Cancer by the Carton," an influential article warning of the dangers of smoking. As other periodicals followed suit and the public began to question whether smoking is as benign as previously thought, tobacco companies responded with "A Frank Statement to Cigarette Smokers" that appeared in the *New York Times* and over four hundred other newspapers on January 4, 1954 (see box 5.1).

Box 5.1
A Frank Statement to Cigarette Smokers

As it appeared in the *New York Times* and
over 400 other newspapers on January 4, 1954

Recent reports on experiments with mice have given wide publicity to a theory that cigarette smoking is in some way linked with lung cancer in human beings.

Although conducted by doctors of professional standing, these experiments are not regarded as conclusive in the field of cancer research. However, we do not believe that any serious medical research, even though its results are inconclusive, should be disregarded or lightly dismissed.

At the same time, we feel it is in the public interest to call attention to the fact that eminent doctors and research scientists have publicly questioned the claimed significance of these experiments.

Distinguished authorities point out:

1. That medical research of recent years indicates many possible causes of lung cancer.
2. That there is no agreement among the authorities regarding what the cause is.
3. That there is no proof that cigarette smoking is one of the causes.
4. That statistics purporting to link cigarette smoking with the disease could apply with equal force to any one of many other aspects of modern life. Indeed the validity of the statistics themselves is questioned by numerous scientists.

We accept an interest in people's heath as a basic responsibility, paramount to every other consideration in our business.

(continued on next page)

In light of what we know now about the close link between smoking and lung cancer, it might be hard to imagine such a "frank statement" appearing in today's leading media, even were such advertising allowed. We must remember that, a half century ago, the case against smoking was based almost entirely on statistical associations that were open to alternative interpretations. Hence tobacco companies were not out of line in

(continued from previous page)

We believe the products we make are not injurious to health.

We always have and always will cooperate closely with those whose task it is to safeguard the public health. For more than 300 years tobacco has given solace, relaxation, and enjoyment to mankind. At one time or another during those years critics have held it responsible for practically every disease of the human body. One by one these charges have been abandoned for lack of evidence.

Regardless for the record of the past, the fact that cigarette smoking today should even be suspected as a cause of a serious disease is a matter of deep concern to us.

Many people have asked us what we are doing to meet the public's concern aroused by the recent reports. Here is the answer:

1. We are pledging aid and assistance to the research effort into all phases of tobacco use and health. This joint financial aid will of course be in addition to what is already being contributed by individual companies.

2. For this purpose we are establishing a joint industry group consisting initially of the undersigned. This group will be known as TOBACCO INDUSTRY RESEARCH COMMITTEE.

3. In charge of the research activities of the Committee will be a scientist of unimpeachable integrity and national repute. In addition there will be an Advisory Board of scientists disinterested in the cigarette industry. A group of distinguished men from medicine, science, and education will be invited to serve on this Board. These scientists will advise the Committee on its research activities.

This statement is being issued because we believe the people are entitled to know where we stand on this matter and what we intend to do about it.

(continued on next page)

1954 to note that "there is no proof that smoking is one of the causes [of lung cancer]." As late as 1959 the eminent and colorful statistician Sir Ronald A. Fisher published a book emphasizing that, in the absence of randomized experiments with human subjects, the correlation of smoking

(continued from previous page)

THE AMERICAN TOBACCO COMPANY, INC.
Paul M. Hahn, President

BURLEY TOBACCO GROWERS COOPERATIVE ASSOCIATION
John W. Jones, President

PHILLIP MORRIS & CO. LTD., INC.
O. Parker McComas, President

BENSON & HEDGES
Joseph F. Cullman, Jr., President
LARUS & BROTHER COMPANY, INC.
W. T. Reed, Jr., President

R. J. REYNOLDS TOBACCO COMPANY
E. A. Darr, President

BRIGHT BELT WAREHOUSE ASSOCIATION
F. S. Royster, President

P. LORILLARD COMPANY
Herbert A. Kent, Chairman

STEPHANO BROTHERS, INC.
C. S. Stephano, D'Sc., Director of Research

BROWN & WILLIAMSON TOBACCO CORPORATION
Timothy V. Hartnett, President

MARLYAND TOBACCO GROWERS ASSOCIATION
Samuel C. Linton, General Manager

TOBACCO ASSOCIATES, INC.
(An organization of free-owned tobacco growers)
J. B. Hutson, President.

BURLEY AUCTION WAREHOUSE ASSOCIATION
Albert Clay, President

UNITED STATES TOBACCO COMPANY
J. W. Peterson, President

---

and cancer does not prove that smoking causes lung cancer (Fisher 1959, cited in Brown 1972). Fisher's essential argument is captured in figure 5.1 above: Some hereditary factor P might predispose some individuals both to smoke *and* to contract lung cancer. Of course, the search for P (hereditary predisposition toward smoking and lung cancer) has proved elusive in the decades since Fisher, and now almost all agree that the evidence is overwhelming that smoking in fact is a causal factor with regard to lung cancer.[2]

Consider again the counterfactual approach to causal inference in light of the smoking-cancer controversy. What we really want to know, for causality, is whether smokers would have had lower cancer rates had they not smoked (and whether nonsmokers would have had higher cancer rates had they smoked). Again, the counterfactual approach is probabilistic: It does not say that if you smoke, you will get lung cancer, nor does it rule out lung cancer among nonsmokers. Rather, to say that smoking causes lung cancer is to say that smoking increases the risk of lung cancer, so individuals who smoke are in greater jeopardy of contracting lung cancer than if they had not smoked.

To take another example, if college education has a positive causal effect on earnings, then the college-educated have higher levels of earnings than they would have had if they were not college-educated. Note the difference between this statement and the finding that there is a positive correlation between college education and earnings. In the correlation between college and earnings we are comparing the earnings of the college-educated with the non-college-educated—as opposed to comparing the earnings of the college-educated with their earnings *if they had not attended college.* The two comparisons would be the same only if we could assume that the non-college-educated earn the same amount as the college-educated would have had they not attended college. That is not a reasonable assumption unless (as described below) individuals are randomly assigned to college, so that the initial differences between those who go to college and those who do not are, on average, zero.

The fundamental concept here—that correlation does not prove causality—holds the key to understanding why it is important to compare like with like. Briefly, the logic is this: In social research we do not directly observe causes at work, but only the results of the causes, that is,

[2] As I write these words, the longstanding controversy over the fluoridation of tap water has been reignited by Harvard professor Chester Douglass's testimony to the National Research Council that there is no significant link between fluoride and osteosarcoma, a rare but deadly form of bone cancer. According to the head toxicologist for a Washington-based environmental group, "His conclusion that there is no link is a lie," and the group has filed an ethics complaint against Douglass (reported in the September 28, 2005 issue of *The Harvard Crimson,* online edition, p. 1).

we observe correlations among variables. To infer causality from those correlations, we must determine in general why it is that correlations do not reflect causality, so that we can know when a correlation between two variables *would* reflect a causal relationship between the two variables. Put simply, correlations do not reflect causality in observational data *because individuals are not assigned randomly to causes*. If individuals were assigned randomly to causes in the real world, then our work as social scientists would be easier because we would be much closer to comparing like with like. It would be much easier, for example, to determine the causal effect of a college education on earnings if individuals had no choice in the matter but were randomly assigned, some to attend college, some not. By removing individual choice from college attendance, random assignment to college would reduce not only the problem of obvious initial differences (such as socioeconomic differences between those who attend college and those who do not) but also the problem of more subtle differences, such as selection-on-Y where individuals self-select college in part on the basis of how much they are likely to benefit from it (resulting in what is known as *selection bias* in observational studies).

That is why random assignment is universally used in controlled experiments with human subjects. Random assignment is designed to compare like with like—we expect the treatment and control groups to differ *only* on the treatment X—so with random assignment to X we can *more readily* demonstrate causality from correlation. In other words, random assignment is the tool social researchers use in controlled experiments to try to thwart the second law of causality ("correlation does not prove causation").

Suppose, for example, that we have all power and no scruples, and we randomly assigned everyone either to a smoking group or to a nonsmoking group. No one is allowed to smoke before age sixteen. On your sixteenth birthday some random method is used to determine whether or not you will smoke. If you are placed in the smoking group you must begin to smoke one pack of cigarettes each day whether you want to or not; likewise, those in the nonsmoking group are prohibited from smoking, whether they want to or not. (We could of course vary the level among smokers—some are required to smoke one-half pack each day, some smoke one pack, some smoke two packs, etc.—on the expectation that heavier smokers are more likely to contract lung cancer than lighter smokers. The same logic holds. For simplicity, we focus on the two-group case.) If we find over a long period of time that the rates of lung cancer are higher for smokers than for nonsmokers, we would claim that smoking indeed causes lung cancer. We would base that claim on the assumption that the cancer rate for the nonsmoking group is a reliable measure of what the cancer rate would have been for the smoking group had they not smoked. That assumption is plausible since by random assignment we have alleviated the effects both of selection bias[3] *and* of initial differences between smokers and nonsmokers that might account for subsequent difference in cancer rates.

To summarize: The problem in estimating causal effects is that we cannot simultaneously observe X and not-X for a given individual. What we would like to have is a reverse-X universe in which, for example, smokers in our universe are nonsmokers in the other universe. In the absence of such a universe we attempt to simulate it. The most obvious simulation method is the controlled experiment, where the researcher randomly assigns subjects to treatment and control groups. But there are other methods, and the remainder of this chapter focuses on them. The idea in each method is to compare like with like.

Types of Strategies for Comparing Like with Like

The objective in causal analysis is to estimate a causal effect from an observed correlation. To estimate a causal effect from an observed correlation, we must compare like with like to rule out other explanations for a correlation between X and Y:

1. Omitted-variables: Individuals' differences on X are related to other causes of Y.
2. Selection: Individuals select X (or others select X for them, as in the case of tracking in schools) on the basis of expectations about Y.

In the classic experimental design we avoid bias, first, by *random selection of units* before the treatment X (to avoid selection bias) and, second, by *random assignment of units* into the treatment (to avoid omitted-variables bias). We also would like a large N, to guarantee that our chances of sampling error are vanishingly small. What we want, in brief, is a research design that *makes individuals in treatment and control groups indistinguishable from each other except for (a) treatment status and (b) completely random shocks to the outcome variable Y.*

So there are three key ingredients in causal analysis: random selection of units, random assignment of units (to a purported cause), and sample size. Chapters 1 and 4 addressed the issue of random selection of units,

---

[3] Selection bias here would mean that individuals base their decision to smoke in part on their actual propensity to contract lung cancer, which seems farfetched. In many other instances, however, selection bias is very likely in observational data, as in the case of college attendance (choosing to go to college is based in part on how likely you are to benefit from college).

and the sample size issue is addressed in those chapters and elsewhere in the book. In this chapter I focus on avoiding omitted-variables bias through the random assignment of units, or through some alternative strategy that mimics the effect of random assignment. Randomization is the means to an end; the end here is the comparison of like with like. Once the subjects are selected, how do we craft our study to try to make individuals in the treatment and control groups indistinguishable except for treatment status and random shocks to Y? The most common method is regression. Regression is a parametric approach, meaning that it tries to compare like with like by using estimated parameters to adjust for differences between treated and nontreated individuals.

Although regression aims, in a very general sense, to "match" on the confounding variables, other methods do so more explicitly by the pairing of similar units. The aim is to compare individuals in the treatment and control group who have the same or very similar values on confounding variables. One way to match individuals is on the basis of measured variables, using either exact matching or matching with propensity scores (described later). A second method is to match a unit on itself through multiple observations (for example, two or more observations per individual for investigations of causal individual-level effects, or observations on two or more family members for causal family effects). For this matching method, unlike the first method, we do not need to measure all the causal variables in order to compare like with like.

A third way to match is through random assignment to the treatment and control groups. Although random assignment is not always included in discussions of matching methods, the matching or "balancing" of treatment and control groups is precisely what random assignment aims to do. Indeed, random assignment is a particularly attractive method for matching because it harnesses the power of probability in the service of matching. To be sure, as researchers we are not always able to randomly assign units. Nonetheless, as we will see subsequently, it is sometimes possible to exploit naturally occurring random assignment.

Matching versus Looking for Differences

Before we consider various matching methods, it is important to note that, depending on our objective, we might not want to match cases in observational studies. If our objective is to examine a range of potential causes, then we want to compare individuals who are dissimilar, not similar, on those hypothesized causes. After we identify likely causes in this manner, then we estimate the *effect of a cause* using matching methods. Until we discover the likely causes, however, we generally want to restrict the matching to nonmanipulable variables such as age and sex.

Consider again the 1928 Lombard-Doering study of the determinants of cancer. That study compared a control group of 217 individuals without cancer with 217 cancer patients, where the two groups were matched on the basis of age and sex. Note that, contrary to the standard experiment, the "control group" in this case is a category of the outcome variable Y, not the treatment variable T. Moreover—and more to the point about looking for differences—the cancer and control groups were *not* matched on the basis of hypothesized causes of cancer. At that time it was thought that cancer might be linked to constipation, carried by vermin, or spread from victim to victim. If those theories are correct, we would expect to find differences between the two groups with regard to laxative use, housing conditions, and contact with cancer victims, respectively. To bring data to bear on the theories, then, we would not want to remove the differences a priori by matching on those characteristics.

The overarching point here is that we need to understand whether our objective is to discover the causes of an effect or to estimate the effect of a cause. If we want to know if T, U, and V are likely causes of some outcome, then we cannot match on T, U, and V. To locate the possible causes of lung cancer, for example, we want to know how lung cancer victims *differ* from those who do not have lung cancer. This harks back to rule 2, "Look for differences that make a difference," as well as to the first law of causality, "No causation without correlation." In exploratory studies, we do not want to match on potential causes.

If, on the other hand, our aim is to estimate the effect of a cause, then we want to match or "compare like with like" to eliminate the confounding effects of *other causes*. In the social sciences, regression analysis is by far the most common strategy for eliminating the effects of other causes. We begin, then, with the regression strategy.

THE STANDARD REGRESSION METHOD FOR COMPARING LIKE WITH LIKE

The standard regression method attempts to compare like with like by including the causes of Y as independent variables in a regression model. Imagine, for example, that Y has two causes, X and Z. To estimate the causal effect of X on Y, we regress Y on X and Z. Alternatively, we could estimate the causal effect of X on Y in two steps: First regress Y on Z and X on Z to create $\hat{Y}_i$ and $\hat{X}_i$ respectively (values of Y and X for individual i, predicted on the basis of Z); then regress $Y_i - \hat{Y}_i$ on $X_i - \hat{X}_i$. Because the residuals $Y_i - \hat{Y}_i$ and $X_i - \hat{X}_i$ are uncorrelated with Z, the effect of $X_i - \hat{X}_i$ on $Y_i - \hat{Y}_i$ is not due to Z. In other words, linear regression has been used as a tool to, in effect, "match" X and Y on Z. By including Z as a regressor, we attempt to compare like with like on Z through regression-based statistical adjustment (as opposed, for example, to a strategy that relies on random assignment to X to remove the confounding effect of Z).

Now imagine that Y has many causes, as is generally the case in social research. Consider the standard linear regression model in the social sciences, with measured causal variables denoted by X, unmeasured causal variables denoted by W, and random disturbances denoted by ε:

$$Y_i = \alpha + \alpha_i + \boldsymbol{\beta} \mathbf{X}_i + \boldsymbol{\gamma} \mathbf{W}_i + \varepsilon_i \tag{5.1}$$

Y_i is the value of the outcome variable for the ith unit (individual, country, etc.), and ε is a random error term that has a mean of zero and is uncorrelated with the Xs and Ws. The term α is an overall constant and α_i, a constant for the ith individual, is a term that captures differences between individuals that are stable over time and not otherwise accounted for by the Xs and Ws. (Although α_i and ε_i are conflated in cross-section data, they are distinguishable with panel data, as we see subsequently.) A bolded Greek letter denotes a row vector of parameters and a bolded Roman letter denotes a column vectors of variables. Thus $\boldsymbol{\beta} \mathbf{X}_i$ is a shorthand way to write $\beta_1 X_{1i} + \beta_2 X_{2i} + \cdots + \beta_P X_{Pi}$, where P is the number of measured causal variables, and $\boldsymbol{\gamma} \mathbf{W}_i$ is shorthand for $\gamma_1 W_{1i} + \gamma_2 W_{2i} + \cdots + \gamma_Q W_{Qi}$, where Q is the number of unmeasured causal variables.

The key feature of this model is the distinction between measured causes, the Xs, and unmeasured causes, the Ws. The model is very generally applicable to regression with observational data since we rarely can measure all the causes of Y. Almost invariably, then, you cannot estimate equation 5.1, and you might resort to estimating the truncated model:

$$Y_i = \phi_0 + \phi_1 X_{1i} + \phi_2 X_{2i} + \cdots + \phi_P X_{Pi} + \nu_i \tag{5.2}$$

Equation 5.2 represents standard linear regression (SLR). The idea is to estimate the causes of Y by trying to include as many of those causes as possible in the model. SLR is the canonical method in most of the social sciences; its use is ubiquitous in nonexperimental social research.

Critique of the Standard Linear Regression Strategy

The problems with the standard linear regression strategy are well known. We rarely know all the causes of Y, and, even when we do, we might not be able to measure all of them. By regressing Y on the measured causes (the Xs) while ignoring the unmeasured Ws, we in effect estimate the wrong coefficients. Instead of estimating β_1, the causal effect of X_1 on Y, we estimate ϕ_1; instead of β_2 we estimate ϕ_2; instead of β_3 we estimate ϕ_3; and so on. Using a regression method that yields unbiased estimates of the ϕs does not help us much, since the ϕs and the βs generally differ ($\phi_1 \neq \beta_1$, etc.) when the Xs and Ws are correlated.

So when the measured and unmeasured causes of Y are correlated, as is almost always the case with observational data, the SLR approach is problematic. The standard practice of regressing Y on its measured causes is, we say, subject to omitted-variables bias. This is all very familiar to researchers: We know that we are all too often estimating truncated models such as model 5.2, and we know that this isn't ideal since our estimates are subject to omitted-variables bias when the Xs and Ws are correlated.

The SLR model continues to dominate many fields of social science despite classic warnings about its limitations. Notable critics of standard regression analyses in social research include econometrician Edward Leamer (1983), who writes about taking the "con" out of "econometrics," and sociologist Stanley Lieberson (1985, chap. 2), who warns about the dangers of the usual control variable approach in regression models. As Lieberson notes, adding control variables willy-nilly or ritualistically, with little thought given to how their addition changes the interpretation of other variables in the model, can have disastrous consequences.

Some observers go further in their criticism of standard regression in social research. Statistician David Freedman, for example, argues that regression—though useful for summarizing linear associations among variables—is ill-suited for finding causal relationships in social research, no matter how much we dress up the method. He writes: "I see no cases in which regression equations, let alone the more complex methods, have succeeded as engines for discovering causal relationships [in social research]. . . . As I read the record, correlational methods have not delivered the goods. We need to work on measurement, design, theory. Fancier statistics are not likely to help much" (1997, pp. 114, 157).

I agree about the "need to work on measurement, design, theory" (the theme of chapter 7), but not with the implication that we would do better to abandon regression methods altogether in causal analysis. The problem lies not in regression itself, but in reliance on *regression control* (residualization) as the primary or only method for matching like with like. The crux of the matter is what to do about the "Ws problem" in equation 5.1. There are two general approaches or grand strategies for trying to minimize omitted-variables bias:

1. *Add-a-regressor approach*: Move variables from W to X, that is, measure more of the causal variables.
2. *Design approach*: Reduce the correlation between the Ws and Xs through research design.

Until recently observational research has relied most heavily on the add-a-regressor approach. In this chapter I suggest that we follow the

lead of recent statistical and econometric work and try something else:
Let's focus our attention on the creation of research designs that reduce
or eliminate the correlation of the Xs with the Ws. On this I think Freedman would agree. Yet, as I show in the examples that follow, regression
may still play an integral role in causal analyses in the social sciences,
since research designs developed to eliminate the correlation of the Xs
with the Ws very often still rely on regression to estimate the key causal
parameters. Importantly, though, this more tailored use of regression
analysis plays to a strength of regression—summarizing the information
in data—rather than to a weakness—matching like with like.

A major shortcoming of the conventional add-a-regressor approach is
that we never know how successful we have been in identifying and measuring all of the causes, or at least most of the important ones. For causal
analysis, then, we would prefer the second option above, the design approach. Random assignment to X is one such design method. Yet random
assignment is not the only possibility and, when random assignment to X
is not feasible—as is frequently the case in anthropology, economics, political science, and sociology—social researchers are prone to scurry back
too quickly to the comfortable add-a-regressor approach. A central message of this chapter is that we need to think more creatively about how to
design our research to compare like with like when classic random assignment is out of the question.

Social researchers have at their disposal a number of strategies that,
whether they realize it or not, are rooted in rule 5. We begin with the
most obvious: Compare individuals with themselves.

COMPARING LIKE WITH LIKE THROUGH FIXED-EFFECTS METHODS

First-Difference Models: Subtracting Out the Effects of Confounding Variables

The first-difference method compares like with like by matching individuals to themselves. To match individuals to themselves, we must have
measures of individuals at two or more points in time, that is, we must
have *panel data* (more on panel models in chapter 6). Consider the elabo-
ration of the standard regression model to permit measures of individual
units (people, corporations, nations, etc.) at multiple time points:

$$Y_{it} = \alpha_t + \alpha_i + \beta_t X_{it} + \gamma_t W_{it} + \varepsilon_{it} \tag{5.3}$$

Note that the panel form of the regression model adds the subscript t
(for "time") to each term in the linear regression model (5.1) except α_i,
which needs no subscript t because it reflects effects that are stable over

time. The subscript t is needed to capture possible change over time. The first term in the panel regression model, α_t, captures differences between measurement points that are the same for all individuals and not otherwise accounted for by the Xs and Ws, or "secular change." (The α_t term is not needed for cross-section data, of course.) By adding the subscript t to Y, X and W, the panel model allows values of the independent and dependent variables to change over time. Similarly, by adding the subscript t to β and γ the model allows the *effects* of the Xs and Ws to change over time.

To illustrate the first-difference model, suppose we measure Y and the Xs at two points in time. Using the notation of the general panel model (5.3) we can write out the separate regression equations for time 1 and time 2 as follows:

$$Y_{i1} = \alpha_1 + \alpha_i + \beta_1 X_{i1} + \gamma_1 W_{i1} + \varepsilon_{i1}$$
$$Y_{i2} = \alpha_2 + \alpha_i + \beta_2 X_{i2} + \gamma_2 W_{i2} + \varepsilon_{i2} \tag{5.3a}$$

The critical advantage of a panel data set is that it allows us to measure individual change over time. Let's exploit that feature by subtracting Y_{i1} from Y_{i2}:

$$
\begin{aligned}
Y_{i2} - Y_{i1} &= (\alpha_2 - \alpha_1) + (\beta_2 X_{i2} - \beta_1 X_{i1}) + (\gamma_2 W_{i2} - \gamma_1 W_{i1}) + (\varepsilon_{i2} - \varepsilon_{i1}) \\
&= (\alpha_2 - \alpha_1) + \beta_2 (X_{i2} - X_{i1}) + (\beta_2 - \beta_1) X_{i1} + \gamma_2 (W_{i2} - W_{i1}) \\
&\quad + (\gamma_2 - \gamma_1) W_{i1} + (\varepsilon_{i2} - \varepsilon_{i1})
\end{aligned}
\tag{5.4}
$$

Equation 5.4 states that change in Y is determined by a constant ($\alpha_2 - \alpha_1$), by change in Y's measured and unmeasured causes ($X_{i2} - X_{i1}$ and $W_{i2} - W_{i1}$, respectively), by change in the *effects* of Y's measured and unmeasured causes ($\beta_2 - \beta_1$ and $\gamma_2 - \gamma_1$), and by a random disturbance term ($\varepsilon_{i2} - \varepsilon_{i1}$). From equation 5.4 we see immediately that the effects of the Ws disappear in the first-difference model when:

- the Ws are constant over time, that is, $W_{i2} = W_{i1}$, *and*
- the *effects* of the Ws are constant over time, that is, $\gamma_2 = \gamma_1$.

In short, a simple first-difference or "change-score" model removes the confounding effects of unmeasured variables that are stable, that is, variables that are constant for a given unit over time, *and* that have constant effects over time. This result is promising, since the most troublesome unmeasured causes very often are the unit-specific traits that are constant, or approximately so, over time. For research on individuals, this might include difficult-to-measure enduring individual traits such as ambition, work ethic, and sense of confidence and personal efficacy. In the field of criminal justice, criminologists have devoted a great deal of attention to individual differences in propensity to commit crime or "criminality," yet criminality remains an elusive trait that is difficult to measure. For research on corporations, there is much talk of the importance of differing "corporate cultures," which presumably are relatively constant, yet difficult to measure. For cross-country research, difficult-to-measure traits include constant or slow-changing national characteristics such as a country's culture, climate, topography, geographical location, access to seaports, and so on. First-difference models remove the effects of these enduring characteristics when the effects of the enduring characteristics are constant over time.

The first-difference method can be viewed as one type of a more general method known as *fixed-effects* (Allison 2005; Halaby 2004; Hsiao 2003). Consider how the fixed-effects method differs from the usual cross-sectional analysis where Y is regressed on Xs. To avoid omitted-variables bias in the cross-sectional regress-Y-on-X method, the unmeasured causes of Y must be uncorrelated with the measured causes of Y. In the case of first-difference models, by contrast, omitted-variables bias is avoided when the unmeasured causes and their effects are stable over the measurement interval. As a general rule, then, first-difference models are better suited for alleviating omitted-variables bias. We might call this the first-difference advantage:

> *First-difference advantage.* The first-difference model replaces the typically unrealistic assumption that the measured and unmeasured causes are uncorrelated with the less restrictive *stability assumption* that the unmeasured causes are constant and have constant effects.

It would be difficult to overstate the importance of the first-difference advantage. Omitted-variables bias is the bane of nonexperimental social research. To avoid this type of bias in standard regression analysis, we must assume either that we have measured all the important causes, or that the causes we have omitted are uncorrelated with the causes we have included. Very often those are heroic assumptions. The first-difference model, by contrast, assumes only *stability* in the level and effects of the unmeasured causes. In many instances the assumption that unmeasured causes are constant over time within units (recall the examples of the criminality of individuals, the culture of corporations, and the topography of countries) is more defensible than the assumption that those causes are uncorrelated with the measured causes across units. This feature gives fixed-effects models a significant edge over Y-on-X regression models in much social research (Allison 2005).

Moreover, first-difference models permit us to test whether the causal effect of X has changed from time 1 to time 2. If we regress $Y_{i2} - Y_{i1}$ on $X_{i2} - X_{i1}$ and X_{i1}, then the coefficient for X_{i1} estimates the difference between β_2 and β_1 (equation 5.4). If the two parameters are the same we can speak of a constant causal effect, but if $\beta_1 \neq \beta_2$ then the causal effect itself changes over time. This might complicate our conclusions, to be sure, but the point is that with first-difference models we can at least test for time-varying causal effects (more on this in chapter 6).

It is surprising, then, that social scientists do not use first-difference and other types of fixed-effects models more often (Allison 2005; Halaby 2004). One likely reason is habit. Until the last few decades cross-section data sets were the norm. As panel data sets become more routine, first-difference and related models should become more standard as well.

As with all methods, the first-difference method is no panacea; there are costs involved. In the first place, first-difference models remove only the stable effects of unchanging Ws. So you cannot rely on differencing as a foolproof method for sweeping away the effects of all types of unmeasured causal variables. First-difference models are designed for instances where there are important causes of Y that are stable and hard to measure.

A second cost is loss of variance on the *measured* causes. First-differencing (and other fixed-effects methods, such as adding dummy variables for individuals) reduces the variance in X. When we regress Y on X for a cross-section of individuals, we use the variance in X across all individuals. When we measure the same individuals at a later point in time, we add change in X over time for individuals $(X_{i2} - X_{i1})$ to the variance in X. Thus when we regress Y on X for a panel of individuals measured at two points in time, the variance in X consists of change in X over time for individuals as well as variance in X across individuals. By removing the variance in X across individuals, first-difference models truncate the variance in X. Truncating variance on independent variables typically is not beneficial since, as noted in rule 2, we need variance to explain variance. Yet truncation may be beneficial here because with first-difference models you generally have less, but "higher-quality," variance. The variance is higher quality because it has been purged of the enduring causal effects of unmeasured fixed traits.

Let me elaborate. Because an individual contributes to variance in $X_{i2} - X_{i1}$ only if X changes for that individual, causal results for first-difference models depend heavily on how much Y changes for individuals whose X changes over time. So the practical implication of variance truncation here is that results for first-difference models depend heavily on how much Y increases (declines) for individuals whose X increases (declines) over time. Consider, for example, the effect of southern residence on racial attitudes. Differencing means that our estimate of the causal effect of southern residence depends on how much (and in what direction) attitudes changed for individuals who moved into or out of the South.

In short, first-difference models might severely reduce the number of cases in the sample that contribute to variance in the causal variable of interest. In the limiting case, $X_{i2} - X_{i1}$ is zero for *everyone* in the sample. This occurs when X is a fixed trait. Ironically, then, the chief virtue of first-difference models—that they eliminate the effects of stable causes—is also one of its weaknesses: First-difference models eliminate the effects of *measured*, as well as unmeasured, causes that are constant over time. Hence first-difference models are problematic if one's objective is to estimate the effect of country of birth, for example, since "change in country of birth" is always zero.[4]

Consider, then, three general classes of variables. At one extreme are ascribed traits that are constant for individuals throughout their lives. You cannot use the first-difference method to estimate causal effects for those variables, though you can use the method to determine whether the association of X and Y has *changed* (shown in chapter 6). At the other extreme are individual traits such as age that change for everyone over time. Most variables fall somewhere between the two extremes. Income tends to fluctuate over time for most individuals, so differencing is often useful for estimating income effects. Differencing is not as useful for estimating education effects for adults, since formal education is fixed for most adults after age thirty. Thus a large sample would generally be required to provide enough variance to estimate education effects for adults with a first-difference model, and in any case the variance you do observe is likely to be beset with measurement error.

In comparing first-difference and other fixed-effects models with alternative methods, then, it is important to pay close attention to the tradeoff of quantity versus quality of variance. Under first-difference models you have less variance, but it may very well be *more telling* variance, since the variance that remains has been purged of the enduring effects of unmeasured (and often hard-to-measure) fixed traits of individuals.

Special Case: Growth-Rate Models

We don't usually think of using growth-rate models to eliminate confounding effects of unmeasured variables, but growth-rate models bear a formal similarity to first difference models. Because $\log Y_{i2} - \log Y_{i1}$ is the rate of growth of Y (where log is the natural logarithm), growth-rate models can be expressed as difference models, where the variables are

---

[4] The point may be moot if, as Paul Holland (1986) argues, it makes no sense to talk about causal effects for variables, such as country of birth, that cannot be manipulated (but see Moffitt 2005, p. 105, for a contrary view).

logged. To simplify notation, suppose Y is caused by just two variables, X and W, where as before X is measured and W is not. We assume further that the effects of $\log X$ and $\log W$ on $\log Y$ are linear. We have then this model for time t:

$$\log Y_{it} = \alpha_t + \alpha_i + \beta_t \log X_{it} + \gamma_t \log W_{it} + \varepsilon_{it} \tag{5.5}$$

It follows that change in log Y from time 1 to time 2 is:

$$
\begin{aligned}
\log Y_{i2} - \log Y_{i1} &= (\alpha_2 - \alpha_1) + (\beta_2 \log X_{i2} - \beta_1 \log X_{i1}) \\
&\quad + (\gamma_2 \log W_{i2} - \gamma_1 \log W_{i1}) + (\varepsilon_{i2} - \varepsilon_{i1}) \\
&= (\alpha_2 - \alpha_1) + \beta_2 \ (\log X_{i2} - \log X_{i1}) + (\beta_2 - \beta_1) \ \log X_{i1} \\
&\quad + \gamma_2 (\log W_{i2} - \log W_{i1}) + (\gamma_2 - \gamma_1) \ \log W_{i1} \\
&\quad + (\varepsilon_{i2} - \varepsilon_{i1})
\end{aligned}
\tag{5.6}
$$

Observe that equation 5.6, a growth rate model, is equation 5.4 applied to logged variables. Hence our conclusions about first-difference models also apply here: Growth-rate models remove the steady effects of constant unmeasured causes that vary across units. In cross-country research, for example, that would include the steady effects of a country's location, topography, history, mineral resources, official language, political and legal systems (to the extent that these systems don't change), access to seaports, and so on. In research on individuals, that would include enduring individual traits whose effects are constant over time.

Applications of growth-rate models sometimes differ from equation 5.6 by regressing growth rate of Y on growth rate of X without including $\log X$ at time 1. These studies assume, then, that $\log X$ is not needed in the model. To assume that $\log X$ is not needed in the growth-rate model is to assume that the rate of growth of X has the same effect on the rate of growth of Y regardless of the initial size of X. Hence the parameter for the effect of growth of X on growth of Y is the same whether we estimate the effect of growth rate forward in time ($\log Y_{i2} - \log Y_{i1}$) or backward in time ($\log Y_{i1} - \log Y_{i2}$). If we estimate backward in time, then our growth rate equation becomes:

$$
\begin{aligned}
\log Y_{i1} - \log Y_{i2} &= (\alpha_1 - \alpha_2) + \beta_1 (\log X_{i1} - \log X_{i2}) + (\beta_1 - \beta_2) \ \log X_{i2} \\
&\quad + \gamma_1 (\log W_{i1} - \log W_{i2}) + (\gamma_1 - \gamma_2) \ \log W_{i2} \\
&\quad + (\varepsilon_{i1} - \varepsilon_{i2})
\end{aligned}
\tag{5.7}
$$

The effect of the growth rate of X on the growth rate of Y is β_2 in equation 5.6 and β_1 in equation 5.7. Because β_1 and β_2 are the same when log X has no effect in the growth equations, then, by including log X in growth rate models, we are testing whether or not the effect of the rate of growth of X on the rate of growth of Y is the same whether we estimate it forward or backward in time.

Sibling Models

Sibling models attempt to compare like with like by matching individuals to strategic other individuals—their siblings—who are likely to be similar in multiple (and often unobservable) ways. Sibling fixed-effects models, or simply sibling models, are used to remove family environment effects that are the same for all children in a family. A sibling model can be thought of as a contextual model where family is the context. Contextual models assume that the characteristics of contexts—families, neighborhoods, schools, and so on—matter, just like individual traits do. By collecting data on individuals with shared environments—children in the same family or in the same neighborhood, for example—we are able to difference out constant unmeasured effects of the shared environment.

Because sibling models are a type of fixed-effect model, the effects of stable confounding variables can be removed without measuring the variables. In light of that feature, Guang Guo and Leah VanWey (1999) use sibling models to determine whether the inverse association between family size and children's intellectual development is causal. In brief, their answer is no, it is not; the "dumber by the dozen" concern (Zajonc 1975) is without merit (see Guo and VanWey 1999 along with commentary by Phillips 1999 and by Downey et al. 1999). (As we note subsequently, Dalton Conley and Rebecca Glauber [2005] investigate the same issue using an instrumental variables approach. Interestingly, Conley and Glauber find causal effects that are smaller than those found in traditional regression approaches but nonetheless are not zero.)

To see how the differencing method works for sibling models, consider again the standard linear regression model (equation 5.1). In addition to distinguishing observed from unobserved causes, we also distinguish family characteristics from individual characteristics, so the sibling model consists of four classes of causal variables: measured and unmeasured individual traits, and measured and unmeasured family characteristics. Of course, if the context were neighborhood instead of family, we would substitute measured and unmeasured neighborhood characteristics for measured and unmeasured family characteristics. Our essential conclusions about sibling models apply to other types of contextual models (neighbor models, school classmate models, etc.) as well.

We add the superscript **Fam** to distinguish family variables and coefficients from individual traits and coefficients. Thus the general sibling model is:

$$Y_i = \alpha + \alpha_i + \beta X_i + \gamma W_i + \beta^{\text{Fam}} X_i^{\text{Fam}} + \gamma^{\text{Fam}} W_i^{\text{Fam}} + \varepsilon_i \qquad (5.8)$$

We can difference out family characteristics for sibling pairs in a manner analogous to the differencing out of individual characteristics with panel data. Although the data demands differ—the differencing out of individual traits requires panel data, whereas the differencing out of family characteristics requires sibling pairs—the logic is the same.

Suppose our sample consists of $i = 1, 2, \ldots, N$ children who have siblings. Call these data sample A. Imagine we collect the same data for one of the siblings (randomly selected) for each of the children in sample A; call these data sample B. We have, then, N matched pairs of (A, B) siblings. (Note that the sibling model rules out only-children—so the population to which we can generalize is children with siblings, not all children.) Now the subscript i indexes a *sibling pair*, not an individual; the individual siblings are denoted iA and iB.

Applying equation 5.8 to samples A and B in turn, we have:

$$Y_{iA} = \alpha_A + \alpha_{iA} + \boldsymbol{\beta}_A X_{iA} + \boldsymbol{\gamma}_A W_{iA} + \boldsymbol{\beta}_A{}^{Fam} X_{iA}{}^{Fam} + \boldsymbol{\gamma}_A{}^{Fam} W_{iA}{}^{Fam} + \varepsilon_{iA}$$

$$Y_{iB} = \alpha_B + \alpha_{iB} + \boldsymbol{\beta}_B X_{iB} + \boldsymbol{\gamma}_B W_{iB} + \boldsymbol{\beta}_B{}^{Fam} X_{iB}{}^{Fam} + \boldsymbol{\gamma}_B{}^{Fam} W_{iB}{}^{Fam} + \varepsilon_{iB} \qquad (5.9)$$

Now subtract Y_{iA} from Y_{iB}:[5]

$$Y_{iB} - Y_{iA} = (\alpha_{iB} - \alpha_{iA}) + (\boldsymbol{\beta}_B X_{iB} - \boldsymbol{\beta}_A X_{iA}) + (\boldsymbol{\beta}_B{}^{Fam} X_{iB}{}^{Fam} - \boldsymbol{\beta}_A{}^{Fam} X_{iA}{}^{Fam}) +$$
$$(\boldsymbol{\gamma}_B W_{iB} - \boldsymbol{\gamma}_A W_{iA}) + (\boldsymbol{\gamma}_B{}^{Fam} W_{iB}{}^{Fam} - \boldsymbol{\gamma}_A{}^{Fam} W_{iA}{}^{Fam}) + (\varepsilon_{iB} - \varepsilon_{iA}) \qquad (5.10)$$

Keep in mind that $Y_{iB} - Y_{iA}$ is the Y difference for the ith *sibling pair*. Thus the differences for the family variables denote differences between siblings in the same family.

We have then a simple first-difference model, similar to the first-difference models described earlier, but with additional terms to distinguish family-level causes from individual-level causes. Proceeding as in equation 5.4 above, rewrite (5.10) as:

$$Y_{iB} - Y_{iA} = (\alpha_{iB} - \alpha_{iA}) + \boldsymbol{\beta}_B (X_{iB} - X_{iA}) + (\boldsymbol{\beta}_B - \boldsymbol{\beta}_A) X_{iA} + \boldsymbol{\gamma}_B (W_{iB} - W_{iA})$$
$$+ (\boldsymbol{\gamma}_B - \boldsymbol{\gamma}_A) W_{iA} + \boldsymbol{\beta}_B{}^{Fam} (X_{iB}{}^{Fam} - X_{iA}{}^{Fam})$$
$$+ (\boldsymbol{\beta}_B{}^{Fam} - \boldsymbol{\beta}_A{}^{Fam}) X_{iA}{}^{Fam} + \boldsymbol{\gamma}_B{}^{Fam} (W_{iB}{}^{Fam} - W_{iA}{}^{Fam})$$
$$+ (\boldsymbol{\gamma}_B{}^{Fam} - \boldsymbol{\gamma}_A{}^{Fam}) W_{iA}{}^{Fam} + (\varepsilon_{iB} - \varepsilon_{iA}) \qquad (5.11)$$

From the last lines of equation 5.11 we see immediately that the effects of unmeasured family characteristics (the $W_i{}^{Fam}$) are eliminated in the sibling model when:

---

[5] To simplify equation 5.10, we assume $\alpha_A = \alpha_B$ since samples A and B are randomly selected. If that assumption is false we could restore the term $\alpha_B - \alpha_A$ without affecting our conclusions.

- W is the same for the sibling pairs, that is, $W_{iB}{}^{Fam} = W_{iA}{}^{Fam}$, *and*
- the effect of W is constant over time, that is, $\gamma_B{}^{Fam} = \gamma_A{}^{Fam}$.

In short, sibling models are most effective at removing confounding family effects when the relevant unmeasured features of the family environment are constant, or nearly so, in their levels and effects. In practice the constant-levels condition that $W_{iB}{}^{Fam} = W_{iA}{}^{Fam}$ is the bigger concern than the constant-effects condition that $\gamma_B{}^{Fam} = \gamma_A{}^{Fam}$. This is the case because, assuming the siblings were selected randomly, there is no reason to expect big differences in γs for the A and B sibling samples. This is not to say that siblings respond the same way to family characteristics. To the contrary, some children might be more sensitive than other children are to parental conflict, for example. But under random selection of siblings, those differences should even out for samples A and B, so $\gamma_B{}^{Fam} = \gamma_A{}^{Fam}$ is generally a reasonable assumption.

The more problematic assumption is that $W_{iB}{}^{Fam} = W_{iA}{}^{Fam}$. Families change over time, so children of different ages are exposed to a "different slice" of family history. Some important but difficult to measure features of the family environment, such as parents' commitment to children and how highly they value academic success, might be relatively constant over time, and thus approximately the same for siblings regardless of age differences between them. Other unmeasured features of family environment, such as how well parents get along, might change over time, or parents might treat their children differently, so in that way different children in the same family are exposed to different family environments (see Conley 2004). Sibling models eliminate only the features of the family environment that are constant across siblings. In evaluating how well sibling models remove the confounding effects of unmeasured differences in family environments, then, researchers need to consider whether the features of the family environment that matter are constant (or nearly so) within families.

What about the confounding effects of unmeasured *individual* traits? Consider the terms $\gamma_B (W_{iB} - W_{iA}) + (\gamma_B - \gamma_A)W_{iA}$ in equation 5.11, where the Ws refer to individual characteristics, not family characteristics. Because we expect γ_A and γ_B to be roughly the same, the second term should be close to zero. It is the sibling difference in unmeasured causes, $W_{iB} - W_{iA}$, that we are more concerned about. Two observations about $W_{iB} - W_{iA}$ are relevant. First, siblings tend to differ less on key individual traits than two randomly-selected children do, so the use of sibling models typically reduces the variance of the unobserved individual-level causes. Second, researchers often use sibling models to estimate the effects of family characteristics, and it might be reasonable to assume that sibling differences in unobserved personal traits ($W_{iB} - W_{iA}$)

are uncorrelated with sibling differences in family characteristics, the causal variables of interest. We might expect siblings' personality differences, for example, to be independent of siblings' differences in level of family income when they were growing up. Sibling models can be useful, then, in alleviating the confounding effect of unobserved family *and individual* characteristics in investigations of the causal effect of *family environment*.

To give substantive flesh to the model, and to illustrate its potential and its limitations, we now consider a study that uses sibling models.

EXAMPLE: THE EFFECT OF FAMILY INCOME ON CHILDREN'S SCHOOLING

In a research article published in the June 1998 issue of the *American Sociological Review*, Greg Duncan, Jean Yeung, Jeanne Brooks-Gunn, and Judith Smith use sibling models to address the question "How much does childhood poverty affect the life chances of children?" As they note, a number of studies have documented an association between family income and children's life chances: For example, children from poorer families tend to do worse on standardized tests of ability and achievement; they tend to drop out of school earlier; and teenage girls from poor families are more likely to experience a nonmarital birth.

The stubborn question is how much of the observed income association is *causal*. To be sure, earlier studies of the income effect typically had included a number of demographic and other control variables in their regressions. Yet skeptics of this prior cross-sectional research (for example, Mayer 1997) remain unconvinced, given the inherent difficulty of measuring all the important family differences that might be related both to parental income and to children's outcomes. As Duncan et al. (1998, p. 409) explain:

> A persistent concern with these kinds of analyses is that the estimated effect of income might be spurious, caused by the mutual association that parental income and the outcomes for children share with some unmeasured "true" causal factor. Suppose, for example, that the mental health of parents is the key ingredient for children's success and that measures of parental mental health were not included in the models. Because positive mental health in parents is likely to make parents more successful in the labor market as well as to lead to fewer problems with their children, the absence of adjustments for differences in parental mental health may produce a serious overstatement of the role income plays in causing children's success.

Observe the policy implications here: If income effects are not causal, then raising the incomes of the poor will be ineffective in improving their children's life chances. So it is important to know whether family income is causal, or whether it is merely correlated with differences in family environment that we have not measured.

Duncan et al. use sibling models to alleviate the problem of unmeasured differences in family environments. Their data consists of 328 sibling pairs in the Panel Study of Income Dynamics. The dependent variable is years of schooling completed, estimated using this model:

$$\Delta \text{SCHOOLING}_i = \beta_0 + \beta_1 \Delta \text{FAMILYINCOME}_i \\ + \beta_2 \Delta \text{CHILDTRAITS}_i + \varepsilon_i \qquad (5.12)$$

where Δ refers to differences between siblings. Thus $\Delta \text{SCHOOLING}_i$ is the difference in the number of years of schooling completed for the ith sibling pair, which is assumed to be a function of the difference between siblings on a number of individual traits, denoted $\Delta \text{CHILDTRAITS}_i$, *and* the difference between siblings on the family's level of income when they were ages 0–15, denoted $\Delta \text{FAMILYINCOME}_i$. In the case of twins there is no difference in family incomes, of course, since twins are the same age. For other siblings, though, $\Delta \text{FAMILYINCOME}_i$ generally is not zero, and we must assume that fluctuation in family incomes over time produces enough variance in family income between older and younger children for reliable estimates of the income effect (more on this assumption below).

Note that, aside from family income, the model has no measure of family environment. The absence of family environment measures is not problematic if in fact differencing on siblings has eliminated the effect of relevant differences in family environments (except for the effect of differences in family income, which is in the model). As shown above, differencing on siblings does eliminate the effects of unmeasured causal family characteristics when $W_{iB}^{\text{Fam}} = W_{iA}^{\text{Fam}}$ and when $\gamma_B^{\text{Fam}} = \gamma_A^{\text{Fam}}$ (equation 5.11). In other words, with sibling models we do not need to measure causal family characteristics when those characteristics are the same for both siblings and have the same average effect on Y for both samples of siblings.

With regard to unmeasured family characteristics, then, we must assume that the family environment was the same for both siblings as they were growing up. As regards the family characteristic of interest, however, the family environment *could not* be the same for both siblings, or there would be no variance on the cause we want to estimate. In the Duncan et al. study of income's effect on children's schooling, for example, we assume one feature of the family environment, income, changed significantly over time, whereas other causal features of the family environment did not.

Suppose some important unmeasured causal family characteristic— let's call it Q—did change, so siblings were reared in different family environments with respect to Q. Then the causal model for Δ SCHOOLING would be:

$$\Delta \text{SCHOOLING}_i = \beta_0 + \beta_1 \Delta \text{FAMILYINCOME}_i + \beta_2 \Delta \text{CHILDTRAITS}_i$$
$$+ \gamma \Delta \text{FAMILYQ}_i + \varepsilon_i \qquad (5.13)$$

where Δ FAMILYQ$_i$ is sibling difference on family characteristic Q. By omitting Δ FAMILYQ$_i$ in equation 5.13, our estimate of the family income effect will be biased when Δ FAMILYINCOME$_i$ is correlated with Δ FAMILYQ$_i$. In general, the greater the correlation, the greater will be the bias.

The same principles apply to the biasing effect of unmeasured *individual-level* causal effects that do not "difference out," that is, $W_{iB} \neq W_{iA}$ in equation 5.11. There may be unmeasured differences in the personal traits of siblings that affect their differences in years of school achieved (perhaps, for example, we have not measured motivation adequately). If those unobserved differences in siblings' personal traits are correlated with differences in their exposure to different levels of family income—which Duncan et al. (p. 411) say is unlikely—then our estimate of the family income effect will be biased.

It is time now to summarize. *The key idea in sibling models (as in standard first-difference models) is to difference out the effects of confounding causes without differencing out the effects you want to investigate.* So you want siblings to be alike *and* different: alike on unobserved causes, and different on the causes you are investigating. Thus sibling models are most effective when your purpose is to estimate the causal effect of some feature of family environments and:

1. Family environments change for the causes you are investigating. Because you cannot explain a variable with a constant (chapter 2), siblings must be exposed to different family environments for the causes you are trying to estimate.
2. Key unobserved features of family environments are stable over time so siblings are exposed to the same features when growing up. The sibling model will difference out these effects ($W_{iB}^{\text{Fam}} - W_{iA}^{\text{Fam}}$).
3. Siblings are randomly assigned to samples A and B so we expect that the average *effects* of unobserved causes will be the same in both samples ($\gamma_B = \gamma_A$ and $\gamma_B^{\text{Fam}} = \gamma_A^{\text{Fam}}$) and that sibling differences in unobserved personal traits ($W_{iB} - W_{iA}$) will be uncorrelated with the family-level characteristics of interest.
4. Sibling differences are the same whether you have one sibling or five (or, if sibling differences do depend on family size, the effect can be modeled).

When these conditions are met, sibling models provide traction in the estimation of family-level causal effects.

COMPARING LIKE WITH LIKE THROUGH MATCHING ON MEASURED VARIABLES

One way to compare like with like is through the use of a fixed-effects model. A second way is through matching on values of measured variables.

There are two common ways to match on measured variables. One method matches individuals from the treatment group with individuals from the control group who are identical on the measured confounding causes. Although straightforward, exact matching generally is feasible only when the number of nontreated units is large relative to the number of treated units, and when the characteristics that need to be matched are relatively few. Because many studies in the social sciences fail to meet these conditions, other methods have been developed that attempt only to equalize the *distributions* of the covariates across the treatment and control groups. These methods make use of *propensity scores* to "balance" the treatment and control groups on measured confounding variables. In this section I describe both approaches, beginning with exact matching.

Exact Matching

The textbook example of exact matching comes from observational biomedical research. Imagine a clinical study where an investigator wants to assess the efficacy of treatment X_0 for alleviating some symptom Y. There is no randomized trial, but the investigator does have access to two sets of individual profiles. One set consists of the demographic characteristics (X_1), health histories (X_2), and current measurement of symptom Y for those who were treated, and the other set consists of the same information for those who were not treated. Matching consists then of strategic subsampling from among the control group to provide matches on X_1 and X_2 for individuals in the treatment group. The treatment effect is estimated by calculating the average difference on Y for the matched units.

In exact matching researchers sift through the controls to find individuals who match those in the treatment group. Because nonmatching cases are discarded, exact matching is most commonly used where there is an abundance of units in the control group from which to form matches with units in the treatment group. In prospective clinical studies the reduction of the data set through the discarding of control units can be cost effective because it permits investigators to follow only the control units that matter (that is, the ones that match) rather than collecting data over time on all the original controls. In those types of studies researchers with limited budgets might decide to use one-to-one exact matching, where each treated unit is matched to exactly one control unit. In general, however, it is better to use all control units that match, since that technique reduces the variance of estimates.

Neither method—exact matching nor one-to-one exact matching—is very common in the social sciences, where the curse of dimensionality makes exact matches problematic. (The term "curse of dimensionality" in statistics refers to the difficulty of fitting a model with many possible explanatory variables.) With regard to the issue of matching, the more variables you have to match on, and the more categories there are for each variable, the more difficult it is to find exact matches. Typically we want to match individuals simultaneously on multiple variables, and often the matching variables have multiple categories (the confounding variables might be continuous, for example). As a result, researchers might end up discarding units in the treated group, as well as units in the control group, for lack of a match. The discarding of cases is so severe in many applications that only a small fraction of the data can be used and, if treated units are among those discarded, the treatment effect of interest might no longer be the treatment effect being estimated. In other words, the wholesale discarding of cases could result in both inefficient *and* biased estimates of the treatment effect.

Fortunately, matching does not require the exact matching of individual units. It suffices instead to match the *distributions* as closely as possible, as we now see.

Propensity-Score Method

The propensity-score method (Rosenbaum and Rubin 1983, 1984, 1985; Rubin and Thomas 1996; see Becker and Ichino 2002 for an overview) attempts to compare like with like by matching individuals on *propensity scores*—summary scores based on observed variables. In effect the method attempts to do by matching on observables what random assignment attempts to do probabilistically—equalize or "balance" the treatment and control groups at the outset, so any subsequent difference in the groups can be attributed to the treatment itself. The propensity-score method is appropriate for estimating the causal effects of categorical variables that are dichotomous (treatment versus control groups) or that can be dichotomized (there is still work to be done to extend the propensity-score method to multivalued Xs). The aim is to *equalize on C* (the confounders) individuals who *differ on X* (the treatment).

Because the goal is to balance the treatment and control groups on the confounders without the benefit of random assignment, we must (in contrast to the fixed-effects approach) have data on the confounders. In this respect propensity scoring is similar to standard regression control with covariates. However, because the use of propensity scores permits us to achieve balance by trial and error, whether or not we know the proper functional form, the method offers an attractive alternative to standard regression in instances where there is uncertainty about the proper functional form of the relationship between Y and its predictors (Harding 2003). Hence the approach is less subject to bias arising from confounding variables that are included, but in the wrong functional form.

The general procedure is to summarize all the measured confounders by a single variable called the *propensity score* and then to match the treated and nontreated units on the basis of the propensity scores. There are four basic steps: (1) use logistic regression (or a similar method) to regress the binary treatment variable X on the confounders to create a variable $\hat{X}$; (2) match treated subjects to controls on the basis of the estimated propensity scores $\hat{X}_i$ for each unit (in "nearest-neighbor matching," for example, each treated unit is matched to the control unit with the most similar value of $\hat{X}$); (3) verify that matching has balanced the treatment and control groups; and (4) draw conclusions about causal effects on the basis of the differences on Y between the treated and control groups for the matched data.

If step 3 tells us that we have not balanced our data, then we try again with a different specification of our regression. That is the cardinal virtue of the propensity-score method: With propensity scores we can try increasingly elaborate specifications (interaction terms, squared terms, and so on) until we find a specification that balances the data. As Daniel Ho et al. (2007) point out, the specification works when it works, and when it doesn't work we keep trying. This is in contrast to standard regression-control-by-residualization, where we are beholden to unverifiable assumptions about proper functional form for balancing our data.

To flesh out the propensity-score method with an example, consider again the effect of childhood poverty on later educational attainment, except this time think about the effect of living in a poor neighborhood rather than the effect of living in a poor family. We know that children who grow up in poor neighborhoods are less likely than other children to complete high school. What we want to know is how much, if any, of this association is causal, that is, how much the graduation prospects would improve for children in poor neighborhoods had they grown up in nonpoor neighborhoods.

As noted earlier in this chapter, the problem is that we cannot observe the counterfactual, since a single individual cannot simultaneously both experience and not experience growing up in a poor neighborhood. Our alternative is to have control subjects serve as the counterfactual. As

David Harding (2003, p. 684) explains in his propensity-score analysis of neighborhood effects:

> The solution used here is to match each treated subject with one or more control subjects such that the treated subjects are, on average, identical to the control subjects on observable characteristics prior to treatment. . . . Treatment and control groups are well matched when subject characteristics that affect the outcome are "balanced" in the treatment and control groups.

To use propensity scores, we first must find measures of the pertinent differences between children who grow up in poor neighborhoods and children in other neighborhoods. We want to measure family income, for example, since children who grow up in poor neighborhoods are more likely to live in poor families, and children from poor families are less likely to finish high school. (We do not want to control for variables that *mediate* the effect of neighborhood poverty on educational attainment, however, since that would bias our estimate of the neighborhood poverty effect.) Then we use logistic regression or some other appropriate estimator to regress the "treatment" (growing up in a poor neighborhood, here denoted X) on family income and other variables associated with living in a poor neighborhood.[6]

The regression of X on the relevant predictors of living in a poor neighborhood yields $\hat{X}$, which we use to match units. We also use the two distributions of $\hat{X}$ (the distribution of $\hat{X}$ for the treatment group and the distribution of $\hat{X}$ for the control group) to check for adequate overlap. In most instances it makes sense to restrict the analysis to the range of values for $\hat{X}$ where the treatment and control groups overlap. Where there is no overlap, estimates of the treatment effect depend on unverifiable assumptions about functional form of the effect—the very situation we are trying to avoid by using propensity scores instead of standard regression control with covariates.

Next we match treatment and control subjects on propensity scores using one of a number of possible matching algorithms (see chapter 4 of Morgan and Winship, 2007, for examples; see Becker and Ichino 2002, for discussion of software). To verify that our matching has produced the desired balance on confounders across treatment and control groups, we can use a quantile-quantile plot (Ho et al., in press) for each of the confounders. Good balance is more critical for variables that have a large

---

[6] Where the pool of potential control cases is large relative to the number of treated cases, Rubin and Thomas (1996, p. 253) advise researchers to include all variables that are likely to be relevant. Again, variables mediating the effect of X on Y should *not* be included, since conditioning on the consequences of X can severely bias our estimate of the causal effect of X.

effect on the outcome variable than it is for variables that have a small effect. If necessary, as noted above, $\hat{X}$ can be reestimated, using a different functional form for the confounders, until balance is achieved.

The final step is to estimate the average treatment effect for the treated (or ATT) for each of the matched groups of individuals as the difference between the treated and control subjects within each of the groups. To calculate the overall effect, it is usually a simple matter to take a weighted average of the treatment effects for each matched group.

The propensity-score method has several advantages over standard regression. First, as I have emphasized, successful balancing of the data on the basis of propensity scores eliminates the need for strong assumptions about the functional form of the relationship between the outcome variables and the regressors. Second, inferences are less likely to be made on the basis of extrapolation from treatment and control cases that do not overlap (note that extrapolation is especially dangerous when we are uncertain about the functional form of relationships). One of the virtues of the propensity-score approach is that it brings the nonoverlapping cases problem out of the closet (in contrast to standard regression analysis, where the problem generally is well hidden). Checking for adequate overlap of the distribution of the treatment group and the distribution of the control group is standard procedure in propensity-score analysis. Under regression, researchers might or might not perform the necessary checks. Third, comparing similar groups of treated and control cases is a more intuitive method for control than the residualization method used by regression. This can be an important advantage when presenting results to a lay audience. Finally, propensity scores can result in smaller standard errors despite the removal of nonoverlapping cases (see Smith 1997 for an example), and in some instances propensity scores can be useful for testing sensitivity to bias from unmeasured confounders (see Harding 2003 for an example).

It is important to stress that neither method—propensity scoring nor regression—solves the Ws problem. Whether we attempt to match by residualization on confounders, as in regression, or by balancing the distributions of the $\hat{X}$ in the treatment and control groups, as in the propensity-score approach, we can match only on observables. Because skeptics can always point to potentially confounding variables that you did not include in your analysis, both methods require strong theory.

The most obvious limitation of propensity-score analysis relative to regression is that the propensity-score method yields no estimates of the confounders' effects on the outcome variable. (Fixed-effects methods are subject to the same criticism.) This limitation is more apparent than real for causal analysis, however, since there is emerging consensus that causal inference is best accomplished by focusing on one cause at a time (Morgan and Winship, 2007). Moreover, the use of propensity scores to balance data does not rule out the subsequent use of regression analysis, as we now see.

Matching as a Preprocessing Strategy for Reducing Model Dependence

Model dependence continues to vex social research. Most estimates of causal effects in social research are model dependent to some degree, since estimates of causal effects usually vary depending on choices researchers make about their model—the variables to include, the functional form to use, the period to analyze or subset of cases to include, and so on. As a result, the estimates that are presented in published research articles generally represent a select subset of the much larger set of estimates possible under alternative (realistic) model assumptions. Because estimates are model-dependent, published findings nearly always are subject to the suspicion of *favored-hypothesis bias* (Firebaugh, in press)—the suspicion that researchers have settled on the estimates that are most congenial with their favored hypotheses rather than those that are most congenial with their data.

Because favored-hypothesis bias pervades observational social research, reducing model dependence should be a primary objective in our research designs. To reduce model dependence, Ho et al. (2007) suggest that researchers use propensity scores to preprocess their data.[7] The first step, which Ho and colleagues call *nonparametric preprocessing*, uses propensity scores to render the treated and control groups as similar a possible; then, to obtain final estimates, researchers can use whatever parametric technique they had planned to use in the first place (linear regression, logit, structural equations, etc.).

Preprocessing with propensity scores reduces model dependence by diminishing the impact of the assumptions we make about our model (Ho et al., 2007). The balancing of the data set (that is, the preprocessing itself) requires fewer assumptions than regression does, and after preprocessing the treatment group is much closer to being independent of the confounding variables than it was before preprocessing. Any subsequent parametric adjustments, then, are less consequential for inferences. The implication is that two investigators who use the same data and variables to address the same research question are more likely to arrive at consonant results if they successfully balance the data by preprocessing than if they do not preprocess the data. And, when we read an article where balancing

---

[7] Ho and colleagues note that their approach is similar in spirit to ideas in Imai and van Dyk (2004), Rosenbaum and Rubin (1984), and Rubin and Thomas (2000), among others.

has been achieved, we can be more confident that small changes in the authors' model specification would not greatly alter the paper's empirical conclusions.

COMPARING LIKE WITH LIKE THROUGH NATURALLY OCCURRING RANDOM ASSIGNMENT

The purpose of random assignment in social research is to create matched groups, so that we can compare apples with apples, like with like. Social scientists in every field understand and appreciate the power of random assignment in controlled experiments. Individuals in an experiment are assigned randomly either to a treatment group that receives X or to a control group that does not receive X. The notion is that we want to vary X to see what happens to some outcome Y. Of course, lots of things can go wrong in an experiment with human subjects because with humans it is hard to hold constant all factors except those under investigation. Even under laboratory conditions, factors that we don't want to vary might vary anyway during the course of the experiment (see Campbell and Stanley's [1966] classic statement on threats to internal and external validity in experiments). In an ideal experiment, though, X varies, other causes of Y do not vary, and—due to random assignment—we expect no initial differences of consequence between the two groups, so we can infer that subsequent group differences on Y are due to the introduction of group differences on X.

Why do we expect random assignment to produce initially equivalent groups? The answer lies in probability theory. In controlled experiments, we attempt to *harness the power of probability* to produce indistinguishable groups. The point I want to make in this section is that random assignment is also found in nature, so in some instances observational studies can also harness the power of probability to compare like with like.

Until recently, discussion of the random assignment of subjects has been largely relegated to experimental research, since observational studies in many areas of social science rarely consider how to incorporate random assignment in the research design. This state of affairs might have come about because of a misimpression that random assignment is outside nature's domain and must be manufactured by researchers: Either we can randomly assign individuals, in which case we do an experiment; or we cannot randomly assign individuals, in which case we don't give the concept of random assignment further thought. As a result, nonexperimental social research has been dominated by less reliable methods for removing the effects of confounding variables. It is time to consider how we might be able to incorporate naturally occurring random assignment more routinely in our research designs.

INSTRUMENTAL VARIABLES: MATCHING THROUGH PARTIAL RANDOM ASSIGNMENT

The instrument variable (IV) method for estimating causal effects involves a sort of partial random assignment. The random assignment is partial because in the IV method it is *incentives to take treatment*, not treatment itself, that is randomized.

To fix ideas, suppose X is a cause of Y, and individuals are randomly assigned to X. Suppose further that X and Y are standardized variables, that is, X and Y each has a mean of zero and a standard deviation of one. Due to random assignment, X is uncorrelated with the other causes of Y. X nevertheless is correlated with Y, since it is a cause of Y. This situation is depicted in figure 5.2, where $X \rightarrow Y$ denotes that X causes Y and $\varepsilon_Y \rightarrow Y$ denotes all the other causes of Y. Figure 5.2 is called a *path diagram* because it shows all the links or paths from X to Y.

Our objective is to estimate β, the causal effect of X on Y. In the case of just two variables X and Y, the slope β equals the correlation of X and Y when (as here) the variables are standardized. So estimating β is equivalent to estimating $r(X,Y)$, the correlation of X and Y. According to the principles of path analysis (Alwin and Hauser 1975), the correlation of X and Y is a function of all the links between X and Y. In figure 5.2 there is just one link, $X \rightarrow Y$. So for the model depicted in figure 5.2 the bivariate correlation *does* reflect the causal effect of X on Y: *correlation implies causality.*

In observational data, however, individuals are not randomly assigned to X, so *in observational data we expect links between X and Y other than $X \rightarrow Y$.* When there are links between X and Y other than $X \rightarrow Y$, correlation does not imply causality (recall the second law of causality). Figure 5.3 depicts that situation. In figure 5.3, X causes Y (as in figure 5.2), but confounding variable C also causes Y, and C is correlated with X, since C causes X. In figure 5.3, then, the correlation of X and Y reflects (1) the causal effect from X to Y and (2) the effect of the confounder C on both X and Y. As a result, in figure 5.3 (unlike figure 5.2) the correlation

Figure 5.2. Example Where Correlation $r(X,Y)$ *Is* Causal Effect of X on Y

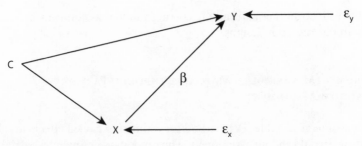

Figure 5.3. Example Where Correlation $r(X,Y)$ Is *Not* Causal Effect of X on Y

of X and Y gives a biased estimate of β, the causal effect of X on Y. (Note that if $\beta = 0$ then figure 5.3 reduces to figure 5.1. So figure 5.1— "correlation of X and Y is [entirely] due to common cause"—is a special case of figure 5.3.)

Random assignment on X alleviates the problem by attempting to remove the empirical link between X and C. If the link is removed so that X and C indeed are independent, then $r(X,Y) = \beta$. The difficulty in observational studies is that X is not randomly assigned. The instrumental variables strategy is to try to find a randomly assigned variable Z that causes X but not Y (except indirectly, through X—see figure 5.4). Because Z is randomly assigned, the correlation of Z with the confounder C is zero (in expected value), so the correlation $r(X,Z)$ is the causal effect $Z \rightarrow X$ (denoted α in figure 5.4). Because Z causes X, we have the causal chain $Z \rightarrow X \rightarrow Y$. That is key to the IV strategy, since in the causal chain $Z \rightarrow X \rightarrow Y$ the correlation of Z and Y is $\alpha\beta$, the product of the causal effect of Z on X and the causal effect of X on Y (we assume

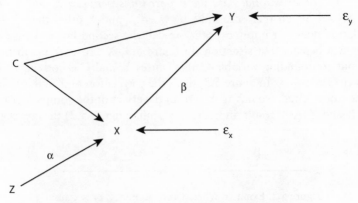

Figure 5.4. Instrumental Variable Method for Estimating β

throughout this discussion that the variables are standardized). Recall that our objective is to estimate β, and note that we can estimate β from the correlations of Z with Y and Z with X, since $r(Y,Z) = \alpha\beta$ and $r(X,Z) = \alpha$.

In short, if we can find a randomly assigned variable Z that affects X but has no direct effect on Y, then $r(Y,Z)$ provides an estimate of $\alpha\beta$, and $r(X,Z)$ provides an estimate of α. For an estimate of β, then, we can simply divide the correlation of Y and Z by the correlation of X and Z: $\beta = r(Y,Z)/r(X,Z)$. In general (whether or not the variables are standardized) the IV estimator is the ratio of the covariance of Y and Z with the covariance of X and Z, that is, $\beta_{IV} = cov(Y,Z)/cov(X,Z)$. Because $cov(Y,Z)/cov(X,Z) = [cov(X,Z)\beta + cov(Z,\varepsilon_Y)]/cov(X,Z)$, it follows that $\beta_{IV} = \beta$ when $cov(Z, \varepsilon_Y) = 0$, as we assume when Z is randomly assigned. Hence if we can find a variable that is randomly assigned yet affects X, then $cov(Y,Z)/cov(X,Z)$ provides a way to estimate the causal effect of X on Y.[8] That is the logic of the IV strategy.

EXAMPLE: EFFECT OF SAME-SEX VERSUS DIFFERENT-SEX SIBLINGS

Intuitively, instrumental variables solve the problem of omitted variables bias by using only part of the variance in the cause—the part that is uncorrelated with the confounding variables. In that sense the IV method is similar to the fixed effects method.[9]

Consider again the example of family size and children's success in school. In dozens of studies since Francis Galton (1874) proclaimed the intellectual advantages of being eldest born, social scientists have debated whether children who come from large families are disadvantaged in cognitive development and academic achievement. Concern that large family size has detrimental effects on children's intellectual development is well expressed by the famous title of Robert Zajonc's 1975 Psychology Today article: "Dumber by the Dozen." As Zajonc (p. 169) advises parents: "If the intellectual growth of your children is important to you, the model predicts that you should have no more than two . . . because the larger the family, the lower the overall level of intellectual functioning."

Researchers consistently find that children from larger families in fact score lower on tests of cognitive ability, do worse in school, and attain fewer years of schooling than do children from smaller families. The

---

[8] In statistical parlance, IV estimates are *consistent* but not *unbiased* (see Angrist and Krueger 2001). An estimator is said to be consistent when estimates converge to the population parameter as the sample size increases.

[9] Because the IV method truncates the variance of the causal variable of interest, the method generally does not work well with small samples.

inverse association between family size and academic performance persists even when socioeconomic status is controlled (Blake 1989; Downey 1995, table 3).

The question, of course, is whether the associations are causal. Skeptics can point to any number of W-variables that are difficult to measure, or to measure adequately, in standard regression approaches (Guo and VanWey 1999). Some potentially confounding factors, such as parents' values and the intellectual climate of the home, are difficult to measure completely. If parents' values and intellectual climate of the home jointly determine children's academic performance *and* decisions about family size, the observed associations are likely to be spurious.

Because of the difficulty of measuring confounders, researchers in this field have sought alternative ways to relieve omitted-variables bias. One possibility is to use sibling models (Guo and VanWey 1999), as described earlier. Another possibility is to use instrumental variables, as described here.

The trick for the instrumental variable approach is to find a randomly assigned Z such that $Z \to X \to Y$. Here Y is school achievement and X is family size. We want to know whether the observed effect of X on Y is causal. To be more concrete, let's suppose Y is measured by failing a grade in school. What we want to know is whether children in large families would be less likely to fail a grade if they were in small families.

The problem is that family size (X) is not randomly assigned, so larger and smaller families are likely to differ on any number of characteristics other than family size. As a result we cannot infer a causal effect of X on Y from an association of X and Y. To make causal inferences we seek a random Z that affects family size yet has no direct effect on a child's probability of failing a grade.

What we would like to find, then, is some sort of nature-provided random assignment mechanism that affects family size but not children's academic success (except indirectly, through its effect on family size). Conley and Glauber (2005) suggest that the sex mix of children provides such a random assignment mechanism Z. Among women with two children, about one-half will have same-sex children and one-half will have mixed-sex children. Importantly, the "assignment" of same-sex versus mixed-sex children is random. So we expect women with two boys or two girls to have the same preferences in general as women with one boy and one girl, with one important exception: If there is an underlying preference for having at least one child of each sex, then women with same-sex children will be more likely to want a third child. In other words, among women with two children, the sex mix of children—a random occurrence—affects decisions about childbearing (so $Z \to X$) but otherwise is independent of family values, the intellectual climate of the home, parents' socioeconomic status, intelligence, and so on (so Z is unrelated to other causes of Y).

The causal leverage provided by sex mix of children depends on two conditions: First, sex mix must be related to family size; second, sex mix must affect academic success *only* through its effects on family size. The first condition can be checked empirically whereas the second is determined on the basis of theory. With regard to the first condition, sex mix *is* related to childbearing. Consider these figures from the U.S. census for 1980 (reported in Angrist and Evans 1998, table 3): Among women with one boy and one girl, 37.2 percent had a third child; among women with two boys or two girls, 43.2 percent had a third child, a difference of 6 percent. If we restrict the analysis to married women, the difference is 6.8 percent. U.S. census figures for 1990 show the same pattern: Among women with one boy and one girl, 34.4 percent had another child; among women with two boys or two girls, 40.7 percent, or 6.3 percent more, had another child (for married women the difference is 7 percent).

The second condition, that Z affects Y only through X, is often more controversial because it must be established on the basis of theory. Consider, for example, Joshua Angrist and William Evans's (1998) use of sex mix of children as an instrument to estimate the causal effect of childbearing (X) on women's labor force participation (Y). While Angrist and Evans argue that there is no compelling reason to expect the sex mix of children to affect labor force participation decisions aside from its effect on childbearing, Mark Rosenzweig and Kenneth Wolpin (2000) are skeptical. It could be the case that there are important differences in the childrearing costs for same-sex and different-sex children (for example, same-sex children might be cheaper because they can wear hand-me-down clothes or share a bedroom), and those costs might affect decisions about whether the mother works.

As the Rosenzweig and Wolpin critique underscores, the instrumental variables strategy is not a panacea for social research. The chief problem is the difficulty of finding randomly assigned Zs that are related to the causal variable of interest. Studies using instrumental variables to relieve omitted variables bias are only as convincing as the instruments they use. It is not always easy to find naturally occurring random assignment mechanisms that provide the sort of leverage one needs to make a compelling case for an instrumental variable Z that measurably affects X *and* that affects Y only through its effect on X. That difficulty does not mean that one should abandon the attempt, however. In observational research we need to do a better job of harnessing the effects of randomization wherever it may be found in nature, and the IV strategy, fallible as it is, at least forces researchers to think more concretely about how one might be able to employ randomization principles to alleviate the inherent limitations of observational data.

MATCHING THROUGH NATURALLY OCCURRING RANDOM ASSIGNMENT TO THE TREATMENT GROUP

In the case of instrumental variables, the *cause of the treatment* is randomly assigned in nature. We would get even more leverage from random assignment if the treatment itself were randomly assigned, as in controlled experiments. This section describes that possibility, which I call *naturally occurring random assignment to the treatment group*. By the term "naturally occurring" I do not mean that nature necessarily made the assignments, but that the assignments were not done deliberately, for the sake of randomization, as one would do in a controlled experiment.

This type of matching strategy is best described by illustration. David Freedman tells the story of John Snow's demonstration, in the 1850s, that cholera is a waterborne infectious disease. Freedman (1991, p. 294) places Snow's achievement in historical context as follows:

> To see his achievement, I ask you to go back in time and forget that germs cause disease. Microscopes are available but their resolution is poor. Most human pathogens cannot be seen. The isolation of such micro-organisms lies decades into the future. The infection theory has some supporters, but the dominant idea is that disease results from "miasmas": minute, inanimate poison particles in the air.

Cholera, which had first appeared in Europe in the early 1800s, came in epidemic waves. Victims became sick suddenly and often died. From his clinical study of the course of the disease, Snow conjectured that cholera was caused by a living organism that humans contracted through food or drink and then passed through the body to infect new victims through the water supply.

Snow did a great deal of detective work to find evidence for his theory. If miasmas in the air cause the disease, then propinquity alone should account for the way the disease spreads. But if the disease is waterborne, he reasoned that the use of a common water supply is the key. It turns out that London at the time presented a naturally occurring random assignment mechanism for testing his theory. Some areas of London were served by more than one water company, so in some districts next-door neighbors received their water from different sources. Of two major water companies in London, the Lambeth company drew its water upstream in the Thames River, above the main sewage discharge points. The Southwark and Vauxhall company, by contrast, drew its water below the sewage discharge points. In his own words, here is how Snow described the experiment:

> Each company supplies both rich and poor, both large houses and small; there is no difference either in the condition or occupation of the persons receiving the water of the different Companies. . . . As there is no difference whatever in the houses or the people receiving the supply of the two Water Companies, or in any of the physical conditions with which they are surrounded, it is obvious that no experiment could have been devised which would more thoroughly test the effect of water supply on the progress of cholera than this, which circumstances placed ready made before the observer.

> The experiment, too, was on the grandest scale. No fewer than three hundred thousand people of both sexes, of every age and occupation, and of every rank and station, from gentlefolks down to the very poor, were divided into two groups without their choice, and in most cases, without their knowledge; one group being supplied with water containing the sewage of London, and amongst it, whatever might have come from the cholera patients, the other group having water quite free from such impurity. (Snow 1855, pp. 74–75, quoted in Freedman 1991, p. 297)

Snow's example is particularly compelling because he was able to find full-blown "natural" random assignment on the cause of interest—a rarity in the social sciences. Social research in this century will become more powerful to the extent that we can more routinely follow Snow's nineteenth-century example in our investigations of human behavior.

COMPARISON OF STRATEGIES FOR COMPARING LIKE WITH LIKE

Confounding variables are the bane of causal analysis with observational data. The methods described in this chapter attempt to deal with the problem by comparing like with like. To evaluate the methods, we contrast the strategies they use for comparison.

In this section the key distinction is between X, the cause of interest, and the Cs, the other causes confounded with X. Earlier I distinguished measured causes (Xs) from unmeasured causes (Ws). Confounding variables can be either measured or unmeasured, which I will denote C_M and C_U, respectively, where boldface is used to denote a vector of variables. So there are three categories of variables to keep in mind: X, the specific cause of interest or "treatment variable"; C_M, measured causes of Y *other than X*; and C_U, unmeasured causes of Y.

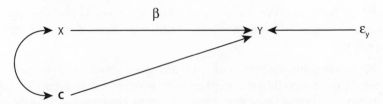

Figure 5.5. Conventional Multivariate Regression Model

Now consider figure 5.5, a stylized example of the confounding variables problem in observational data. We want to estimate β, the (average) causal effect of X on Y. The regression of Y on X does not yield a good estimate of β since that method fails to separate the causal effect of X on Y from the causal effects of C on Y, where C is bolded to emphasize that it denotes a vector of confounding variables (virtually always there is more than one confounding variable). Figure 5.5 is a generalization of figure 5.3 to the typical case of multiple confounding variables. In the general case X and C are correlated, as indicated by the curved arrow between X and C in figure 5.5. The curved arrow means that there are causal effects from C to X, or common causes of X and C, or both.

The key to estimating β lies in removing the confounding effects of the variables in C. The standard regression strategy is to regress Y on X and C_M, the measured variables in C. Alternatively, we obtain the same regression coefficients by (1) regressing Y on C_M, and X on C_M, to create $\hat{Y}_i$ and $\hat{X}_i$—values of Y and X for individuals, predicted on the basis of the measured Cs—and (2) regressing $Y_i - \hat{Y}_i$ on $X_i - \hat{X}_i$. Thus the standard regression strategy can be thought of as removing the effect of the measured confounding variables through *residualization*. Because the residuals $Y_i - \hat{Y}_i$ and $X_i - \hat{X}_i$ are uncorrelated with those confounders, any association between $Y_i - \hat{Y}_i$ and $X_i - \hat{X}_i$ could not be due to the confounders that we have measured. So if we can accurately measure all the confounders, we can use standard regression to obtain an unbiased estimate of the causal effect of X on Y. That is the basic logic of the standard regression approach (table 5.1).

In the case of propensity scores, as in standard regression, we must measure confounders to control for their effects. Instead of controlling through residualization, however, we control through matching on propensity scores, where propensity scores refer to the predicted probabilities of selection into the treatment group. Propensity scores provide an attractive alternative to residualization because propensity scores typically eliminate the need for strong assumptions about the functional form of effects and very often result in smaller standard errors despite the loss of cases.

TABLE 5.1
Comparison of Strategies for Alleviating the Effects of Confounders
in Observational Studies

Strategy and Model	Central Assumption(s)
Regression with control variables $(Y_i - \hat{Y}_i) = \hat{\alpha} + \hat{\beta}(X_i - \hat{X}_i) + \varepsilon_i$, where $\hat{Y}$ and $\hat{X}$ are linear functions of C_M	$C_M = C$ [thus $(Y_i - \hat{Y}_i)$ and $(X_i - \hat{X}_i)$ are uncorrelated with C, so any effect of $(X_i - \hat{X}_i)$ on $(Y_i - \hat{Y}_i)$ is not due to C].
Propensity scores $\hat{\beta} = \mu_T - \mu_C$, where μ_T is the mean of Y for the treatment group $(X = 1)$ and μ_C is the mean of Y for the control group $(X = 0)$	That treatment and control groups are balanced on C.
Instrumental variables $Y_i = \hat{\alpha} + \hat{\beta}\hat{X}_i + \varepsilon_i$, where $\hat{X}$ is a function of Z.	That Z is correlated with X but not with C nor with the error term of Y (thus Z has no direct effect on Y).
Fixed-effects models (illustrated here with differencing method) $\Delta Y_i = \hat{\alpha} + \hat{\beta}\,\Delta X_i + \varepsilon_i$, where: $\Delta Y_i = \begin{cases} Y_{i2} - Y_{i1} \text{ for the } ith \text{ unit in change models} \\ \log Y_{i2} - \log Y_{i1} \text{ for the } ith \text{ unit (nation, etc.)} \\ \quad \text{in growth-rate models} \\ Y_{iB} - Y_{iA} \text{ for the } ith \text{ sibling pair in sibling} \\ \quad \text{models} \end{cases}$ ΔX_i is defined in the same way.	That the confounders are constant (over time for change models, across sibling pairs for sibling models, etc.) *and* have constant effects on Y.

Key: β is the causal effect of X on Y.
    X is the causal variable of interest.
    Y is an outcome variable.
    Z is an instrumental variable.
    C is vector of confounder variables, measured or not.
    C_M is vector of measured confounder variables (a subset of C).

Because measuring all confounders, or even the most crucial ones, is not always feasible, one of the most pressing issues in applied statistics has been to develop alternative strategies for alleviating the effects of confounders in observational studies. One strategy is to use an instrumental variable—a randomly assigned variable Z that affects X but not C and affects Y only indirectly, through its effect on X. In the IV strategy we regress Y on $\hat{X}$, where $\hat{X}$ is a linear function of Z (table 5.1). The effect of $\hat{X}$ on Y is independent of the other causes of Y because $\hat{X}$ is a linear function of Z, where Z is independent of the other causes of Y (that is, the causes of Y other than X). Moreover, because Z has no causal effect on Y except through its effect on X, the substitution of $\hat{X}$ for X does not bias our estimate by mixing together the causal effects of X and Z. There is no independent causal effect of Z to mix with the effect of X.

In principle the instrumental variable approach is a very attractive alternative to standard regression control, since it suggests a way to avoid omitted-variables bias without the need to measure the confounding causal variables. (In that sense, the promise of the IV approach is similar to the promise of controlled experiments and of fixed-effects models.) In practice, though, it is often difficult to find defensible instrumental variables.

Another strategy for alleviating the effects of unobserved confounding variables is to use change models, growth-rate models, or sibling models. I group these three methods because they can be thought of as belonging to a class of models called fixed-effects models. Fixed-effects models provide traction for eliminating the effects of confounding variables by providing two or more individual observations where X varies but C is constant. When we know that two or more observations have the same values on C we in effect can match individuals on the confounding variables (for example, two siblings are matched on family environment since they have the same family environment; or the same individual at two points in time is matched with herself on permanent individual traits). By using subtraction or some other method (Allison 2005) we can eliminate the confounding effect of unmeasured variables that are the same for the matched observations (table 5.1).

Because fixed-effects models can alleviate the effects of unobserved confounding variables, they are attractive in a number of social science applications. Indeed, as Charles Halaby (2004) argues, fixed-effects models are probably underutilized in social research. It is important to note, however, that the fixed-effects strategy assumes that X differs for the matched units (the matched units are siblings in the case of sibling models, individuals measured at two points in time in the case of panel models, and so on), but that the variables in C are the same for the matched units. The fixed-effect method generally is most effective, then, in applications where the causal variables of interest change over time (or differ across siblings, etc.) while the unmeasured confounders are stable.

Conclusion

The idea in causal analysis is to find ways to circumvent the second law of causality, that correlation does not prove causation. We want a design or method that permits us to infer causality from correlation because correlation is all we have (we cannot observe causality directly). That's what this chapter has been about. We discovered that, under specific conditions, correlation does imply causality. The trick in causal analysis is to create those conditions by comparing like with like—through investigator-produced random assignment (as in a controlled experiment), through naturally occurring random assignment, or through some other means of matching.

Consider again the question of whether smoking causes lung cancer. When we say that "smoking causes lung cancer," we do not mean that all smokers will be victims of lung cancer, nor that all nonsmokers will avoid it. Rather, the claim "smoking causes lung cancer" means that smokers are more likely to contract lung cancer than if they had not smoked and, similarly, that nonsmokers are less likely to contract lung cancer than if they had smoked. To investigate the causal effect of smoking on lung cancer, then, what we really want to know is what the cancer rate would have been for smokers if they had not smoked, and for nonsmokers if they had smoked. Both of these rates are, by definition, unobserved, so they must be estimated. The first strategy that comes to mind is to use the observed cancer rates for nonsmokers to infer the cancer rates for smokers had they not smoked, and similarly to use the observed cancer rates for smokers to infer the cancer rates for nonsmokers had they smoked. In effect we use smokers as proxies for nonsmokers and nonsmokers as proxies for smokers. The reliability of the proxy method obviously depends on the reliability of the proxies—we must assume that smokers and nonsmokers are alike with respect to the factors (other than smoking) that lead to lung cancer.

In the laboratory, we try to make the treatment and control groups indistinguishable at the outset through random assignment. In other words, units are *randomly assigned to the cause*—some units receive the treatment and some don't, and the placement of units into one group or the other is solely on the basis of chance. Outside psychology, however, social researchers typically use observational data, and random assignment to the cause is rarely found in observational data. Thus we need to find alternative methods to investigator-produced random assignment. The most common method is regression using covariates; that is, researchers attempt to remove the contaminating effects of other variables by adding a set of causal variables to the regression equation for Y, thus residualizing both X (the causal variable of interest) and Y (the outcome of interest) on the other causal variables. In effect we try to make dissimilar individuals similar by modeling the effects of the causal variables (other than X) that distinguish them. The limitations of this method are well known. Even if we can discern the other causes, we might not be able to measure them reliably; even if we can measure them reliably, we might not be confident about the proper functional form of their effects on Y (for example, whether the effects are linear); and even in the case of perfect knowledge and measurement, we might need a large sample for reliable estimates, especially when the other causes are numerous and highly correlated.

In light of the problems with standard regression analysis, modern causal analysis in the social sciences has focused on the search for methods to supplement or replace regression as a tool for estimating causal relationships in observational data. The aim in each case is to compare like with like. One general strategy is the matching of units exactly, or matching on the basis of propensity scores. Another strategy is matching through repeated measurement: We use repeated measures of the same unit over time, or the same measures of similar units, such as siblings. A third strategy is to use naturally occurring random assignment either on the treatment itself or on a cause of the treatment.

By using one or more of the analytic strategies above—regression, exact matching or matching with propensity scores, fixed-effects models, or methods that exploit naturally occurring random assignment—our aim is to reduce the uncertainty of causal inference from observational data. In addition to the threats posed by sampling and nonsampling error linked to data collection (discussed in chapter 4)—problems endemic to experiments as well—unmeasured confounding variables greatly complicate causal inference from observational data. As our data sets become larger, sampling error contributes relatively less to uncertainty, and the other sources contribute relatively more. Hence forward-looking social scientists will shift their attention to the other threats to the accuracy of inferences in social research. Omitted-variables bias and selection bias are chief among these other threats.

Finally, observe that the strategies for employing rule 5 generally involve better research design. This observation underscores a central theme of this book: that, to improve social research, we need to focus on better conceptualization and design of our research, not on more sophisticated statistical estimation methods. Indeed, I would argue that causal analysis in the social sciences is largely an issue of proper research design. If the design is faulty, powerful estimation methods cannot be counted on to salvage the project. Sophisticated statistical estimation methods may result only in more precise estimates of the wrong thing (a theme that I will take up again in chapter 7). In addition, I want to stress that, although rule 5 itself is universally applicable, there is no single all-purpose *method* (for example, fixed-effects) that is appropriate for all causal analyses. The methods described in this chapter are tools. As with all tools, the value of the tool depends on the skill of the worker in knowing when and how to use the tool.

Student Exercises on Rule 5

MARITAL STATUS, HEALTH, AND HAPPINESS: CROSS-SECTIONAL VERSUS FIXED-EFFECTS MODELS

The assignment for chapter 5 investigates the effects of health and marital status on happiness. Recall that we also examined those effects in the exercises at the end of chapter 2. You should review your answers to the questions in the earlier assignment before beginning this one.

The assignment for chapter 5 differs because we use fixed-effects (FE) models. We could not use FE methods in chapter 2 because the 1972–2004 GSS consists of repeated cross-sectional, not panel, data. The dataset we use this time is called Aging, Status, and Sense of Control (ASOC), provided by sociologists John Mirowsky and Catherine Ross (1999). ASOC is a national probability sample of American adults in 1995 with an oversampling of those who were sixty years or older in 1995. (Nearly half the respondents are age sixty or older.) Respondents were interviewed in 1995 and reinterviewed in 1998 and in 2001.

The data are available through the Inter-University Consortium for Political and Social Research (ICPSR) at the University of Michigan. The ICPSR is a tremendous resource for social research, and one purpose of this assignment is to introduce you to this resource. Moreover, ICPSR has its own SDA site with an interface identical to that of the Berkeley SDA site, so you do not need to learn a new computer program to complete this assignment.

You can access ICPSR data only from a network provided by a university that is a member of ICPSR. Many universities belong to ICPSR. If you do not have access to the network, then unfortunately you will not be able to complete this assignment.

To access the ASOC data, go to the ICPSR homepage at http://www.icpsr.umich.edu, enter "3334" in the "Search" box, and click "Search." This will bring up the dataset, with a list of options underneath the name. Click "online analysis." When the page labeled "Analyze and Subset—Study No. 3334" comes up, go to the section titled "Online Analysis Using SDA" and click on the link indicated to bring up the SDA interface. Before the SDA interface appears, you must log in and agree to a confidentiality statement. (You will need to create an ICPSR account if you do not already have one.)

The directions for recoding variables should be familiar by now; if you need a refresher, refer to previous chapters. As before, all variable names appear in **boldface**.

Cross-sectional Relationships between Marital Status, Health, and Happiness (1995 Data)

Our dependent variable, **happy**, is a count of the number of days in the past week respondents felt happy. Note that **happy** refers to the 1995 data, **happy2** refers to the 1998 data, and **happy3** refers to the 2001 data. The other variables are similarly named. This protocol is important for the subsequent FE analysis because it enables us to create change scores for individuals simply by subtracting variables (e.g., **happydiff=happy3-happy**).

The frequency distributions of **happy**, **happy2**, and **happy3** show that ASOC respondents are generally a happy bunch. In all three years the vast majority of respondents report being happy all seven days of the past week, and only a tiny fraction say that they did not feel happy at all over that period.

We first estimate a model using the 1995 cross-section. In this analysis we regress **happy** on marital status and health. Strictly speaking, **happy** is not a continuous variable since it is bounded by 0 and 7. The more important problem, however, is that the distribution of **happy** is heavily skewed—as just noted, the vast majority of respondents are in the highest category, "happy all 7 days." So ordinarily we might dichotomize **happy** and use logit or probit regression. For the sake of simplicity here, however, we use ordinary least squares (OLS) regression.

We need to tidy up **happy** a bit before we can use it, since the variable treats missing-data codes (98 and 99) as valid responses. Because it is impossible to have been happy for 98 or 99 of the past 7 days, we need to recode this variable to eliminate those values. Select "Recode variables" under the "Create new variables" menu, enter **happy_re** as the name of your new variable (make sure that you select the option to replace any existing variable with the same name if it already exists), and enter **happy** as the name of the variable to recode. In the first row enter "0" for "Value," "no happy days" for "Label," and "0" for "Var 1." (You need to fill in rows 2–8 for values 1–7 only if you want the value labels on your printout.) Select "assign the value of input variable #1" in the "What to do with unspecified combinations of input variables (if any)" option (this is important). Then scroll down to the "Optional specifications for the new variable" section, where you should enter "0" in the "Minimum valid value" box and then "7" in the "Maximum valid value" box. Click "Start Recoding." You should now have 1,130 valid cases, with a valid range of 0 to 7.

Now recode **marstat**—the marital status variable—into a dichotomous variable called **married** denoting whether a respondent is currently married (coded as 1). Your entries into the "Recoding Rules" boxes should read: 1, married, 1; 0, not married, 2–6. Make sure that everything else is converted to MD code, and click "Start Recoding." You should have 1,142 valid cases.

Finally, recode **health** ("In general, would you say your health is very good, good, satisfactory, poor, or very poor?") into a new variable called **health_re** so that higher values represent better health. Your entries into the "Recoding Rules" boxes should read: 5, very good, 1; 4, good, 2; 3, satisfactory, 3; 2, poor, 4; 1, very poor, 5. Make sure that everything else is converted to MD code, and click "Start Recoding." Although **health_re** is an ordinal variable, we will treat it as an interval-level variable for simplicity. You should have 1,138 valid cases.

We can now run the regression on the data for 1995. Select "Multiple regression" from the "Analysis" menu. Enter **happy_re** in the "Dependent" box, then **married** and **health_re** in the "Independent" boxes. Click "Run regression." You should have 1,122 valid cases.

Question 1. (a) Do marital status and health affect happiness in this sample of mostly older Americans? If so, describe the direction of the effects. (b) Describe how omitted variables might be biasing these estimates of the causal effects of marriage and health. Be specific—in each case, list two or more omitted variables that are likely to have confounding effects.

Critics might point to the potential endogeneity of the independent variables: whether because of genetic inheritance or because of the enduring effects of early childhood socialization, perhaps some individuals are just "naturally" happy and others are naturally unhappy. And perhaps these happier people are more likely to have had the efficacy and energy to maintain a stable marriage and good health over their lives.

Our cross-sectional regression cannot rule out this possibility. However, we can take advantage of the 2001 follow-up wave to investigate whether *change* in marital status or health is associated with *change* in happiness. By restricting the analysis to within-individual variation in happiness we eliminate the effect of any stable underlying tendency of some individuals to be happier than others.

Marital Status, Health, and Happiness: A Fixed-effects Model

For the 1995 ASOC data, as well as for the GSS data (see chapter 2 exercises), we find that Americans who are married tend to be happier than Americans who are not, and that those in good health are happier than those who are in poor health. However, as noted in chapter 1 and again in the current chapter, association does not prove causation. Perhaps there are hidden variables that cause both health and happiness, or both marriage and happiness. Or perhaps there is reverse causation, as just noted in the discussion of endogeneity bias.

With FE methods we can gain leverage on the hidden variables issue as well as on the reverse causation issue. The cost of FE models is that they truncate variance because they use only the within-unit variance. In the case of panel data for individuals, "within-unit variance" means individual change over time. Here individual change over time refers to change in marital status and health status among Americans, with an oversampling of those age 60 and older. Because the possibility of failing health and the death of one's spouse is greater among the elderly, this sample likely provides more over-time variance on the key variables than would, for example, a sample that focused on adults who are age 30 to 50.

The first step is to alter the variables in the 2001 wave as above. The recoding and computing techniques are the same; only the variable names differ. Recode **happy3** into **happy3_re** (you should have 1,128 valid cases), **marstat3** into **married3** (you should have 1,118 valid cases), and **health3** into **health3_re** (you should have 1,137 valid cases).

Next, compute difference scores for happiness and health. Click on "Compute a new variable" under the "Create variables" menu. In the "Expression to define the new variable" box, type **happydiff**=**happy3 _re** – **happy_re**. Select the option to replace the variable if it already exists, make sure that the "No" option is checked beside "Include numeric missing-data values in computations?," and leave everything else the same. Click "Start Computing." You should have 1,114 valid cases. Repeat this procedure for **marrdiff**=**married3** – **married** (this should give you 1,116 valid cases) and for **healthdiff**=**health3_re** – **health_re** (this should yield 1,131 valid cases). Keep a copy of the output because you will need it for question 4 below.

Observe that **marrdiff** has three values: –1 for those who lost a spouse (due to death or divorce) from 1995 to 2001; 0 for those who did not change marital status (that is, remained married or unmarried); and 1 for those who gained a spouse. To make that clearer in the analysis, let's create two dummy variables from the **marrdiff** variable—one for being married in 1995 but not married in 2001 (**nolongermarried**), and another for being married in 2001 but not married in 1995 (**newlymarried**). Our reference group is those whose marital status did not change.

To create the dummy variables, return to the "Recode variables" screen. Recode **marrdiff** into **nolongermarried**: you should recode scores of –1 on **marrdiff** to scores of 1 on **nolongermarried**, and then **marrdiff** scores of 0 or 1 to **nolongermarried** scores of 0. Then create **newlymarried**: codes of 1 on **marrdiff** should remain 1 on **newlymarried**, but codes of 0 or –1 on **marrdiff** should become codes of 0 on **newlymarried**. You should have 1,116 valid cases on both new dummy variables—the same as for **marrdiff**.

Now run the fixed-effects model. Click on "Multiple regression" under the "Analysis" menu, then enter **happydiff** as the dependent variable and **nolongermarried, newlymarried,** and **healthdiff** as the independent variables. Click "Run regression." You should have 1,091 valid cases.

Question 2. On the basis of your results for the FE model:
(a) Does health still have a statistically significant, positive effect on happiness? Compare the FE slope with the slope in the cross-section model: Is one slope notably steeper, or are they roughly the same size? Is this result reassuring?
(b) Does marriage still have a statistically significant, positive effect on happiness? Do you find a positive effect for **newlymarried** and a negative effect for **nolongermarried**? Given the positive effect of marriage on happiness in the cross-section analysis, are you surprised by the FE results? In a few sentences of plain English, summarize the apparent effect of marriage on happiness.
(c) Refer back to your answer to question 1(b), above. For each of the omitted variables that you listed, explain how the use of the FE method here alleviates (or fails to alleviate) their confounding effects.
(d) On the basis of the FE results, are you more confident that the effects of marital status and physical health on happiness are causal? Explain.

Question 3. Compare the R^2 values for the cross-section and FE models. How do you account for the fact that the FE model explains less variance?

Question 4. (a) What percentage of the respondents experience change in reported health from 1995 to 2001? On average, did the health improve or get worse? What percentage report better health? What percentage report worse health?
(b) What percentage of respondents report a change in marital status from 1995 to 2001? What percentage changed from married to not married? What percentage changed from not married to married?
(c) Do the results for (a) and (b) seem plausible, given the age of the respondents? Explain.

OPTIONAL FIXED-EFFECTS EXERCISE FOR STUDENTS
WHO USE SAS

This exercise is designed for students who have access to SAS. Paul Allison's excellent book *Fixed Effects Regression Methods for Longitudi-*

nal Data Using SAS summarizes fixed-effects models and how to estimate them with SAS. Chapter 2 of Allison's book contains a running example of the use of fixed-effects methods to estimate the effect of family poverty (a dichotomy) and child's self-esteem (a scale) on antisocial behavior (a 7-point scale) using a sample of 581 children who were interviewed in 1990, 1992, and 1994.

Assignment: Read chapters 1 and 2 of Allison. Then replicate the results reported by Allison in outputs 2.1, 2.2, and 2.4 through 2.9. (See Allison's page 11 for the web site for downloading the data. He provides SAS codes in chapter 2.) Does family poverty appear to affect children's antisocial behavior, controlling for child's self-esteem?

Selected Further Reading

On the counterfactual approach to causal inference:

Holland, Paul W. 1986. "Statistics and causal inference." *Journal of the American Statistical Association* 81:945–70.

Morgan, Stephen L., and Christopher Winship. 2007. *Counterfactuals and Causal Inference: Methods and Principles for Social Research.* Cambridge: Cambridge University Press.

Winship, Christopher, and Stephen L. Morgan. 1999. "The estimation of causal effects from observational data." *Annual Review of Sociology* 25:659–706.

On experiments and quasi-experiments:

Campbell, Donald T., and Julian C. Stanley. 1966. *Experimental and Quasi-Experimental Designs for Research.* Boston: Houghton-Mifflin.

Ghosh, S., and C. R. Rao (editors). 1996. *Handbook of Statistics 13: Design and Analysis of Experiments.* Amsterdam: Elsevier Science.

On fixed-effects models:

Allison, Paul. 2005. *Fixed Effects Regression Methods for Longitudinal Data Using SAS.* Cary, NC: SAS Press.

Halaby, Charles N. 2004. "Panel models in sociological research: Theory into practice." *Annual Review of Sociology* 30:507–44.

On instrumental variables:

Angrist, Joshua D., and Alan B. Krueger. 2001. "Instrumental variables and the search for identification: From supply and demand to natural experiments." *Journal of Economic Perspectives* 15:69–85.

On matching methods:

Becker, S. O., and A. Ichino. 2002. "Estimation of average treatment effects based on propensity scores." *The STATA Journal* 2:358–77.

Ho, Daniel E., Kosuke Imai, Gary King, and Elizabeth A. Stuart. 2007. "Matching as nonparametric preprocessing for reducing model dependence in parametric causal inference." *Political Analysis* 15:199–236.

Morgan, Stephen L., and David J. Harding. 2006. "Matching estimators of causal effects: Prospects and pitfalls in theory and practice." *Sociological Methods and Research* 35:3–60.

Rubin, Donald B. 1973. "The use of matched samples and regression adjustment to remove bias in observational studies." *Biometrics* 29:185–203.

———. 1979. "Using multivariate matched sampling and regression adjustment to control bias in observational studies." *Journal of the American Statistical Association* 74:318–28.

The Sixth Rule

USE PANEL DATA TO STUDY INDIVIDUAL CHANGE AND
REPEATED CROSS-SECTION DATA TO STUDY SOCIAL CHANGE

Chapter 5 focused on causal effects—what they are, and how we might estimate them as social scientists. Investigating causes is not the only aim of social research. Sometimes the primary aim of research in the social sciences is to describe key features of the social world, and how those features are changing. This chapter focuses on the question of how to study change. Although researchers frequently study change at the individual level in order to investigate causal relationships, the study of broad social change most often is descriptive. Generally the aim in aggregate-level studies is to describe broad change and its correlates—to get the basic facts right. Both types of studies are needed. Indeed, I see description and explanation as complementary, since we need to know what there is to explain before we set about to provide an explanation.

Rule 6 states that you should use panel data to study change at the individual level and repeated cross-section data to study broad social change, such as change in societies. An example of the repeated cross-section design is the repeated survey, where the same questions are asked from survey to survey, but a new sample is selected for each survey. Many repeated surveys, such as the American National Election Study, are spaced at regular intervals (usually every year or every other year). Other repeated surveys, such as the Gallup and Roper polls on the Equal Rights Amendment, are spaced at irregular intervals (see assignment 1 in chapter 4).

Unlike repeated surveys, panel surveys follow the same individuals over time. Although repeated surveys and panel surveys both enable researchers to study change over time, they are designed for different purposes (Duncan and Kalton 1987). Panel surveys track how individuals change over time—for example, whether an individual has switched her political allegiance from Republican to Democrat, or vice versa—whereas repeated surveys track aggregate change over time—for example, change in the proportion of Americans who identify themselves as Democrats.

Repeated surveys and panel surveys have become staples of modern social research. One of the best-known repeated surveys in the United States is the General Social Survey, an omnibus survey of attitude change since

1972. From 1972 to 1993 the survey was done annually (with a few missing years); since 1994 it has been done every other year. To remain representative of the changing U.S. adult population, the GSS selects a fresh sample for each new survey. Otherwise the GSS would lose its value for tracking change in U.S. society. The youngest respondents in the original 1972 GSS sample were eighteen years old in 1972; that is, they were born in 1954. So if the GSS were still based on the 1972 sample, the 2004 GSS would consist only of individuals who are age fifty and older.

By selecting a fresh sample for each survey, the GSS cannot follow specific individuals over time. As a result, repeated surveys are ill-suited for monitoring individual change. That's what panel data are designed to do, and large panel data sets are becoming increasingly prominent in social research.

In view of the limitations of pure panel and pure repeated cross-section designs, the best data sets often contain elements of each. Thus some panel data sets routinely add individuals to the sample to maintain a representative sample; some repeated surveys contain a panel component so some of the respondents are followed over time; and some data sets employ various other hybrid designs. In using the terms "panel" and "repeated cross-section," I am referring to the core feature of the sample design: Does the study primarily reinterview the same individuals or select new respondents each time? The best empirical studies in the social sciences today very often rely on panel data or repeated survey data or data from hybrid designs, so there is good reason to be familiar with these research designs even if you are not interested in the study of change per se.

This chapter presents a number of regression models designed to exploit the panel and repeated cross-section data sets that are increasingly available in the social sciences. The models are simple and flexible. Most of the models can be estimated using ordinary least squares regression. The next section sets up the discussion of the models by formalizing a key difference between panel and repeated survey designs.

ANALYTIC DIFFERENCES BETWEEN PANEL AND REPEATED CROSS-SECTION DATA

Suppose we want to estimate the relationship between X and Y from data on X and Y for a sample of N_1 individuals at time 1 and N_2 individuals at time 2. What analytic leverage do we gain by following the same individuals over time, as in the panel design?

The panel design offers two important advantages over the repeated cross-section design. First, with panel data we can measure *gross* individual change; that is, we can measure all the change that is taking place for individuals (for example, how many individuals marry or remarry, and how many divorce, over some period). With repeated surveys we observe only *net* individual change, for example, change in the overall percentage married or divorced (though of course we can ask people about their marital histories).

The second advantage is that panel designs provide two or more degrees of freedom for each individual in the study. As a result, panel designs enable us to use fixed-effects models for individuals. Recall that with fixed effects we are able to remove the constant effects of enduring individual traits, as described in chapter 5. This is an important virtue of panel data because with fixed-effects methods (for example, differencing) we can very often remove the effects of significant confounding variables even when we don't know what those variables are. Because we cannot apply those methods when we have only one data point for each individual, in the case of repeated cross-section data we must actually measure enduring individual traits in order to remove their confounding effects. This point harks back to what was called, in chapter 5, the "first-difference advantage": The first-difference model replaces the standard regression assumption that measured and unmeasured causes are uncorrelated with the less restrictive assumption of stability in the unmeasured causes and their effects.

In short, panel data sets, but not repeated cross-section data sets, permit you to use fixed-effects methods to control for unmeasured traits of individuals (Liker, Augustyniak, and Duncan 1985). Because this point is central to what follows, it is useful to write out a model that demonstrates the panel advantage more formally and provides a point of comparison for repeated cross-section models.

Consider the simple case where X, one of the causes of Y, changes over time for individuals, while the other causes of Y are constant over time. To simplify notation, imagine that these constant traits—the ones that confound our estimation of the effect of X on Y—can be captured by a single variable F ("fixed traits") and that the effect of F on Y is constant over time. Then we have a simple two-regressor model where Y is a function of a variable X that changes over time (or a set of variables that change over time—the model readily generalizes to multiple Xs) and a variable F that does not change over time:

$$Y_{it} = \alpha + \alpha_t + \gamma F_i + \beta_t X_{it} + \varepsilon_{it} \qquad (6.1)$$

Y_{it} is the value of Y for the ith individual at time t, F_i is the value of F for the ith individual (there is no subscript t since F is the same for individual i regardless of the time of measurement), X_{it} is the value of X for the ith individual at time t, and ε_{it} is the error for the ith individual at time t. The other terms are parameters: α is an overall constant, α_t is a constant specific to time t (capturing change in Y that is constant across individuals and not otherwise accounted for by the regressors), γ is the effect of F on Y, and β_t is the effect of X on Y at time t. Our aim is to estimate β_t. (If the effect of X on Y does not vary over time, then $\beta_t = \beta$, and we could drop the subscript t.)

The term γF_i holds the key. Because γ is a constant and F_i is a constant for the ith individual, γF_i can be captured by a dummy variable for the ith individual. In other words, we don't need to measure F at all *if* we have enough degrees of freedom to capture γF_i by the use of dummy variables for each individual in the study. With panel data we have the needed degrees of freedom to do that. With repeated cross-section data we do not. To illustrate, suppose we have three waves of panel data consisting of 1,000 individuals each. Because there are 1,000 individuals, we need $N-1$ or 999 dummy variables[1] to capture the effect of the γF_i. Because we have $1,000 \times 3 = 3,000$ data points, we have plenty of degrees of freedom to estimate equation 6.1 without measuring F. In the analogous case for repeated cross-section data, however, there are 3,000 separate individuals, requiring 2,999 dummy variables. In the case of repeated cross-section data, then, to control for the effect of F_i we must actually measure it since we cannot remove its effects through dummy variables or other fixed-effects methods.

Three General Questions about Change

Chapter 6 is organized around three general questions about change over time. One question focuses on individual-level change, one focuses on social change (aggregate-level change), and one bridges individual change and social change by asking how individual-level change "adds up" to social change.

1. *Changing-effect models for panel and repeated cross-section data.* The question addressed here is: Has the association of X and Y changed over time?
2. *Convergence/divergence models for repeated cross-section data.* The question here is: Has Y changed over time for societies, and has it changed in the same direction and at the same pace for all groups?

---

[1] With more than one observation per individual, you have several options for capturing γF_i (so you don't literally need to enter 999 dummies). For two waves of panel data, for example, you could use a first-difference equation, as described in chapter 5. I use the example of dummy variables here because I assume most readers are familiar with dummy variables.

3. *Bridging individual and social change.* The question here is: How much of the aggregate change in Y can be accounted for by change in the population composition?

The models differ in the way time is treated. Time is treated as categorical in changing-effect models and serves as the key subscript for variables in the models. In convergence models, time is treated as continuous and serves as the primary X-axis. In models that bridge individual and social change, time serves as a subscript to obtain parameter estimates that are used in a second step to estimate overall change over the time interval.

CHANGING-EFFECT MODELS, PART 1: TWO POINTS IN TIME

Changing-effect (or changing-parameter) models ask whether the association of X and Y has changed over time. For example, has education become a more important predictor of individuals' earnings? What about the association of race and earnings—are racial differences diminishing? Do Catholics still tend to have larger-than-average families, or has that fertility difference disappeared? To fix basic concepts, we begin with the case of data collected at just two points in time.

Case 1: Two-Wave Panel Data with Time-Varying Xs

Imagine you have two waves of panel data, and you are especially interested in the effect of a particular individual trait that changes over time. We denote that trait as X to distinguish it from the other observed variables, Vs (not to be confused with Ws, the *unobserved* causal variables discussed in chapter 5). With two waves of panel data we can regress change in Y from time 1 to time 2 on change in X and change in V from time 1 to time 2, as in standard first-difference models. The aim in a changing-effect analysis (as the name suggests) is to determine whether the effect of X has *changed* from time 1 to time 2. To find out, we add X_{i1} to the first-difference model:

$$Y_{i2} - Y_{i1} = (\alpha_2 - \alpha_1) + \beta_2 (X_{i2} - X_{i1}) + (\beta_2 - \beta_1)X_{i1}$$
$$+ \gamma(V_{i2} - V_{i1}) + (\varepsilon_{i2} - \varepsilon_{i1}) \tag{6.2}$$

To simplify we assume only one X and one control variable V; the model easily generalizes to multiple Xs and Vs. X and V are time-varying regressors (later we consider the case where X is constant) that can be either continuous or discrete; nonetheless, it is convenient to speak of the α parameters in equation 6.2 as y-intercepts in a regression plane, so we assume that at least one of the regressors is continuous. (This assumption is for convenience only; it does not affect our conclusions.) In equation 6.2, then, α_1 is the y-intercept at time 1 and α_2 is the y-intercept at time 2. The parameter β_1 is the effect of X on Y at time 1, β_2 is the effect of X on Y at time 2, and γ is the effect of V on Y, which we assume does not change over time. (These models may be for descriptive purposes only, that is, we do not necessarily assume that the effects we observe are causal.) Note that the coefficient for X_{i1} is $\beta_2 - \beta_1$, the *change* in the effect of X on Y from time 1 to time 2. Hence including X at time 1 in a first-difference model provides a ready-made test for changing effects.

A statistically significant coefficient for the X_{i1} term indicates that the effect of X on Y has changed from time 1 to time 2. To illustrate, consider again the example of southern residence and racial attitudes. In chapter 5 we noted that difference models can be used to estimate the effect of southern residence on racial attitudes. Here the issue is whether that effect has *changed*. Historically, segregationist attitudes have been strongest in the South. It is frequently claimed, however, that the association of region and segregationist attitudes has weakened in recent decades. To determine if the South-Nonsouth difference indeed has diminished we can, with two waves of panel data, regress change in segregationist attitudes on change in region and on initial region. A statistically significant coefficient *for initial region* indicates that regional differences in segregationist attitudes have in fact changed. If we code region as a dummy variable for the South, we expect the coefficient for initial region to be negative (that is, we expect $\beta_2 < \beta_1$), in line with our hypothesis that the effect of region on segregationist attitudes is weaker now than earlier.

With panel data, then, we can test whether effects change over time for our measured variables. By using change scores, as in equation 6.2, we purge X and Y of the persistent effects of unmeasured causes (the chief virtue of first-difference models, as noted earlier). The promise of that purging is a better estimate of the true causal effect of X. Also as noted in chapter 5, however, there is a price to pay for the purging: reduced variance on the independent variables. Consider again the effect of southern residence on racial attitudes. In the first-difference model our estimate of the effect of southern residence depends on attitude change among individuals who moved into or out of the South. We cannot use first-difference models to estimate the effect of southern residence on racial attitudes at time 1 or time 2 in the absence of migration into or out of the South since, in the absence of migration, change in southern residence would be constant (zero) for everyone. Interestingly, though, in the absence of migration we *can* use first-difference models to determine whether the effect of southern residence on racial attitudes *changed* from time 1 to time 2. That is the topic of the next section.

Case 2: Two-Wave Panel Data with Time-Invariant Xs

Equation 6.2, like equation 6.1, removes the confounding effects of the F_i— the constant effects of fixed individual traits—without measuring those traits. This is the feature of fixed-effects methods that makes them attractive: We can use fixed-effects methods to remove the effects of fixed individual differences, even when we do not measure those differences. It turns out, however, that in some instances those are the effects of interest—and we cannot estimate the effects of individual differences if we have removed them.

In other words, differencing will not work if we are interested in the enduring effects of fixed traits because differencing removes the variance of interest. But if we are interested in estimating *change* in effects— which *is* the objective in the case of changing-effect models—then fixed-effects methods can be used even when the traits of interest are fixed.

To illustrate, suppose we hypothesized (1) that Americans who are "born Catholic" (that is, Americans who grow up in a Catholic home) are more likely to disapprove of abortion and (2) that the effect has weakened over time, reflecting the declining influence of official church doctrine among American Catholics. Fixed-effects methods can be used to examine the second hypothesis but not the first. Let Y be a measure of attitude about abortion, coded so that high values reflect disapproval of abortion and low values reflect approval. Let X be a dummy variable for Catholic-born ($X_{i1} = X_{i2} = 1$ for those reared Catholic, 0 otherwise). Because the term ($X_{i2} - X_{i1}$) drops out in equation 6.2, we cannot use equation 6.2 to test the hypothesis that Americans who grew up Catholic are more likely to disapprove of abortion. The equation does shed light, however, on whether the effect of Catholic upbringing changed from time 1 to time 2. The coefficient for X_{i1} estimates ($\beta_2 - \beta_1$), so a negative coefficient for X_{i1} is consistent with our hypothesis that the effect of Catholic upbringing on anti-abortion attitudes is weaker now (assuming the effect was positive in the first place).[2]

---

[2] Because Catholic upbringing is a fixed trait for individuals, the term ($X_{i2} - X_{i1}$) drops out in equation 6.2 and we have:

$$Y_{i2} - Y_{i1} = (\alpha_2 - \alpha_1) + (\beta_2 - \beta_1)\, X_{i1} + \gamma(V_{i2} - V_{i1}) + (\varepsilon_{i2} - \varepsilon_{i1}),$$

where α_2 is the y-intercept for non-Catholics at time 2 and α_1 is the y-intercept for non-Catholics at time 1. β_1 is the difference in y-intercepts for Catholics and non-Catholics at time 1—the Catholic-upbringing effect at time 1—and β_2 is the difference in y-intercepts for Catholics and non-Catholics at time 2. Hence $\beta_2 - \beta_1$, the parameter for X, is the difference in

In short: Although we cannot estimate the effects of fixed traits such as gender or Catholic upbringing with differencing methods, we can use differencing methods to estimate the *changing* effect of such variables. Thus if we are interested in estimating changes in the effect of gender, we can use the differencing model of equation 6.2 when we have panel data. Equation 6.2 also can be used to estimate the changing effects of variables that vary over time. Fixed-effects models such as equation 6.2 do not work for repeated survey data, however, since repeated surveys do not follow individuals over time. As we now see, an interaction model is more appropriate for investigating changing effects with repeated survey data.

Case 3: Repeated Cross-section Data

One way to think about the question of whether the association of X and Y has changed over time is to think of time as a variable that moderates the effect of X on Y. Instead of using time as the basis for differencing, we include time in the model as a variable and interact it with the variable(s) of interest.

Imagine we have two repeated surveys, one administered at time 1 and the other administered at time 2. To simplify the model we assume a single focal variable X and a single control variable V; the model easily generalizes to multiple Xs and Vs. The variables X and V can be either continuous or discrete; nonetheless, so that we can speak of the α parameters as y-intercepts in a regression plane, it is often convenient to think of at least one of the regressors as continuous.

We could estimate the effects separately for time 1 and time 2 as follows:

$$Y_{i1} = \alpha_1 + \beta_1 X_{i1} + \gamma V_{i1} + \varepsilon_{i1} \tag{6.3a}$$

$$Y_{i2} = \alpha_2 + \beta_2 X_{i2} + \gamma V_{i2} + \varepsilon_{i2} \tag{6.3b}$$

The subscript i indexes individual, so Y_{it} is the value of Y for the ith respondent in the tth survey ($t = 1, 2$). Note that these equations assume that the effect of X on Y might have changed over time: the effect of X on Y at time 1 is denoted β_1 and the effect of X on Y at time 2 is denoted β_2.

---

the Catholic-upbringing effect on abortion attitudes at time 2 versus time 1. A nonzero parameter for X, then, indicates that the Catholic-upbringing *effect* has changed; that is, the *difference* between Catholics and others (with V controlled) has changed with regard to abortion attitudes. The size of the change in the effect depends on how much Catholics change and how much others change. If change in attitudes toward abortion is the same for Catholics and non-Catholics, then the Catholic-upbringing *effect* does not change, and $\beta_2 - \beta_1$ is zero.

One way to determine whether the effect has changed, then, is to estimate separate models and compare coefficients. But there is a simpler way. Consider again the issue of Catholic upbringing and abortion attitudes. To determine whether the association of Catholic upbringing and attitude toward abortion has changed from one survey to the next, we can estimate the parameters for both equations in a single step by regressing a measure of abortion attitudes on a dummy variable for time (T_2, coded 1 for time 2), a dummy variable for Catholic upbringing (X), a dummy variable representing the interaction of Catholic upbringing and time ($X \times T_2$), and a measure of the control variable V:

$$Y_{it} = \alpha_1 + (\alpha_2 - \alpha_1)T_2 + \beta_1 X_{it} + (\beta_2 - \beta_1)(X_{it} \times T_2) + \gamma V_{it} + \varepsilon_{it} \tag{6.4}$$

Equation 6.4 subsumes equations 6.3a and 6.3b (as you can see by substituting $T_2 = 0$ into equation 6.4 to reproduce 6.3a and $T_2 = 1$ into equation 6.4 to reproduce 6.3b). No important information is lost by estimating 6.4 in place of 6.3a and 6.3b—in fact, equation 6.4 is better because it gives you an easy way to determine whether or not observed change in the effect of X is statistically significant. Note that equation 6.4 contains terms for the focal variable X, for time (T_2), and for the interaction of X and time.[3]

The aim of equation 6.4 is to determine whether the effect of X on Y has changed over time. The key is the interaction term, $X \times T_2$. The parameter for this interaction term is $(\beta_2 - \beta_1)$, change in the effect of X from time 1 to time 2. Hence a statistically-significant coefficient for the interaction term indicates a change in the effect of X over the time period examined. In the language of interaction effects, the effect of X on Y is "moderated" by time.

In the case of Catholic upbringing and abortion, the parameter for the interaction term indicates whether or not the effect of Catholic upbringing has changed over time. Recall that equation 6.2 also estimates $\beta_2 - \beta_1$, except that equation 6.2 has the advantage of differencing out the effects of the confounder V without measuring it. Even if we measure V perfectly in equation 6.4, we do not expect this equation and equation 6.2 to yield the same value for $\beta_2 - \beta_1$ because the meaning of $\beta_2 - \beta_1$ differs for the two methods, as the next paragraph explains.

The interaction model of equation 6.4 and the differencing model of 6.2 both can be used to investigate changing effects of X on Y. But the two models ask somewhat different questions about changing effects.

---

[3] A note on notation: α typically denotes y-intercept and β typically denotes slope. Equations 6.3 and 6.4 use α as the parameter for T and not X because T is always a categorical variable in changing-effect models, whereas X could be either categorical or continuous.

With panel data we can ask whether the effect of X on Y has changed for a given set of individuals. With repeated cross-section data we can ask whether the effect of X on Y has changed in the general population. Thus if we are interested in describing change in some association in the general population, the repeated survey/interaction method is the more appropriate. This result should not be surprising since, by selecting a fresh sample for each survey, repeated surveys generally provide a more representative sample of changing populations. If we are interested in change in the *causal* effect of X on Y, however, the panel/differencing method is likely the better choice, since differencing removes the enduring effects of confounding variables.

For repeated cross-section data where X is continuous, the changing-effects test $\beta_2 \neq \beta_1$ is the test for nonparallel slopes in analysis of covariance models as described in statistics texts (for example, Agresti and Finlay 1997, chap. 13). In standard analysis of covariance models we might want to know, for example, whether the income return to education is the same for all groups, that is, whether the effect of years of education on income is the same for men and women, for whites and nonwhites, for southerners and nonsoutherners, and so on. In the case of equation 6.4, "group" does not refer to gender categories or race categories or regional categories, but to time—there is a time 1 group and a time 2 group. What we want to know is whether the effect of X on Y is the same for the time 1 and time 2 groups, in the same way that we might want to know whether education has the same effect on income for African Americans and Hispanic Americans as it does for white Americans.

Suppose we find that the effect of X on Y has changed. Why did it change? In the case of repeated cross-section data, one possibility is changing population composition—the population membership changes from time 1 to time 2, especially if the time interval is large. For example, in investigating changes in the determinants of voting behavior in the United States in 1970 versus 2000, we would need to bear in mind the substantial change in the U.S. electorate over the period. The use of panel data rules out such effects since the same individuals are followed over time (though compositional effects on a small scale might occur due to differential attrition). In the case of repeated cross-section data, however, changing population composition might account for some or all of the observed change in the effects of the Xs.

We consider the effect of changing population composition in more detail later in the chapter, when we examine cohort replacement effects. Here the important point to note about changing population composition is that it can change the observed association of one variable with another. To determine if that has happened we can, with repeated cross-section data, reestimate the association using a sample restricted to the birth-cohorts present in the population at the initial measurement point.[4] (The term "birth-cohort" refers to people born the same year.) Later in this chapter I describe a method that isolates the contribution of changing population composition to *societal trends*. As I show there, the method can be used to estimate how much changing population composition contributes to any trend in society, from declining voting rates to rising rates of online shopping to change in norms about sex (to cite just a few examples).

In short: We can do quite a bit with data for just two points in time. That holds for both panel data and repeated cross-section data. Certainly two points in time is better than one. But multiple data waves are better still.[5] The next section takes up that issue.

CHANGING-EFFECT MODELS, PART 2: MULTILEVEL MODELS WITH TIME AS THE CONTEXT

This section describes how to use multiple waves of data to examine the *correlates* of changing parameters. The question of how to exploit multiple waves of data is becoming more relevant as we cumulate longer time-series in the social sciences.

The two-wave changing-effect models described above are limited in what they can do. The models are designed to detect, not explain, change in individual-level associations or causal effects. The major advantage of the two-wave models above is that they make few data demands: Two surveys suffice. Increasingly in the social sciences, however, we have multiple surveys to exploit. The changing-effect models above quickly become unwieldy as we add waves of data. If we want to study how the effect of X varies over (say) thirty surveys, we would have thirty regression coefficients to compare, one for each survey. To summarize those

---

[4] To illustrate, suppose we found a steadily rising gender gap in voting for Democratic versus Republican candidates from the 1984 national election to the 2004 national election. Part or all of this growth in the gender gap could be due to greater gender differences in voting among the new cohorts of voters (those who became eligible to vote between 1984 and 2004, that is, citizens born from 1967 to 1986). To examine the effect of changing population composition, then, we could examine the gender gap with and without the new birth cohorts. If gender differences diminish significantly when we remove the new cohorts, we would infer that the cohorts recently added to the U.S. electorate contributed to the growth in the gender gap.

[5] With three or more waves of panel data it is possible to bring evidence to bear on the issue of whether the treatment effect in an experiment is better estimated by using change in Y (that is, $Y_2 - Y_1$) as the outcome variable or by using regression to control for the initial value of Y (that is, by including Y_1 as a control variable in a model of Y_2). See Allison (1990) and Morgan and Winship (2007, chap. 9).

thirty coefficients, we might very well correlate the coefficients themselves with macro-level variables for the thirty measurement points—a step toward multilevel analysis.

What We Want to Know

What are the macro changes that matter for the X-Y relationship, that is, what conditions have changed over time to cause the X-Y relationship to change over time? We might want to know, for example, why racial differences in rates of imprisonment have grown, or why the gender gap in voting for Democratic candidates has grown. Or we might want to know why the effect of education on earnings has increased in the United States.

These sorts of questions lead naturally to a multilevel model with time-varying macro-level conditions as the contextual variables. Although multilevel analysis was developed initially to study the effects of school contexts, it has proved useful for the study of other contexts as well. To apply the method here we think of time as a context, so we can wheel in the multilevel machinery, including multilevel software, to apply to change. The multilevel approach inspired by the school-effects literature can, with some modification (see DiPrete and Grusky 1990a, 1990b), be applied to the changing-effect situation where it is time, not school, that forms the context.

The General Multilevel Model

To introduce the general multilevel model, let us focus on two levels of aggregation, where individuals are nested in time. (The multilevel model can be extended to more than two levels—for example, students nested in classrooms nested in schools nested in school districts, or four levels. Most applications of the model employ two levels, however.) The two-level model consists of a "level 1" (micro) equation and a "level 2" (macro) equation. To fix basic concepts, consider the simple case of one level 1 regressor (X) and two level 2 regressors (Z_1 and Z_2, reflecting macro-level conditions).

LEVEL 1 (MICRO) EQUATION

The level 1 equation is:

$$Y_{ij} = \beta_{0j} + \beta_{1j} X_{ij} + \varepsilon_{ij} \quad (j = 1, 2, \ldots, J \; contexts) \tag{6.5}$$

Y_{ij} is the value of Y for the ith individual in the jth context and X_{ij} is the value of X for the ith individual in the jth context. Equation 6.5 differs from the standard regression model in that effects are permitted to differ across contexts, as reflected by the subscript j attached to the parameters (not just the variables). Thus β_{0j} is the y-intercept for the jth survey and β_{1j} is the slope (the effect of X on Y) for the jth survey.

Because equation 6.5 permits effects to vary across contexts, it is natural to use the multilevel framework for changing-effect models where we have measurements at multiple points in time. The key is to think of *time as the context*. With multiwave panel or repeated cross-section data, then, we specify survey wave as the "group" and apply the multilevel modeling approach to estimate the βs in equation 6.5 that reflect the changing effects over time.

To simplify matters, multilevel models generally use deviation scores to center X on zero. By centering X on zero, the y-intercepts in equation 6.5 are $\bar{Y}$s (Y-means).[6] Thus β_{01} is the mean of Y for the first survey, β_{02} is the mean of Y for the second survey, and so on.

LEVEL 2 (MACRO) EQUATION

Because we are modeling both intercepts and slopes, we have an equation for each. For two Zs, the equations are:

$$\beta_{0j} = \gamma_{00} + \gamma_{01}Z_{1j} + \gamma_{02}Z_{2j} + \nu_{0j} \quad \text{(intercepts)} \tag{6.6a}$$

$$\beta_{1j} = \gamma_{10} + \gamma_{11}Z_{1j} + \gamma_{12}Z_{2j} + \nu_{1j} \quad \text{(slopes)} \tag{6.6b}$$

Note that the dependent variables in the level 2 equations are coefficients from the level 1 equations. The first equation models the level 1 intercepts as functions of the two Zs. The second equation models the level 1 slopes as functions of the two Zs. I follow standard multilevel notation (Bryk and Raudenbush 1992), where the first subscript for γ identifies the level 1 coefficient being used as the dependent variable (0 for intercept, 1 for the slope for the first micro-level regressor, and so on), and the second subscript for gamma is the conventional notation of 0 for intercept *in that equation*, 1 for the slope for Z_1, and so on. Substantively, then:

- γ_{01} is the effect of macro-level variable Z_1 on the $\bar{Y}$s across surveys, and γ_{02} is the effect of macro-level variable Z_2 on the $\bar{Y}$s across surveys.
- γ_{11} is the effect of variance in macrolevel variable Z_1 on variance in the regression slopes, that is, on variance in the effect of X on Y over time. Similarly, γ_{12} is the effect of variance in Z_2 on variance in the effect of X on Y over time. In short, the model is designed to tell us whether *change in the effect* of X on Y over time is associated with change in macro conditions Z_1 and Z_2

Because the level 2 equations involve clustering effects that violate key assumptions about the error term, ordinary least squares is not appropriate

---

[6] This follows from the fact that a regression line goes through the point $(\bar{X}, \bar{Y})$, so when X is centered on zero the y-intercept is the point $(0, \bar{Y})$.

for estimating multilevel models (DiPrete and Grusky 1990a; Bryk and Raudenbush 1992). Several computer packages are available that employ appropriate methods for estimating coefficients and their standard errors in multilevel models (for example, Raudenbush 2004).

Although multilevel analyses of replicated surveys will become increasingly practical as we continue to cumulate such surveys over time, it is important to emphasize that our macro-level models nonetheless will continue to lack power for some time to come. The number of time contexts is still limited in the most popular replicated surveys in the social sciences, and a paucity of time contexts in turn limits the macro equation to just a few variables. In the case of the cumulative General Social Survey, for example, there are 46,510 respondents (as of the 2004 survey) but only 25 time contexts (surveys), and the surveys are being added at the rate of only one every two years. In effect, $N = 25$ for GSS macro-level equations where time is the context. At the macro level, then, our changing-effect analyses still lack power.

We turn our attention now to the second general question posed in the chapter, the convergence question. Are significant economic, social, and political indicators changing in the same direction and pace for all groups in a society?

CONVERGENCE MODELS

Social scientists have an abiding interest in divisions in societies—race and ethnic divisions, gender gaps, differences based on religion, "blue states" versus "red states," disparities in health outcomes for the rich and the poor, and so on. For example, there is talk these days about deepening divisions in the United States on the basis of age ("age polarization"), moral values and religion ("culture wars"), and perhaps race and gender. By "deepening divisions" I am referring to divisions at the societal level, so repeated cross-section data are appropriate, as dictated by rule 6.

To find out if divergence is indeed taking place in a society we can, with repeated cross-section data, estimate a regression model that permits unique regression coefficients to capture the time trends for each of the groups. (Alternatively, we could estimate separate regressions for each group. A single model with interaction terms is more convenient, however, since a single model provides a ready-made test for whether differences in the group trends are statistically significant.) The distinctive feature of this model is that time is the X-axis, so the regression line for each group reflects the group's linear time trend. Because time itself is not thought of as a cause, the model is descriptive. The model nonetheless is useful for addressing a wide range of issues including, most notably, issues related to fissures in society.

The convergence model provides a simple way to test hypotheses about the reduction or deepening of social divisions in a society. For two groups the model can be expressed as follows, with T (time) and G (group) as the independent variables:

$$Y_{it} = \alpha + \beta T + \delta_2 G_2 + \phi_2 (T \times G_2) + \varepsilon_{it} \tag{6.7}$$

The first two terms in equation 6.7, $\alpha + \beta T$, refer to the baseline or reference group, where α and β are the y-intercept and slope, respectively. In contrast to the changing-effect model, the convergence model treats time as continuous. Because time is continuous in the convergence model, T has no subscript in equation 6.7. The groups, however, are discrete, and numerical subscripts are used to distinguish them. Thus G_2 is a dummy variable coded 1 for the second group. The parameter β is the linear time trend for the baseline group, δ_2 is the difference in y-intercepts between the second group and the baseline group, and ϕ_2 is the difference in the slope for the second group and the baseline group.

The convergence model generalizes to multiple groups $(1, 2, \ldots, G$ groups) in a straightforward manner:

$$Y_{it} = \alpha + \beta T + \delta_2 G_2 + \delta_3 G_3 + \cdots + \delta_G G_G + \phi_2 (T \times G_2) \\ + \phi_3 (T \times G_3) + \cdots + \phi_G (T \times G_G) + \varepsilon_{it} \tag{6.8}$$

In equation 6.8, as in equation 6.7, group 1 is the baseline group. Thus the parameters for the other groups are in comparison to group 1.

The Sign Test for Convergence: Comparing Your ϕs and δs

To accommodate additional groups, equation 6.8 adds dummy variables $(G_3$, etc.) to capture differences in intercepts, and interaction terms $(T \times G_3$, etc.) to capture differences in time trends. It is convenient to code T as zero for the first measurement, so α is the predicted value of Y for the baseline group at the first measurement or wave of data. The δs are differences in y-intercepts between the baseline group and the other groups, so δ_2 is the difference in y-intercepts between the first group and the second group, δ_3 is the difference in y-intercepts between the first group and the third group, and so on. In other words, the δs reflect *initial group differences on Y* (fitted by linear regression).

Similarly, the ϕs are differences in slopes (linear time trends) between the first group and the other groups. Thus ϕ_2 is the difference in linear trends for the first and second groups, ϕ_3 is the difference in trends for the first and third group, and so on.

The question of convergence and divergence of trends turns on the signs of the ϕs and the δs. When ϕ and δ have the same sign for a group, Y is diverging between that group and the baseline group. When ϕ_2 and δ_2 are both positive, for example, then the second group was higher than the baseline group on Y initially, and that initial relative advantage is increasing over time—divergence. When ϕ and δ have different signs for a group, Y is converging between that group and the baseline group (or possibly the trends have crossed).

Different group comparisons can be made by reestimating the model with different baseline groups. To determine if groups 2 and 3 are converging, for example, you can rerun the model with group 2 or group 3 as the baseline group. By repeating this process it is possible to test for convergence or divergence for all pairs of groups.

ILLUSTRATION: ATTITUDES OF WORKERS AND RETIREES TOWARD
SPENDING ON EDUCATION AND SOCIAL SECURITY

Some observers argue that, with the rise of other sources of division in American society—such as "culture wars," racial/ethnic "balkanization" in America, or generational divisions—the class war envisioned by Karl Marx has been supplanted by a culture war or a war between generations. The convergence model is designed to test just such notions. In the case of generational wars, for example, growing division between the young and the old should show up in diverging attitudes on contentious issues such as funding for Social Security and funding for public education. Consider this question in the General Social Survey:

> We are faced with many problems in this country, none of which can be solved easily or inexpensively. I'm going to name some of these problems, and for each one I'd like you to tell me whether you think we're spending too much money on it, too little money, or about the right amount. . . . Are we spending too much, too little, or about the right amount on . . . Improving the nation's education system? On Social Security?

These items invite us to bring data to bear on the question of deepening divisions across generations in the United States. The question about spending on education (**nateduc**) has been asked in the General Social Survey since 1973, while the question about spending on Social Security (**natsoc**) has been asked since 1984. It turns out that the vast majority of Americans believe either that the right amount of money or that too little money is spent on education and on Social Security; fewer than 10 percent believe that too much is spent on either, and in both cases this percentage has been declining over time. But does this overall pattern obscure diverging attitudes for the young and the old?

To find out, we apply the convergence model of equation 6.7 to **nateduc** and **natsoc**. Because those in the paid labor force are paying into Social Security while retirees are withdrawing from it, a comparison of the attitudes of paid workers and retirees toward Social Security should be especially telling. A comparison of those two groups is strategic in the case of spending on public education as well, since both groups pay school taxes even though retirees are much less likely than paid workers are to have children in public schools. If attitudes are determined by self-interest, then, we expect retirees will be more likely than workers to favor increased spending for Social Security and less likely than workers to favor increased spending for education. Moreover, if the deepening-divisions argument has merit, we should find an exacerbation of these differences over time.

Table 6.1 reports results for spending on public education. I use logit models. In a logit or "log-odds" model, the dependent variable is expressed as the natural logarithm of the odds of Y, where Y is a dichotomy

TABLE 6.1
Changing Attitudes toward Spending on U.S. Public Education:
Retirees versus Workers, 1973–2004

	Too much spending versus about right or too little spending (logit)	Too little spending versus about right or too much spending (logit)
Convergence coefficients		
Retirees – workers, initial year ($\hat{\delta}_2$)	+0.919	−0.613
	(.099)	(.069)
Retirees – workers, trends ($\hat{\phi}_2$)	−0.012	−0.001
	(.007)	(.004)
Baseline group		
Intercept for workers ($\hat{\alpha}$)	−2.29	+0.127
	(.051)	(.028)
Trend for workers ($\hat{\beta}$)	−0.028	+0.038
	(.003)	(.002)

$N = 19,816$. Standard errors are in parentheses.

Data: 1973–2004 General Social Survey, adjusted for black oversamples in 1982 and 1987. Dependent variable is GSS variable **nateduc**. Workers are respondents who are working full-time or part-time in the paid labor force (codes 1 and 2 on the GSS variable **wrkstat**), and retirees are those coded 5 on **wrkstat**.

Model: $\text{logit}(Y_{it}) = \alpha + \beta T + \delta_2 G_2 + \phi_2 (T \times G_2)$

The subscript "2" denotes group 2. Year is coded 1973 = 0 so the intercepts pertain to 1973. "Workers" is the baseline category and "retirees" is group 2, so $\hat{\delta}_2$ is the estimated difference between retirees and workers in 1973 and $\hat{\phi}_2$ is the estimated difference in the linear time trends for retirees versus workers. Trends are reported as average annual change.

and "natural logarithm" refers to the use of the base e instead of the base 10. To convert a logit back to an odds, you take the antilog of the logit. A logit coefficient of 0.919, for example, implies an odds of $e^{0.919} = 2.51$.

Because the dependent variable consists of three categories (too much spending, spending is about right, and too little spending), I dichotomize Y two different ways and report results for both. In the first model the dependent variable is dichotomized as "too much spending" versus "about right" or "too little." In the second model the contrast is "too little spending" versus "about right" or "too much."

Retirees in fact are more likely than workers to say that we are spending too much on public education in the United States (column 1 of table 6.1) and less likely to say that we are spending too little (column 2). The observed differences between retirees and workers are statistically significant and large. The y-intercept for retirees is 0.919 logits above the y-intercept for workers on "too much spending" and 0.613 logits below on "too little spending." The y-intercepts refer to values in 1973, the first survey that asks the question about spending on public education. The findings indicate that, in 1973, the odds that a retiree believes that we spend too much on public education is $e^{0.919} = 2.5$ times the odds that a worker believes that we spend too much on public education, and the odds that a retiree believes that we spend too little on education is only about half the odds ($e^{-0.613} = 0.54$) that a worker believes that we spend too little.

With regard to spending on education, then, there does appear to be a substantial generational difference, as least as of 1973. But is it growing? The results in table 6.1 suggest not. Among workers there was growing support for spending for public education, as indicated by the negative trend (slope) for "too much spending" and the positive slope for "too little spending" (last row of table 6.1). In other words, over the time period here workers became less likely to believe that we are spending too much on education and more likely to believe that we are spending too little. But retirees exhibit the same trends, as indicated by the nonsignificance of the trend differences ($\hat{\phi}_2 s$).

In short: Over the past three decades there has been growing support for more spending on public education in the United States. And there are generational differences: Thirty years ago retirees tended to be less supportive than workers for such spending, and retirees are still less supportive today. Yet there is no evidence that the generational division is widening.

Now let's look at the trend in attitudes about spending on Social Security (table 6.2). If there is generational polarization, as some have suggested, then we should observe an increasing gap between retirees and workers over the past two decades. As expected, we find that in 1984

TABLE 6.2
Changing Attitudes toward Spending on Social Security: Retirees versus Workers, 1984–2004

	Too much spending versus about right or too little spending (logit)	Too little spending versus about right or too much spending (logit)
Convergence coefficients		
Retirees – workers, initial year ($\hat{\delta}_2$)	–0.882	–0.345
	(.171)	(.069)
Retirees – workers, trends ($\hat{\phi}_2$)	+0.014	–0.003
	(.014)	(.006)
Baseline group		
Intercept for workers ($\hat{\alpha}$)	–2.31	+0.062
	(.053)	(.029)
Trend for workers ($\hat{\beta}$)	–0.021	+0.022
	(.005)	(.002)

N=22,098. Standard errors are in parentheses.
Data: 1984–2004 General Social Survey, adjusted for black oversamples in 1987. Dependent variable is GSS variable **natsoc**. Workers are respondents who are working full-time or part-time in the paid labor force (codes 1 and 2 on the GSS variable **wrkstat**), and retirees are those coded 5 on **wrkstat**.
Model: $\text{logit}(Y_{it}) = \alpha + \beta T + \delta_2 G_2 + \hat{\phi}_2 (T \times G_2)$
The subscript "2" denotes group 2. Year is coded 1984=0 so the intercepts pertain to 1984. "Workers" is the baseline category and "retirees" is group 2, so $\hat{\delta}_2$ is the estimated difference between retirees and workers in 1984 and $\hat{\phi}_2$ is the estimated difference in the linear time trends for retirees versus workers. Trends are reported as average annual change.

retirees were less likely than workers to believe that we spend too much on Social Security: According to the table 6.2 estimates, in 1984 the odds that a retiree believes that we spend too much on Social Security were less than half the odds that a worker believes that we spend too much on Social Security ($e^{-0.882} = 0.4$). Contrary to the polarization thesis, however, this gap did not grow over the next two decades, since $\hat{\phi}_2$ is not statistically significant. We conclude, then, that the time trends for retirees and workers are parallel.

An interesting wrinkle appears in our results when the dependent variable is coded as spending too little on Social Security. Recall that retirees in 1984 were less likely to say that we spend too much on Social Security. The wrinkle is that retirees were also less likely than workers to say that we spend *too little* on Social Security. In other words, retirees were more likely than workers to say that spending on Social Security is about right, whereas workers were more likely than retirees to say that the spending is off one way or the other, either too high or too low.[7] Interestingly, workers over the past two decades have become more likely to say that we spend too little on Social Security ($\hat{\beta} = 0.022$, highly significant). Yet retirees have also become more likely to say we spend too little, and the *gap* between retirees and workers has remained stable from 1984 to 2004 ($\hat{\phi}_2 = -0.003$, not significant). As we saw, the gap is constant also in the case of "spend too much." In other words, there is neither divergence nor convergence; the trends are parallel for workers and retirees.

We find no evidence at all, then, for the notion that generational divisions are growing in the United States. We do find evidence of growing support for increased spending for both public education and Social Security in the United States, at least over the time periods examined here (1973–2004 in the case of public education and 1984–2004 in the case of Social Security). Critically, though, this support has increased in tandem for retirees and workers. Even with a sample size close to 20,000 for both issues, we found no statistically significant differences in the trends for workers and retirees. There appears to be no generational war around the corner.

Finally, it is important to stress that convergence models should not be estimated blindly, without first becoming familiar with one's data and building reality checks into one's research, as dictated by rule 3. It is possible, for example, that change in Y is not monotonic over the time interval—Y might exhibit a secular increase over the first part of the interval and a secular decline over the second part of the interval. Or Y might change monotonically for some groups but not for others. It is a good idea, then, to graph the mean of Y over time before estimating convergence models. In some instances these graphs will show that the time interval needs to be broken into smaller periods or "periodized" for analysis.

Convergence Model versus Changing-Effect Model

It is useful to review what we have learned so far about the study of change. Rule 6 dictates that you use panel data to study individual change and repeated cross-section data to study social change. Panel data can used to investigate whether the association of X and Y has changed for a fixed cohort of individuals. Repeated cross-section data can be used to investigate

---

[7] The tendency of retirees to say that Social Security spending is "about right" might be an example of the psychological principle that people seek to reduce their cognitive dissonance. Because retirees are more likely than workers to be the recipients of Social Security benefits, retirees are more subject to the dissonance that would result if they were *not* to believe that spending on Social Security is about right.

whether the association of X and Y has changed for society in general. Repeated cross-section data can be analyzed using either changing-effect models or (if there are enough measurement points) convergence models. Changing-effect models treat time as categorical and use regression models of the individual-level relationship of X and Y to ask whether the effect of X on Y has changed over time. Changing-effect models can be descriptive (has the association of X and Y changed over time?) or causal (has the causal effect of X on Y changed over time?). Convergence models are descriptive models that focus on change in Y at the aggregate level. Convergence models treat time as continuous, not categorical, and use regression to model the trend in Y over time. As the name suggests, convergence models ask whether different groups are converging (or diverging) on Y.

When applied to social divisions, the convergence question (are group trends converging or diverging?) and the changing-effects question (have group differences changed?) are similar but not identical. A changing-effect test is often a natural supplement to a convergence test. For the education and Social Security examples above it would be useful to know whether we would have reached the same conclusions about the stability of generational differences had we used a two-wave changing-effect model instead of a convergence model based on all the relevant waves of GSS data. On the basis of data for the two endpoints, a changing-effect test tells us whether the difference in attitudes between workers and retirees is larger or smaller in the initial and final years. Although the two-wave changing-effect model discards data for intervening years, it can still be a powerful method because it is based on individual-level data.

The convergence and changing-effect tests are not redundant. The convergence model uses data for intermediate years, as well as the endpoints, to determine if there is linear convergence or divergence. If there is linear convergence, the difference between retirees and workers will be smaller in the final year than in the initial year. If there is linear divergence, the difference will be larger. The converse is not true. A larger difference at the final year (changing-effect model) does not necessarily mean that the trends are still diverging, since the trends might be nonlinear, with the divergence occurring earlier in the period. For the same reasons, a smaller difference at the final year does not necessarily mean that the trends are still converging. In other words, while the results of a two-wave changing-effect model can tell you whether the effect of X on Y has changed over time, it cannot tell you when the change occurred, and whether it is continuing.

Consider again the issue of generational differences in support for public education in the United States, this time investigated using a changing-effect model. To enlarge the sample for the changing-effect analysis, I combine the data for 1973–75 (the first three surveys in which the spending on public education question appeared) as well as the 2002 and 2004 surveys (there was no 2003 survey). A quick inspection of the percentages suggests that a changing-effect analysis will yield the same story as the results reported above. In the combined 1973–75 surveys, for example, 53.8 percent of workers and 38.8 percent of retirees thought that we spend too little on public education, a difference of 15 percentage points between workers and retirees. In the combined 2002 and 2004 surveys, those figures had jumped to 76.0 percent for workers and 62.0 percent for retirees, a difference of 14 percentage points between workers and retirees. Although there is much greater support today for increased spending on public education than there was three decades ago, the change in that support has increased equally among retirees and workers.

These impressions can be tested more formally. Because the General Social Survey consists of repeated surveys, I employ the interaction form of the changing-effect model:

$$Y_{it} = \alpha_1 + (\alpha_2 - \alpha_1)T_2 + \beta_1 X_{it} + (\beta_2 - \beta_1)(X_{it} \times T_2) + \varepsilon_{it} \qquad (6.9)$$

Recall that the subscripts 1 and 2 refer to time in the changing-effect model. The independent variable X in equation 6.9 can be either continuous or discrete. In the example under consideration here, X is discrete. If we code X as a dummy variable for retirees ($X = 1$ for retirees) we have this model:

$$Y_{it} = \alpha_1 + (\alpha_2 - \alpha_1)T_2 + \beta_1 retirees + (\beta_2 - \beta_1)(retirees \times T_2) + \varepsilon_{it} \qquad (6.10)$$

Table 6.3 reports results for the application of equation 6.10 to the GSS data on attitudes toward spending on public education in the United States. As before, the dependent variables is dichotomized as too much spending versus about right or too little, and too little versus about right or too much. Results closely resemble those for the convergence model. The changing-effect model indicates that workers' support for spending on public education was substantially higher in 2002–04 than it had been in 1973–75—workers in 2002–04 were less likely to say that we spend too much on education and more likely to say that we spend too little ($\hat{\alpha}_2 - \hat{\alpha}_1$, columns 1 and 2). This result squares with the trends observed in the convergence model. Results for the retirees dummy variable in equation 6.10 also square with results from the convergence model. Retirees in the mid-1970s were significantly more likely than workers to say that we spend too much on public education and significantly less likely than workers to say that we spend too little.

The key finding in table 6.3 is that ($\hat{\beta}_2 - \hat{\beta}_1$), the coefficient for the interaction term $retirees \times T_2$, falls well short of statistical significance, indicating that the difference between workers and retirees in 2002–04 is the same as it was thirty years earlier. On the basis of this finding we conclude,

TABLE 6.3
Changing Attitudes toward Spending on U.S. Public Education: Results for
Changing-Effect Model, 1973–75 versus 2002–04.

	Too much spending versus about right or too little spending (logit)	Too little spending versus about right or too much spending (logit)
Convergence coefficients		
Retirees–workers, initial year ($\hat{\beta}_1$)	+0.767	−0.610
	(.140)	(.106)
Retirees–workers, trends ($\hat{\beta}_2 - \hat{\beta}_1$)	−0.013	−0.002
	(.009)	(.006)
Baseline group		
Intercept for workers ($\hat{\alpha}_1$)	−2.21	+0.154
	(.071)	(.043)
Trend for workers ($\hat{\alpha}_2 - \hat{\alpha}_1$)	−0.022	+0.034
	(.004)	(.002)

$N = 4{,}761$. Standard errors are in parentheses.

Data: 1973–75 and 2002–04 General Social Surveys. Dependent variable is GSS variable **nateduc**. Workers are respondents who are working full-time or part-time in the paid labor force (codes 1 and 2 on the GSS variable **wrkstat**), and retirees are those coded 5 on **wrkstat**.

Model: logit $(Y_{it}) = \alpha_1 + (\alpha_2 - \alpha_1)T_2 + \beta_1 retirees + (\beta_2 - \beta_1)retirees \times T_2$, where *retirees* is a dummy variable coded 1 for retirees.

In the changing-effect model, the subscripts 1 and 2 denote *time*. Year is coded 1973–75 = 0 so the intercepts pertain to time 1. Note that all the variables, including time, are dummy variables, so "linear trend" here is reflected by differences in intercepts. To facilitate comparison with results from the convergence model (table 6.1), coefficients for workers' trend $(\hat{\alpha}_2 - \hat{\alpha}_1)$ and trend difference $(\hat{\beta}_2 - \hat{\beta}_1)$ were divided by 29 to convert from total to average annual change over the period 1973–75 to 2002–04.

as before, that the trends for workers and retirees are neither converging nor diverging. With the changing-effect model, however, the evidence is less direct since we do not know what the trend was between 1975 and 2002—something that we can readily examine under the convergence model. The evidence from the changing-effect model is also based on a smaller sample.

In this instance, then, the changing-effect model and the convergence model tell the same story, with effect sizes that are roughly similar (table 6.4). This will not always be the case. Because it uses all the waves of data, the convergence model provides a more direct test of whether trends are converging or diverging. On the other hand, changing-effect models are more widely applicable in the social sciences since they require only two waves of data. They ask whether effects are the same at two different points in time—a more delimited issue than the issue of convergence. Convergence

TABLE 6.4

Changing Attitudes toward Spending on U.S. Public Education: Comparing Results for Convergence and Changing-Effect Models

	Too *much* spending versus about right or too little spending (logit)	Too *little* spending versus about right or too little spending (logit)
Convergence coefficients (both models)		
Retirees – workers, initial year		
Convergence model	+0.919	−0.613
Changing-effect model	+0.767	−0.610
Retirees – workers, trend difference		
Convergence model	—[a]	—
Changing-effect model	—	—
Baseline group (both models)		
Intercept for workers		
Convergence model	−2.29	+0.127
Changing-effect model	−2.21	+0.154
Trend for workers (annual change)		
Convergence model	−0.028	+0.038
Changing-effect model	−0.022	+0.034

Note: Results from tables 6.1 and 6.3. N = 19,816 for convergence model and 4,761 for changing-effect model.

[a] Not statistically significant.

models will become increasingly useful in the social sciences as we accumulate more and more measurement points in our data sets. In the meantime, with changing-effect models we can often learn quite a bit from just two waves of data, particularly if the measurement interval is appropriate for the change in question.

BRIDGING INDIVIDUAL AND SOCIAL CHANGE: ESTIMATING COHORT REPLACEMENT EFFECTS

Where does social change come from? By social change I am referring to change on some aggregate attribute for a society, such as change in percentage of people who vote or percentage of people who attend church regularly. There are two major proximate sources: Individuals can change, and the composition of a population can change (Ryder 1965). In other words, change in public attitudes could be due to changing public opinion or to *changing publics*.

The effect of changing publics—changing population composition due to population turnover—is often ignored in discussions of social change. For example, popular discussions of the rise of political conservatism and the increased popularity of the Republican party in the United States in the 1980s were often framed in terms of questions such as "Why are people converting to the Republican party?" Because of population turnover, however, percentage Republican could rise during a period when no one switched to the Republican party. The composition of the U.S. electorate changes over time as older birth-cohorts gradually die off and are replaced by younger birth-cohorts. This type of population turnover, called *cohort replacement* or *cohort succession*, leads to societal change when the attitudes and beliefs of the cohorts entering the electorate differ from the attitudes and beliefs of the birth-cohorts that are dying off.[8]

It turns out that cohort replacement in fact accounted for a large part of the 1980s' rise in Republicanism, as cohorts entering the electorate in the 1980s tended to be more Republican than the older cohorts they were replacing (Norpoth 1987). Similarly, by decomposing the change in segregationist attitudes among U.S. whites in the 1970s and early 1980s, we find that growing acceptance of interracial marriage in the United States in that period was driven primarily by cohort replacement—reflecting generational differences—whereas change in other racial attitudes resulted largely from individual change across a broad swath of society (Firebaugh and Davis 1988).

Separating the effect of population turnover from the effect of aggregated individual change is strategic in the study of social change. By identifying the proximate sources of social change, we know better where to look for underlying causes. When we know that changing attitudes toward interracial marriage are due to cohort replacement rather than to aggregated individual change, the question "Why are the younger cohorts more tolerant?" replaces the question "Why are people's attitudes changing?" Those two questions may point in very different directions with respect to underlying causes.

Because pure panel designs do not have a mechanism for adding new cohorts as they enter a population, panel data alone cannot be used to investigate cohort replacement effects. Repeated surveys, by contrast, are well suited for investigating cohort replacement effects. With repeated survey data it is possible to estimate how much of the observed social change is due to aggregated individual change and how much is due to cohort re-

---

[8] Population turnover effects consist of more than just cohort replacement effects, since populations can also change because of migration. Typically, however, the cohort succession process dominates the population turnover effect, so studies generally speak of separating the effect of cohort replacement from the effect of aggregated individual change.

placement. The next sections describe a straightforward method for such a partitioning.

An Accounting Scheme for Social Change

Suppose we are investigating social change on some variable Y. Overall social change from survey 1 to survey T is $\bar{Y}_T - \bar{Y}_1$, where $\bar{Y}$ is the mean of Y. Our aim is to determine how much of $\bar{Y}_T - \bar{Y}_1$ (for example, change in percent Republican) is due to aggregated individual change and how much is due to the effect of cohort replacement. (Note that the mean of Y subsumes percentages and proportions, since a proportion is the mean of a binary variable coded 0, 1 and a percentage is the mean of a binary variable coded 0, 100.)

With repeated survey data we cannot follow individuals over time, so we cannot follow the change in racial attitudes for particular individuals as they age. We can, however, follow *birth-cohorts* over time, so we can follow the change in racial attitudes for cohorts as they age; we call this *within-cohort* or *intracohort change*. We begin the decomposition of societal change by separating intracohort change from cross-cohort or intercohort change, where cross-cohort change refers to cohort differences on the mean of Y. Cohort differences are necessary for cohort replacement effects: If all cohorts had the same mean on Y, then substituting one cohort for another would have no effect on the overall Y-mean.

Cross-cohort change, then, bears on the contribution of cohort replacement to social change. As noted earlier, panel data alone cannot be used for estimating cohort replacement effects, since the effect of entering cohorts is not captured in panel data.

Within-cohort change bears on the contribution of aggregated individual change to social change. Although individuals are not followed over time with repeated survey data (so change for specific individuals is unobserved), the net effect of individual change on social change *is* observed. Suppose we find that political party preference (percentage Republican, Democrat, and Independent) remained the same over time within cohorts. With repeated surveys, we do not know how much party switching occurred over the period. But we do know that, to the extent that there was party switching, the changes canceled each other out within the cohorts, so party switching resulted in no net change within cohorts. As a result, individual change (if any) produced no social change in this instance.

With repeated cross-section data, we can glean the effect of aggregated individual change from change in the Y-mean within birth cohorts over time. This strategy is not foolproof, since change in Y-mean within a cohort might reflect more than the effect of individuals changing on Y: It can also reflect migration effects or the effect of differential cohort mortality. Imagine, for example, that party preference is fixed for all individuals after age eighteen: Once a Republican always a Republican, and similarly for Democrats and Independents. Percent Republican could nonetheless increase within birth-cohorts if Republicans tend to outlive others. Similarly, the average education of a cohort could rise over time simply because the less-educated tend to die younger than the better-educated. We could detect this sort of effect with panel data but not with repeated cross-section data. Thus in instances where there is reason to believe that differential mortality or migration is related to Y, it is a good idea if possible to compare the within-cohort trend in repeated surveys with the comparable trend in panel data.

Linear Decomposition Method

The cohort replacement accounting scheme divides total social change over some time period into (i) the part due to cohort replacement and (ii) the part due to aggregated individual change. The magnitude of the cohort replacement effect is determined by the *size* of cohort differences for the cohorts rotating in versus those dying off and the *rate* of cohort replacement. The contribution of aggregated individual change to social change is determined by the intracohort trend, that is, by the average change over time within cohorts.

Partitioning of this type makes sense only when the pace of cohort replacement is commensurate with the pace of social change, so that cohort replacement is a plausible source of the change. It would be pointless to investigate the contribution of cohort replacement to the weekly or monthly swings in the popularity of a sitting U.S. president, for example, since the ups and downs of presidential popularity happen at a much faster pace than the pace of cohort succession. It would also be pointless, at the other extreme, to investigate the contribution of cohort replacement to change in voting patterns from, say, 1910 to today, since there is no overlap of voting cohorts—in a vacuous sense all change since 1910 is attributable to cohort replacement because the replacement is complete. In the discussion that follows, we assume that the pace of the social change of interest is in fact commensurate with the pace of cohort replacement, so that cohort replacement could sensibly account for some or all of the observed social change. We also assume that measurement intervals for the data are appropriate for the pace of social change under investigation, so that the data indeed capture the change.

Linear decomposition provides a way to separate out the cohort replacement component of overall social change. It is called linear decomposition because it assumes linear within- and cross-cohort change; other methods are possible when linearity assumptions are not met (Firebaugh 1989, 1997).

Suppose we have repeated survey data consisting of T surveys with N_t units (individuals) in the tth survey. Such data sets are increasingly common in the social sciences, and generally the surveys come ready-made for analysis as cumulated data files; that is, the T surveys are already merged. Linear decomposition is attractive in part because it is so easy to do with merged data, and the data requirements are so minimal: It requires only three variables (age, year of survey, and an outcome variable Y).

The first step is to create a birth-cohort variable. With data on survey year and respondent's age, we calculate birth-year as year minus age. For the sake of data display, it might be useful sometimes to collapse birth-cohort into broader intervals (e.g., five-year or ten-year intervals), particularly if the surveys are five years or ten years apart. For the decomposition itself, however, one-year intervals generally are most appropriate, and for shorthand I will refer to the cohort variable as birth-year. We assume year as the appropriate metric for surveys as well, so cohort is measured as birth-year and survey is measured as survey-year. To facilitate interpretation of the y-intercept, it is useful to code survey-year as zero for the first survey and birth-year as zero for the oldest birth-cohort.

The next step is to regress Y on individual's birth-year and date of survey (year that the individual was surveyed):

$$Y_{it} = \beta_{0t} + \beta_{1t} SurveyYear_{it} + \beta_{2t} BirthYear_{it} + \varepsilon_{it} \qquad (6.11)$$

Equation 6.11 is meant to be descriptive, not causal. It states that the value of Y for an individual is a linear and additive function of the year the individual was surveyed and the year the individual was born.

From the results of this very simple model we can decompose social change on Y. To assist intuition, note that social change on Y from survey 1 to survey T is defined as $\overline{Y}_T - \overline{Y}_1$, and that we can determine both of those means by taking the expected value of equation 6.11 for the first and last surveys as follows:

$$E(Y_{i1}) = \overline{Y}_1 = \beta_{01} + \beta_{11} SurveyYear_1 + \beta_{21} \overline{BirthYear}_1 \qquad (6.12)$$

$$E(Y_{iT}) = \overline{Y}_T = \beta_{0T} + \beta_{1T} SurveyYear_T + \beta_{2T} \overline{BirthYear}_T \qquad (6.13)$$

$SurveyYear_1$ is the year the first survey was administered and $\overline{BirthYear}_1$ is the average year of birth for respondents in the first survey, and similarly for the Tth survey.

Social change in Y from the first survey to the Tth survey is change in $\overline{Y}$ from time 1 to time T, or equation 6.13 minus equation 6.12:

$$\Delta \overline{Y} = \overline{Y}_T - \overline{Y}_1 = \beta_1 \Delta SurveyYear + \beta_2 \Delta \overline{BirthYear}, \qquad (6.14)$$

where Δ denotes change, and we assume the βs are the same at time 1 and time T (for example, $\beta_{11} = \beta_{1T}$).

Equation 6.14 is the key equation in linear decomposition. On the basis of equation 6.14 we can partition social change into two components:

- The first component, $\beta_1 \Delta SurveyYear$, is the contribution of aggregated individual change to overall social change from survey 1 to survey T. Recall that β_1 is the linear within-cohort slope (a weighted average of all the within-cohort slopes), or average annual change in Y within cohorts. To get the total contribution of aggregated individual change to social change over the entire time interval, then, we weight the average change per year (β_1) by $\Delta SurveyYear$, the number of years from the first survey to the last survey.

- The second component, $\beta_2 \Delta \overline{BirthYear}$, is the contribution of cohort replacement to overall social change from the first survey to the last survey. β_2 is the linear cross-cohort slope, or average difference in Y from one cohort to the next. To get the total contribution of cohort replacement to social change over the entire time interval, then, we weight the average cross-cohort change (β_2) by $\Delta \overline{BirthYear}$, the difference between the average year of birth for respondents in the first survey and the last survey. To illustrate, suppose the average age for respondents is forty for a survey taken in 1980 and forty-two for a survey taken in 2005. The 1980 respondents on average were born in 1940, and 2005 respondents on average were born in 1963, so $\Delta \overline{BirthYear} = 1963 - 1940 = 23$ years. To estimate the contribution of cohort replacement to social change in Y from 1980 to 2005, then, we would multiply β_2 by 23.

The linear decomposition method has been used in a number of recent investigations of social change (for example, Alwin 1996; Brewster and Padavic 2000). The key assumption is that the effects are linear and additive. In particular, equation 6.14 assumes the same intracohort and intercohort slopes at times 1 and T (compare equations 6.12 and 6.13). We can check the plausibility of our assumptions by summing the two components. Generally the two components do not sum exactly to the difference between $\overline{Y}_1$ and $\overline{Y}_T$, but the discrepancy should not be large. If the components do not sum approximately to $\overline{Y}_T - \overline{Y}_1$, the problem could be survey-to-survey bounciness in the $\overline{Y}$-trend. In that case perhaps more reliable estimates of the overall change in Y might be obtained by using regression or moving averages to smooth the trend in the $\overline{Y}$. If a large discrepancy remains after smoothing, the underlying assumptions of the linear decomposition model are dubious, and another decomposition method should be used.

The linear decomposition method is simple—making very few data demands—and elegant. It applies to the study of social change for binary variables (change in proportions or percentages) as well as to the study of change for continuous variables.

Finally, let me stress again that the accounting scheme here locates proximate sources of change, not the underlying causes. Partitioning social change using linear decomposition does, however, provide insight about where to look for the underlying causes of change. Knowing whether the change lies in individual conversion (individuals actually changing) or in changing population composition (as older cohorts die off and are replaced by newer cohorts) is an important first step in locating the root causes of the change.

SUMMARY

Rule 6 dictates the use of panel data to study individual change and the use of repeated cross-section data to study social change. Panel data are useful for both descriptive and causal studies. By tracking individuals over time, panel data enable researchers to describe individual change and to remove the enduring effects of unmeasured individual heterogeneity in causal models.

Panel data and repeated cross-section data both can be used to investigate the first general question posed in this chapter, the changing-effect question: Has the effect of X on Y changed over time? With panel data we ask whether the effect of X on Y has changed for a given set of individuals. With repeated cross-section data we ask whether the effect of X on Y has changed in the general population. Because only two measurement points are required to estimate a changing-effect model, we need only two waves or two cross-sections of data to determine whether the $X - Y$ association changed from time 1 to time 2. To identify the aggregate-level causes or correlates of the change, however, we need multiple measurement points. With enough measurement points we can estimate multilevel models with time as the context.

By collecting updated samples of the population at each measurement point, repeated cross-section data sets are especially well-suited for investigating social change. Hence repeated cross-section data are recommended for addressing the second and third questions posed in this chapter: the convergence question (Has $\bar{Y}$ changed in the same direction and pace for all groups?) and the cohort replacement question (How much of the change in $\bar{Y}$ can be accounted for by change in the cohort composition of the population?). The convergence model uses time as the X-axis and includes interaction terms to determine whether groups are converging or diverging on Y. The contribution of cohort replacement to social change can be estimated using the regression coefficient for cohort obtained in the regression of Y on birth-cohort and year of survey.

The issues in this chapter are timely for social research. Prospects for the quantitative study of social change have never been better, and they should continue to improve in the future as ongoing panel and repeated survey data sets steadily add new waves of data. It is likely, then, that the issues of this chapter—the investigation of change or stability in individual-level effects, the investigation of convergence and divergence of groups, and the investigation of cohort replacement's contribution to social change—will be central to social research in the twenty-first century.

Student Exercises on Rule 6

The exercises again use the 1972–2004 data from the General Social Survey. Go to the web site http://sda.berkeley.edu and follow the instructions below. By following the instructions you should be able to generate all the statistics you need to answer the questions. Variable names are in **boldface**.

Note: Recall that the figures given below are for the 1972–2004 GSS, the most recent GSS data available when this book was written. Thus if you are working with more recent data, to replicate the figures exactly you will need to use the "selection filter" in the SDA program to remove years after 2004. Also recall that the format in the SDA web site might have changed somewhat since these directions were written, so some of the specific directions below might be out of date. You nonetheless should be able to follow the logic below to obtain the tables you need to answer the questions.

ASSIGNMENT 1: COHORT REPLACEMENT'S CONTRIBUTION TO CHANGE IN ATTITUDES ABOUT INTERRACIAL MARRIAGE

In most of the surveys from 1972 to 2002 the GSS asked this question, labeled **racmar:**

> Do you think there should be laws against marriages between (Negroes/Blacks/African Americans) and whites? (yes/no)

Beginning in 1980, the question was posed to African Americans as well as to white Americans. However, only about 6 percent of African Americans say that they favor laws against black-white intermarriage, so in this exercise we focus on the trend for whites.

As we will see shortly, the GSS results indicate that the percentage of white adults who say they favor such laws has declined sharply over the last three decades, from 4 in 10 in 1972 to 1 in 10 today, one of the steepest trends observed in the GSS. It is important to determine whether the decline was driven primarily by cohort replacement or by individuals changing their views on interracial marriage. Our aim in this exercise is to answer that question.

The exercise consists of five steps: Recode **racmar;** look at the **racmar** trend from 1972 to 2002 (the question was not asked in 2004); create a variable called **birthcohort** and calculate change in the mean of **birthcohort** from 1972 to 2002; regress **racmar** (recoded) on **birthcohort** and **year** (year of survey); finally, estimate the contributions of cohort replacement and aggregated individual change by inserting the appropriate values into equation 6.14, above. Here is some help on how to do that:

- Use the recode command (found in the pull-down menu under "Create Variables") to create a new variable **racmar2** that is coded 100 for those who think there should be laws against interracial marriage and 0 for those who think there should not be such laws. (We use 100 instead of 1 because we want to use percentages instead of proportions—percentages are more convenient for the decomposition later.) For the 1972–2004 cumulative data set, you should find 22,155 respondents who say they oppose such laws, and 6,629 who say they favor such laws.
- The second step is to examine the trend over time by crosstabulating **racmar2** (row variable) with **year** (column variable). Because we want to restrict the analysis to whites, enter "**race**(1)" in the box beside "Selection filter(s)." Select "No weight," and run the table. Note the decline in the percentage of those who think there should be laws against black-white intermarriage.
- Now use the "Compute a new variable" command under "Create Variables" to create a variable called **birthcohort**, as follows: **birthcohort**=**year**–**age**–1883. The value "1883" is added to set **birthcohort** at zero for the first birth-cohort in the sample. (The oldest people in the GSS cumulative data were born in 1883.) We do this for convenience in interpreting the y-intercept.
- Next we need to find the mean of birth-cohort for 1972 and 2002, the first and last years we are examining. Go to "Comparison of means" under "Analysis." Enter **birthcohort** as the dependent variable and **year** as the row variable. Again use the filter "**race**(1)" to restrict your analysis to whites. Also enter **racmar2**(0–100), **birthcohort**(0–103), and **year**(1972–2002) as filters. These filters are necessary to make the sample here consistent with the sample you will use in the next step, the regression. Your sample size should be 24,671.
- Now go to "Multiple regression" under "Analysis." Estimate equation 6.11 by regressing **racmar2** (dependent variable) on **year** and **birthcohort**.[9] Remember to use the filter "**race**(1)" to restrict your analysis to whites. Select "No weight," then "Run regression." You

[9] In this case we arrive at the same conclusion whether we use logistic regression or OLS regression so, to simplify matters, the assignment asks for OLS even though the outcome variable is dichotomous.

should obtain a regression coefficient of −0.318 for **year** and −0.722 for **birthcohort**.

Question 1. How do you interpret the coefficients −0.318 and −0.722? Which one reflects within-cohort change and which one reflects cross-cohort change? Explain what these coefficients mean, in plain English.

Question 2. (a) Use equation 6.14 and a hand calculator to estimate the contributions of cohort replacement and aggregated individual change to the 1972–2002 decline in support for laws prohibiting black-white intermarriage. Round off your estimates to the nearest one-tenth of a percent. What do you find? (HINT: You should find that cohort replacement accounts for about two-thirds of the decline and that aggregated individual change accounts for about one-third of the decline.)

(b) Do the two components sum approximately to the observed decline in the percentages for **racmar2** from 1972 to 2002? Explain why this result is important.

(c) Summarize your results in a paragraph. Are you surprised that cohort replacement is the larger contributor to the decline? Why or why not?

ASSIGNMENT 2: CHANGING ATTITUDES TOWARD SPENDING ON U.S. PUBLIC EDUCATION: RETIREES VERSUS WORKERS, 1973–2004

The challenge in this assignment is to use the information given in this chapter and in the notes to table 6.1 to reproduce the coefficients in that table. You can use the Berkeley SDA web site to do the assignment since logit analysis is one of the options (it's on the pull-down menu under "Analysis"). Make sure that your sample size is 19,816, and that you code the dummy variables the way I did.

Hints

- You will need to recode the dependent variable, **nateduc**, twice, to create two dummy variables. The first—let's call it **toomuchspend**—is coded 1 for "spend too much" and 0 for "about right" and "spend too little." The second, **toolittlespend**, is coded 1 for "spend too little" and 0 for "about right" or "spend too much."
- Recode **wrkstat** to create a dummy variable **retiree**, where **retiree**=1 for **wrkstat**=5 and **retiree**=0 for **wrkstat**=1–2.
- Create a new variable **trend**=**year**−**1973** (so the y-intercept pertains to the first year, 1973).
- Create the interaction term **retireextrend**=**retiree*trend**.

This gives you the variables you need to reproduce the results in table 6.1.

Question 3. (a) What are your estimates for **retiree**? Is either coefficient statistically significant? In plain English, describe what your result means.
(b) What are your estimates for **trend**? Is either coefficient statistically significant? In plain English, describe what your result means.
(c) What are your estimates for the interaction term? Is either coefficient statistically significant? In plain English, describe what your result means.
(d) What are your estimates for the y-intercepts? Interpret.

CHAPTER 7

The Seventh Rule

LET METHOD BE THE SERVANT, NOT THE MASTER

Statistical estimation methods should serve as the handmaiden to theory and research design, not the other way around. You fit the research design to the research question, and then fit the estimation method in turn to the design and question. While we all agree to this rule in principle, in practice method can become master because we become so enamored with a particular method that our research is designed around the method rather than the method designed to fit the research.

In this book I have not said much about statistical estimation methods but have focused more heavily on research design issues. The emphasis on design over estimation is deliberate. In the first place, there is little value in precise estimates of the wrong thing. Until we get the design right—so we are estimating the right thing—there is little point in refining our estimation. Second, there are already many excellent statistics and econometrics texts covering estimation methods for social research. Finally, the emphasis on design reflects my belief that unimaginative research design is the greatest bottleneck in social research these days. Our statistical methods very often are better than our research designs. The greatest potential for breakthroughs in social research today lies in better research design, or in better research design in conjunction with appropriate estimation, rather than in better estimation methods per se.[1]

In that light, rule 7 is a fitting conclusion for the book. Although rule 7 is implicit in much of what has come before, I include it as a separate rule to serve as a counterweight to the "technification" (Collier, Brady, and Seawright 2004, p. 266) assumption that more complex methodology equals better research. Sometimes complex is better, and sometimes not. Those who worship at the altar of complex methods are prone to the error of thinking that technical sophistication can substitute for knowledge of the

---

[1] It is important to stress that there is no sharp boundary between design and estimation method. The fixed-effects model, for example, could be thought of either as a type of research design or as a type of statistical estimation method. Either way, we underscore the importance of design, since fixed-effects methods dictate the use of certain types of research designs (panel data, sibling data, etc.).

subject matter, careful theorizing, and appropriate research design.[2] As social researchers our aim should not be research with the most bedazzling estimation method—in effect making method the master—but research with the most appropriate research design and estimation method for the question at hand. Often simplest is best. If percentages will do, then use percentages.

There are two ways that statistical estimation can become the master in social research. The first is through the hegemony of a single statistical technique or set of closely related techniques. Although social scientists give lip service to the principle that the tool should fit the research design and objective, in practice there is a remarkable sameness in the tools used in much nonexperimental research. To determine the causes of some outcome variable Y, researchers routinely regress Y on some set of other variables. The problem is not regression itself, but the routine use of regression, as if regression were the only tool available. When there is only a hammer in the toolbox, then everything begins to look like a nail. The danger is that social researchers will adjust their questions to fit the method, instead of the other way around.

A second way that statistical method can become the master is through unrealistic expectations about what statistics can do. Statistics becomes the master when we begin to believe that fancy statistics can substitute for hard thinking about data collection and research design. The danger here is that false hope in the remedial power of statistics can undercut careful thinking about design. Consulting statisticians often complain about being contacted for statistical advice too late—after the data are collected. We cannot rely on statistical wizardry to overcome faulty data and research design.

Unfortunately, social science methods too often have become impediments to social research today, along the lines just described. The knee-jerk use of regression methods and false hope in the remedial power of statistical estimation methods both limit our imagination in research. Quantitative research in the social sciences today tends to be longer on statistical sophistication than on imagination.

My aim in this chapter is to provide examples to serve as a counterweight to the privileged position of the standard stand-alone regression strategy in social research. The examples are meant to be suggestive, not exhaustive. They barely scratch the surface with regard to the options we should be considering in social research. I intend the examples to be positive—examples of what to do, not of what not to do. I want the book

---

[2] In addition, there is the danger that reliance on statistical fixes can lead to a deterioration of research quality as researchers are beholden to techniques that they can easily use (due to user-friendly computer software) but don't fully understand.

to end on a positive note. Before discussing those examples, though, I describe the dominance of regression analysis in one social science discipline, sociology.

OBSESSION WITH REGRESSION

To gauge the predilection for regression methods among sociologists, I counted the use of regression in the articles published in the *American Sociological Review* in 1999, the last year I was editor. Of the thirty-eight quantitative articles published that year, all but four employed regression or regression-like methods (for example, event-history analysis) in their study.

In chapter 5 I noted the problem with relying on standard linear regression as the primary, or only, tool for comparing like with like. As I mentioned there, Freedman (1991, 1997), Leamer (1983), and Lieberson (1985) have made similar points about the limited ability of regression to "deliver the goods." Here I want to make a somewhat different point: that, even if always done well, the dominance of the regression model in social research can be stultifying; it limits our imagination. In some lines of social research the regression approach is so domineering that practitioners might be hard-pressed even to conceptualize research outside of the "regress Y on X" box. Cleverness and originality are the casualties of the hegemony of a single method. When the automatic routine is to regress Y on X, social researchers quit looking for natural experiments and quit thinking about other options—computer simulation, decomposition analysis, decision-tree methods, network analysis, and so on. That trained incapacity to think outside the regression box is among the most pernicious effects of our over-reliance on standard linear regression in the social sciences.

Again, I stress that the fault lies not with regression itself, but in the unthinking use of regression, as if it were the only game in town. Often a different approach would be better. Some of the most promising empirical work in the social sciences uses something other than regression per se to do the heavy lifting, as we now see.

NATURALLY OCCURRING RANDOM ASSIGNMENT, AGAIN

Natural experiments are potential gold mines for social research. Yet social researchers rarely mine natural experiments. At first blush it might seem that natural experiments are seldom exploited because they are in fact rare. But interruptions of various sorts are commonplace in the social realm—new laws or policies, natural or human-made disasters, and so on—and many of these interruptions, with a little imagination, might be exploited as natural experiments or quasi-experiments. More than a half century ago, Trygve Haavelmo (1944) noted the "stream of experiments that nature is steadily turning out from her own enormous laboratory." Arguably, the relative scarcity of natural experiments in social research is due to the lack of imagination of researchers more than it is due to the lack of raw material in the social world.

We first encountered naturally occurring random assignment in the discussion of rule 5, where we noted that natural experiments are strategic for creating instrumental variables. Recall that the term "naturally occurring" does not necessarily mean that nature made the assignments, but that the assignments were not done for the sake of randomization, as one would do in a controlled experiment. In this section I describe more examples of naturally occurring random assignment that social researchers have been able to exploit. From these examples I hope to convince you of the value of thinking hard about what a relevant natural experiment would look like, and of doing this thinking early in your research project. I do not mean to suggest that you will always find an appropriate natural experiment (though of course you are more likely to find a natural experiment if you are looking for one). But the exercise itself is worthwhile: Even "dry searches" are useful because the discipline of thinking about natural experiments helps to sharpen your thinking about threats to the reliability of your research findings.

To stimulate thinking along these lines, I describe four investigations that have used natural experiments of some sort to gain leverage on a significant issue in the social sciences. The first investigation addresses the question of how marital instability is transmitted across generations, the second addresses the question of birth-cohort effects, the third estimates peer effects in schools, and the fourth addresses the question of whether schooling in America is an equalizing force or merely a mechanism for reproducing class privilege across generations. The issues are diverse in substance; what the examples have in common is their use of some type of natural experiment (along with regression methods) to gain analytic traction on a question that has proved difficult to answer using more conventional methods.

Random Assignment Based on National Tragedy: Post–World War II Germany

The first example uses family structure in post–World War II Germany to gain leverage on the causes of divorce. Divorce feeds divorce, that is, children whose parents are divorced are more likely themselves to end their marriages in divorce. Observers have offered various explanations for the transmission of marital instability across generations. Some of these focus on divorce itself as the factor that increases the risk of divorce in the next generation. For example, respondents from divorced families might place less investment in their own marriages because of more negative attitudes toward marriage that they acquired while growing up. In addition, since we can expect children to learn conflict-resolution behaviors from observing their parents, children of divorce are more likely to acquire behaviors that reduce the chances of success in their own marriages.

Other explanations identify the absence of a parent, not divorce itself, as the principal factor. These explanations place less emphasis on social learning and more emphasis on the obstacles faced by single parents. As a general rule single parents have less time and money to invest in their children. Less time often means less supervision and control; less money often means lower investment in a child's education. Along with less education, financial pressure in the home can lead to earlier marriage, thus increasing the risk of divorce.

The decimation of the German World War II male population provides a natural experiment to test whether it is divorce or the absence of a parent that is the key transmitting mechanism. About one-fourth of German men ages eighteen to forty were killed in the war. With such a stunning mortality rate for young men, it is plausible to assume that death can be treated as a relatively random event, or at least that the men who died and the men who survived did not differ greatly with respect to things that matter here, such as their parenting skills. Thus the assignment of children to the treatment category—growing up in a single-parent family due to widowhood—can be viewed as random, or nearly so.

German children of the World War II generation have now grown up and formed families of their own. Andreas Diekmann and Henriette Engelhardt (1999) use marital data from a 1988 random sample of the West German population ages eighteen to fifty-five to investigate how those children have fared in their own marriages. For those born between 1933 and 1945, 77 percent grew up in two-parent families, 16 percent grew up in single-parent families due to war deaths, and 2 percent grew up in single-parent families due to parental divorce (5 percent grew up with no parents). Diekmann and Engelhardt (table 2) report the results of a multivariate model using children who grew up in a two-parent family as the baseline. Other things equal, they find no difference in the risk of divorce for respondents from a two-parent family and respondents from a single-parent family, *if* the absence of the parent is due to death. For respondents who grew up in a single-parent household due to divorce, however, the risk of divorce was increased by 180 percent. Thus divorce risk depends on the reason for a parent's absence; "risks are higher for children of divorce than for respondents who grow up with a widowed parent" (p. 792). This evidence suggests, then, that it *is* divorce that is transmitted.

Random Assignment Based on National Laws: Voting in Post–Nineteenth Amendment America

A venerable body of work in the social sciences asserts that historical conditions present when one "comes of age" have lasting effects on one's attitudes and behaviors (Mannheim 1927; Ryder 1965). Because different birth-cohorts are subjected to different "slices of history" as they come of age, cohort differences arise. As Norman Ryder (p. 844) explains, "Each new cohort makes fresh contact with the contemporary social heritage and carries the impress of the encounter through life." Or as Ron Lesthaeghe and Johan Surkyn (1988, p. 40) put it, "Cohorts develop distinctive meaning-giving universes early in life and seem to maintain them throughout adulthood." We call this embedding of history in cohorts a *cohort effect*: "Cohort effects occur whenever the past history of individuals exerts an influence on their current behavior in a way that is not fully captured by an age variable" (Hobcraft, Menken, and Preston 1982, p. 10).

Yet it is very difficult to determine how much cohort effects matter, or even whether they exist at all. The problem turns on separating cohort effects from age effects. People who come of age at the same time are the same age, and age together. So if we find, for example, that people who were born in the 1940s differ from those who were born in the 1960s, it is hard to know whether the difference is due to their age differences or to their cohort differences (arising from their experience of different historical conditions during their formative years). Adding data for other time periods only complicates the problem, since that introduces the possibility of what is called *period effects*, and cohort (year of birth) equals period (year of measurement) minus age (Glenn 2005).

Note that the operative mechanism for cohort effects is historical conditioning: Different cohorts have different tastes or values or worldviews because they were exposed to different historical conditions during the formative period of their lives. To separate cohort effects from age effects, then, we need to imagine circumstances in which individuals in a given society are randomly assigned to different historical conditions as they come of age. By framing the issues this way, we see immediately that the effects of historical conditioning—cohort effects—could be isolated from age effects through a controlled experiment in which people of the same age were randomly assigned to different historical conditions during their formative years.

Can we find something resembling such an experiment in the real world? Consider the passage of the Nineteenth Amendment to the U.S.

Constitution, which extended voting rights to women in all states. Before women were eligible to vote, sex randomly separated children at birth into two groups—a group that would be eligible to vote upon reaching voting age, and a group that would not be eligible to vote. The Nineteenth Amendment changed the historical conditions. To compare the lasting effect of historical conditioning on birth cohorts, then, we can compare the voting rates of women who came of age before women were eligible to vote with the voting rates of women who came of age after passage of the amendment in 1920. By comparing the voting rates of women with the voting rates of men who are the same age, we can separate out the effect of age on voting. If Nineteenth Amendment women—women who came of age before women could vote—are less likely to vote than their same-age male counterparts, *and* this gender gap disappears for later cohorts, we have strong evidence for the enduring effects of a cohort's conditioning.

First it is useful to know whether, in the 1920s, women were less likely to vote than men. Scattered evidence suggests that Nineteenth Amendment women in fact were less likely to vote (than men) when first eligible to do so. In the "first sample survey recorded in the annals of American political science" (Bennett and Bennett 1987, p. 158), Charles E. Merriam and Harold F. Gosnell (1924) discovered a substantial gender gap in the 1923 mayoral election in Chicago—a result consistent with turnout data for the whole of Illinois for the 1920 national election (Kleppner 1982, table 2; Illinois was the only state to report vote turnout separately for men and women).

The key questions are (1) whether women of the amendment era continued to exhibit lower voting rates than men thirty to forty years later, and (2) whether the disparity disappeared among later birth cohorts. As Kevin Chen and I explain (1995, p. 978): "After passage of the Nineteenth Amendment, historical conditions no longer 'taught' young women the impropriety of voting. So if historical conditioning is the telling factor, postamendment cohorts should exhibit no sex differences in vote turnout."

Moreover, we expect a pattern of disappearing gender gaps across cohorts that is keyed to the passage of the Nineteenth Amendment. In the language of experiments, there are several levels of the "treatment effect": Some women in fact were denied the right to vote, others were adolescents during disenfranchisement, others were children, and others have no memory of disenfranchisement. If historical conditioning has an enduring effect on cohorts, the effect should be greatest for cohorts with the greatest exposure to the conditioning; hence disenfranchisement should have "the greatest lasting effect on women actually denied the right to vote, with a lesser effect on women who were adolescents during the disenfranchisement era, followed by those who were children during that era" (Firebaugh and Chen 1995, p. 979).

Data from the 1952–1988 American National Election Study strongly confirm these predictions. Even though the right to vote had been extended to women more than thirty years—and in some instances, more than fifty years—before the elections examined here, women who came of age before or during the Nineteenth Amendment era continued to vote at lower rates than their male counterparts. And the stronger the historical "treatment," the greater the difference. For men and women born before 1905, the odds that a man voted is twice the odds that a woman did, controlling for age and age-squared, education, family income, region, party partisanship, marital status, and election year (Firebaugh and Chen 1995, table 2). For those born from 1906 to 1915, the odds were 43 percent greater for men; for those born from 1916 to 1925, the odds were 28 percent greater for men.[9] Voting rates are the same for men and women born after 1925.

In short, the ratification of the Nineteenth Amendment provided a natural experiment to test the concept that the values of birth-cohorts are shaped by their common youthful experiences—a central social science concept that is often assumed but hard to demonstrate empirically.

School Reassignments in North Carolina

Our third example of the use of natural experiments in social research comes from an econometric investigation of peer effects on student achievement by Caroline Hoxby and Gretchen Weingarth (2005). Peer effects, like cohort effects, are often surmised but seldom proved. In addition to the usual concerns about measurement error and omitted-variables bias, the empirical search for peer effects is complicated by the possibility of self-selection on the dependent variable. For example, adolescents who have an unmeasured propensity for delinquency might befriend other delinquency-prone adolescents, resulting in a positive association between individual's delinquency and peers' delinquency. The unwary researcher might interpret this association as indicating a peer effect when in fact the delinquency-prone individual would have committed the same acts of delinquency without the peers. There is also the possibility of a "reflection" (Manski 1993) or "social multiplier" (Glaeser, Sacerdote, and Scheinkman 2003) effect. Because I am a peer to my peers, if there is a peer effect, then my outcomes will affect their outcomes, which in turn will affect my outcome, and so on in a continuing loop. This loop further complicates the analysis of peer effects.

---

[9] Moreover, this pattern of gender differences occurred only for voting, not for other measures of political involvement.

Classrooms provide a strategic place to search for peer effects because classmates spend a great deal of time together. The challenge is to separate true peer effects from selection effects and other types of biases. It is helpful to conceptualize this in terms of an experiment where peer composition is the treatment effect. What we want to know is whether a student's outcome would have been different had she been embedded in a group of peers who were different on the characteristics of interest (such as race, if one's interest is in the effects of race segregation on some outcome).

The massive reassignment of students in the Wake County (North Carolina) School District provides a grand natural experiment for studying how student achievement is affected by the peer composition of the class. In an effort to balance its schools on the basis of race and family income (as measured by percentage of students participating in the free or reduced-price lunch program) in the face of a rapidly growing student population, the district has, each year for more than a decade, assigned up to 5 percent of its students to different schools.[3] For students, the result of the constant reshuffling is changing peer composition: 62 percent of students in the district have experienced a change in their peer composition due either to the reassignment of others or to their own reassignment (Hoxby and Weingarth 2005, p. 15).

For researchers, the reshuffling presents a unique opportunity to investigate peer effects because of the "very large number of natural experiments in which students experience new peers in the classroom" (Hoxby and Weingarth, abstract). Hoxby and Weingarth use panel data for students in the third through eighth grade in the Wake County district for the 1994–95 school year through the 2002–03 school year. The dependent variable is student achievement, as measured by scores on North Carolina's end-of-grade tests in reading and mathematics. The panel data permit the examination of students' scores before and after they experience changes in peer composition. In addition to students' test scores, the dataset includes measures of race, gender, participation in the free or reduced-price lunch program, and parents' education. The dataset also includes information to identify each child's classroom.

Because the purpose of the reassignment is to relieve overcrowding and prevent (or at least alleviate) segregation of schools by race and income, the reassignments are not random. Specifically, students in more-crowded grades in crowded schools are more likely to be reassigned than students in less-crowded situations. And, given the aim of racial and income

---

[3] The reassignment strategy for balancing schools could be sabotaged if parents removed reassigned students from the public schools (they might switch to private schools, for example, or to home-schooling). The procedures used by the school district make noncompliance difficult, however (see Hoxby and Weingarth 2005, p. 14), and most families in fact comply with the reassignment.

balance, in any given year students of a particular race or a particular income category are more likely to be reassigned.

The reassignments are, however, *conditionally* random: Conditional on a student's race, ethnicity, lunch participation (the income measure), school, and grade level—variables included in the dataset—students are equally likely to be reassigned. In other words, for two students of the same race with the same level of family income, those in the same school and grade are equally likely to be reassigned. In particular, as Hoxby and Weingarth (table 2) show, once the reassignment variables (crowdedness of school and so on) are controlled for, the probability of reassignment is independent of students' initial test scores. This independence is critical to their investigation, since their aim is to determine what effect peers' achievement has on one's own achievement, and how that effect might differ across groups (perhaps, for example, the presence of high-achieving peers benefits only other high achievers and has no effect or even a negative effect on low-achieving students).

Hoxby and Weingarth conclude that there *are* peer effects on students' achievements, but these effects hinge on peers' achievement levels, not on their income level or their race. Quoting Hoxby and Weingarth (p. 28; bracketed clause was added for clarification):

> The vast majority of the apparent impact of a concentration of racial minorities, ethnic minorities, or poor students [that is, students in the free or reduced lunch program] is really the effect of their achievement. Put another way, if we see two schools with the same *distribution* of achievement (not merely the same mean), we should expect their students' achievement to evolve similarly in the future, even if the schools have quite different racial, ethnic, and income compositions.

In short, on the basis of the natural experiments provided by the Wake County reassignments, Hoxby and Weingarth find that what matters for school achievement is the *achievement composition* of one's peers, not whether they are black or white or poor or not poor. It remains to be seen whether other researchers are able to replicate their findings with other data, but the important point here is Hoxby and Weingarth's imaginative use of a school district's reassignment plan to provide analytic leverage on the difficult issue of peer effects in schools.

Using Seasonal Comparisons to Assess Schooling's Impact on Inequality

The fourth example, a study by Douglas Downey, Beckett Broh, and Paul von Hippel (2004), also involves schools: "Are schools the great equalizer?"

Cognitive inequality during the summer months and the school year." It is well documented that, in the United States and other Western nations, children from families with higher SES (socioeconomic status) tend to obtain more education than children from lower SES families. And one's education, in turn, is a major determinant of one's own SES. So we have this general SES transmission model: Parents' SES → Children's education → Children's SES.

In addition to obtaining more years of schooling on average, children from higher SES families also tend to receive *better* education. Higher SES students generally attend schools with better resources, they are assigned to higher ability groups, and they and their parents typically have more favorable interactions with teachers. Due to what one author calls "savage inequalities" in public education in the United States (Kozol 1991), some observers have concluded that education in the United States, far from serving as an equalizing force, serves instead to reproduce or even exacerbate inequalities. Indeed, some scholars argue that schooling represents one of the most important channels by which parents transmit their SES advantage (or disadvantage) to their children. In that way schools serve the interests primarily of those at the top of the SES hierarchy (Bowles and Gintis 1976).

No one disputes the fact that children from higher SES families tend to receive more and better schooling. The issue is whether schools function to *transmit* class differences from parents to children or *reduce* such class differences. Despite large disparities in resources, schools might nonetheless function to reduce disparities in skills between higher and lower SES students. As Downey, Broh, and von Hippel (2004, pp. 613--14) explain:

> Even if schools are unfair, they may serve as equalizers if the variation in school environments is smaller than the variation in non-school environments. Some children may have relatively poor school experiences, but the disadvantages in their non-school environments may be even more severe. As a result, a disadvantaged child attending a low-quality school can enjoy a larger "school boost" than an advantaged child attending a high-quality school. In this way schools can favor advantaged students, yet still serve as equalizers.

In short, to determine whether or not schools serve as equalizers, we must consider two learning environments: in school and out of school. In an ideal experiment, we would randomly assign children to various school and nonschool conditions to try to separate their effects. The claim that schools fail to level the playing field would be supported if we found that inequality in learning tended to be just as high under the school conditions as it is under the nonschool conditions.

Although such an experiment is not feasible, we can use summer vacation for students as a natural experiment to separate the effects of school
and nonschool environments on learning. During the school year, children
are exposed both to school and nonschool environments. During the summer, the large majority of children are exposed only to nonschool environments. To separate out the school effect on learning, then, we can
compare rates of learning over the summer with rates of learning when
school is in session. As Downey, Broh, and von Hippel (p. 616) observe,
this design is "analogous to a crossover design in health research, where
the same patients are exposed to different treatments in different periods."

To compare students' learning in the summer and during the school year,
Downey, Broh, and von Hippel use test score data from a nationally representative sample of about 20,000 children who entered kindergarten in the
United States in 1998. By beginning when formal education first begins,
Downey, Broh and von Hippel are able to examine differences across children that are relatively uncontaminated by school processes. Consistent with
prior research, they find significant differences in the reading and mathematics skills of higher and lower SES children as they begin their schooling careers. On the first day of kindergarten a child whose family SES is one
standard deviation higher than that of another child will, on average, have
nearly a two-month school head start on that other child (p. 624).

The question is whether schools tend to exacerbate those SES disparities. By comparing learning rates during kindergarten and first grade with
learning rates during the intervening summer, Downey, Broh, and von
Hippel find that schools in fact *reduce* the inequality among students of
differing SES backgrounds. Children learn at much more equal rates during the school year than they do during summer vacation. As a result,
even though the learning gap between SES groups grew during kindergarten and first grade, the gap grew much more slowly when school was
in session than when it was not. In the language of an experiment, exposure to the "treatment" (school) reduced the disparity in learning rates for
higher and lower SES children. In that sense, schools are "great equalizers" in America (Downey, Broh, and von Hippel, p. 633). Apparently the
disadvantages that lower SES children face in school, as savage as they
might be, are less consequential for their learning than are the disadvantages they face in their homes and neighborhoods.

Decomposition Work in the Social Sciences

Regression analysis produces coefficients (slopes) that summarize the associations among variables. Under certain conditions these slopes are
estimates of the average causal effects across individuals in some population.

On the basis of these slopes, then, we can predict how much an outcome variable Y will change on average for a one-unit change in a causal variable X.

Decomposition analysis, by contrast, accounts for the observed change or variance in some outcome variable Y by isolating the contributions of subpopulations to the overall change or variance in Y. The accounting procedures will vary depending on the nature of the change or variance under investigation, but the objective is the same: to determine the proximate sources of the variance in Y. The proximate sources might not constitute the causes per se of the variance, but proximate sources can point us to the underlying causes. There are an endless number of ways that overall change and variance can be partitioned, of course, so the subpopulations should be groups of particular theoretical, substantive, or policy interest. The first step, then, is to identify the strategic subpopulations: The more strategic the subpopulations, the more telling the decomposition.

To give a simple example of decomposition, suppose the U.S. poverty rate rises over some period. As a first step toward understanding the cause of that rise, we want to determine its source: Is the growth in poverty primarily among blacks or whites or Latinos? Is it among the young or the old? Is the increase concentrated in certain regions of the country? And so on.

Decomposition is underutilized in social research, perhaps because it is seen as merely descriptive. As social scientists we are apt to explain, not just to describe. But first we must get the facts right, so that we know what there is to explain. Good decomposition work helps us know what the facts are. It also points us toward likely explanations.

Decomposition has proved its mettle in the analysis of change in means or rates, or what we might call "decomposition of first-moments"; in the analysis of variances ("decomposition of second-moments"); in the analysis of inequality, a special type of variance; and in the analysis of segregation. The well-known Blinder-Oaxaca decomposition of differences in *group means* (Blinder 1973; Oaxaca 1973) is an example of first-moments decomposition. The linear decomposition model described in chapter 6— dividing social change over some time period into the part due to cohort replacement and the part due to aggregated individual change—is another example; the "group means" in this case are the means on Y at different points in time, since it is change over time that is decomposed. Some methods, such as the Blinder-Oaxaca decomposition and linear decomposition (as described in chapter 6), employ regression; others, such as the decomposition of inequality and segregation indexes (below), do not.

Because chapter 6 describes a method to decompose means or rates, in this chapter I focus on the decomposition of variances and the decomposition of segregation. In keeping with the theme of this chapter, the methods for the most part are not fancy, but they are appropriate for the task at hand. I rely on examples from prior research, beginning with the decomposition of variance and inequality.

Decomposition of Variance and Inequality

Some of the most compelling examples of decomposition in social research involve the partitioning of variance or inequality into successively smaller subpopulations, each contained or "nested" within a larger population. The citizens of the world, for example, can be partitioned geographically: Individuals are nested in local communities; local communities are nested in larger jurisdictions or regions; regions are nested in countries; and countries are nested in the world. Likewise, students are nested in classrooms that are nested in schools that are nested in school districts, and so on.

The decomposition of variance or inequality within and across nested groups is often very telling. Some inequality measures, for example, have the property of *additive decomposability* (Jenkins 1991), meaning that total inequality can be partitioned exactly into its within- and between-group components (for nested groups). This property has been used, for example, to partition global income inequality into the part due to within-nation inequality and the part due to between-nation inequality (recall the discussion of global income inequality in box 1.1 of chapter 1).

As another example, Weeden et al. (2007) additively decompose the growth of earnings inequality in the United States over recent decades, 1973–2004. Earlier analyses in economics and sociology have focused on the causes of growing inequality. Weeden and her colleagues, in contrast, investigate the *consequences* of growing inequality for the class structure in the United States. Nested-group decomposition is appropriate here, since individual workers are nested in occupations that are nested in larger categories that Weeden and colleagues call "big classes." The question is whether growing inequality is strengthening or weakening the big-class structure in the United States. More rapid growth in between big-class as opposed to within big-class inequality would indicate an inclining importance of class for earnings in the United States, that is, a lumpier earnings distribution with relatively stronger class distinctions. More rapid growth of the within-class component would indicate a declining relative importance of class for earnings in the United States.

Weeden and colleagues use two standard measures of inequality to study the trend in earnings inequality. The first measure is simply the variance of logged earnings. The variance of the log is often used as a measure of inequality because it meets the essential requirements for inequality measures. In particular, the variance of the log is constant when the rate of change is the same for everyone—consistent with the standard way of conceptualizing inequality (Allison 1978). The measure is attractive here because there is a ready-made method, analysis-of-variance (ANOVA), for decomposing variance. It is a relatively straightforward matter, then, to use off-the-shelf computer packages to decompose the variance of log(earnings) into its between-class and within-class components. And, since variance of log(earnings) is a measure of inequality, the between-class and within-class components reflect between- and within-class inequality, respectively.

Weeden and colleagues also use the Theil index to measure inequality. The Theil index is appropriate here because it is additively decomposable using algebra (Jenkins 1995; Firebaugh 2003, pp. 127–28). Both sets of decompositions (of the variance of logged earnings, and of the Theil) indicate that inequality within occupations remains the source of most of the wage inequality in the United States. Between-class inequality has grown more rapidly, however; as a result, the labor market is becoming lumpier as well as more unequal.

As the example of earnings inequality demonstrates, decomposition work in the social sciences can be used to shed new light on observed changes by apportioning the whole into its constituent parts. Sometimes we can use the logic in reverse, to try to estimate the whole from the parts. Consider, for example, how one might estimate income inequality across all individuals in the world. If we had income data for everyone, then (with a fast computer) we could estimate global income inequality by calculating some measure of inequality such as the Theil index. Of course we do not have that data, but we do have estimates of the average income for all the populous nations in the world (to estimate between-nation inequality), and estimates of within-nation inequality for many of them. The strategy in this instance, then, is to sum up to the total by using decomposition equations to estimate the whole from the parts (for example, Goesling 2001; Schultz 1998).

Finally, consider inequality in individuals' life spans—"arguably the most fundamental inequality that exists among human populations" (Edwards and Tuljapurkar 2005, p. 665). Life expectancy at birth (that is, *average* life span for all individuals) converged among twenty-one industrialized countries over the second half of the twentieth century (White 2002). However, *variance* in adult life span, as measured by variance in the age at death among those who live to age ten, has not converged (Edwards and Tuljapurkar 2005). Variance in the adult life span is higher in the United States than it is in other high-income countries, such as Britain, Canada, Denmark, France, Japan, and Sweden (Edwards and Tuljapurkar 2005, fig. 5).

What is the source of this U.S. exceptionalism? We know, from the classic study of differential mortality by Evelyn Kitagawa and Philip

Hauser (1973), that there are substantial differences in mortality rates across social classes and racial categories in the United States. As Kitagawa and Hauser (1973, p. 4) note, "The importance of socioeconomic differentials in mortality is that they point to the possibilities of reducing mortality through the betterment of socioeconomic conditions in the population." In addition, socioeconomic and race/ethnic differences in mortality might help explain the puzzle of the greater heterogeneity in adult life spans in the United States. Greater heterogeneity in adult life spans might be tied to greater heterogeneity in the U.S. population, since the United States tends be more racially heterogeneous than other rich nations. To test this conjecture, we could decompose the variance in adult life span by race. What we want to know is whether the variance in adult life span within race/ethnic groups in the United States is similar in size to the variance for racially homogeneous groups in other nations. Whatever we discover regarding variance in age at death within racial groups, we could probe further by decomposing the within-nation, within-race variances along other key dimensions such as sex, social class, and cause of death. The point is that successive partitioning of the variance is likely to tell us quite a bit about heterogeneity in adult life spans and reveal where we should look—and not look—for explanations of the greater life span uncertainty in the United States.

Decomposition of Segregation Indexes

Segregation refers to the extent to which individuals' local environments differ on the composition of some population trait (such as race or socioeconomic status). School racial segregation, for example, refers to the extent to which racial composition varies across schools. The more that racial composition varies across schools, the more that a student's local racial environment depends on the school that he or she attends, so school racial segregation can also be thought of as the association between race and school. From the raw data we can tell immediately when school racial segregation is zero—that would occur when racial composition is the same for all schools, so race and school are not related. We could also tell immediately when there is maximum or complete segregation—all schools would be monoracial, with whites attending all-white schools, blacks attending all-black schools, Latinos attending all-Latino schools, and so on.

In virtually all cases, of course, the racial segregation of schools is neither zero nor complete but falls somewhere between the two extremes. In that case it may not be obvious, from the raw data, whether school segregation is greater in city A or in city B. A number of segregation indexes have been developed to solve this problem, including multigroup indexes

(Reardon and Firebaugh 2002). Segregation indexes measure the extent to which the local environments of individuals differ, on average, on race or some other population characteristic.

If our aim is to reduce the overall racial segregation of schools, we must first determine where the segregation is located—between city schools and suburban schools? Between school districts within cities or suburbs? Within school districts in central cities or in suburbs? Obviously the reduction of segregation within school districts will have limited effect if most school segregation lies between school districts. Likewise reducing segregation across suburban school districts will have little impact on overall school segregation in a metropolitan area if most of the segregation lies within the central city, or between the central city and the suburbs.

In fashioning policies to alleviate school segregation, then, it is helpful first to decompose segregation indexes to pinpoint the principal sources of the segregation, so that you know where to concentrate your effort. Sean Reardon, John Yun, and Tamela McNulty Eitle (2000) show that Theil's entropy index of segregation (H) can be additively decomposed, so overall segregation can be expressed as a sum of within-aggregate and between-aggregate segregation, where "aggregate" refers to an organizational unit, such as school district, or to a demographic group, such as racial group. Very often the within-aggregate component can be decomposed further; thus, for example, segregation within a suburb can be further partitioned into the part that is due to segregation across school districts in the suburb, and the part that is due to segregation across schools within school districts.

Consider figure 7.1, a five-part decomposition of school segregation in U.S. metropolitan areas. In this scheme overall school segregation for

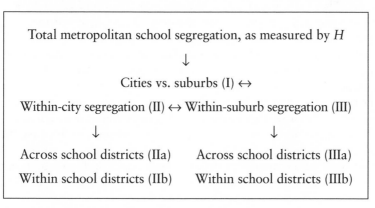

Figure 7.1. Decomposition of School Segregation in U.S. Metropolitan Areas. *Source*: Reardon, Yun, and Eitle (2000).

metropolitan areas is first partitioned into three components: the part that is due to differences in racial composition of the central city as a whole versus suburbs as a whole, the part that is due to differences in racial composition across schools within central cities, and the part that is due to differences in racial composition across schools within suburbs. The second and third parts—within-city and within-suburb segregation—are further apportioned into segregation due to differing racial compositions across *school districts* and segregation due to differing racial compositions across *schools* within school districts. So there are five components in all (I, IIa, IIb, IIIa, IIIb), and they sum to total segregation for the metropolitan area.

Note the differing policy implications for the components. Component I can be reduced only by convergence in racial compositions of cities and suburbs as a whole. Component II is reduced by convergence in the racial composition of schools within central cities. By decomposing II further, we can determine whether significant reductions in school segregation are possible by changing the racial composition of schools within school districts (IIb), or whether changes across school districts will be required (IIa). The same reasoning applies of course for reducing school segregation within suburban areas, where components IIIa and IIIb are strategic.

Simultaneous decomposition along two dimensions is also possible with H. For example, in their analysis of average school segregation in 217 metropolitan areas in the United States in 1995, Reardon, Yun, and Eitle (2000) partition simultaneously by the five-part scheme above and by race. In the case of race, they want to know how much of the total school segregation is due to the white-minority divide and how much is due to segregation among minorities themselves (blacks, Hispanics, and Asians). There are two race components (segregation of whites from minorities, and segregation across minorities[4]) in their scheme, so the Reardon-Yun-Eitle two-way decomposition yields $2 \times 5 = 10$ components of school segregation in U.S. metropolitan areas. Because their results so nicely illustrate the value of decomposition work in the social sciences, I reproduce them in table 7.1.

From this two-way decomposition we see, first, that about four-fifths of the overall school segregation in the 217 metropolitan areas arises from the segregation of whites and minorities. This means that eliminating all segregation among black, Hispanic, and Asian students would reduce overall segregation on average only by about one-fifth. Reardon, Yun, and Eitle (2000, p. 358) note that the contribution of black/Hispanic/Asian

[4] Because whites are considered a single race, there is a within-group segregation component only for minorities (blacks, Hispanics, and Asians), and not for whites.

TABLE 7.1

Components of School Segregation in the United States: Averages for 217 Metropolitan Areas

	White/Minority Segregation (percent)	Black/Hispanic/Asian Segregation (percent)
I. Segregation of city vs. suburbs	36.9	3.9
II. Within-city segregation		
IIa. Across school districts	6.5	1.8
IIb. Within school districts	17.1	7.4
III. Within-suburb segregation		
IIIa. Across school districts	14.2	4.4
IIIb. Within school districts	5.5	2.2
	$\Sigma = 80.2$	$\Sigma = 19.7$

Source: Reardon, Yun, and Eitle (2000), table 3.

segregation to the total is small in part because these groups constitute less than one-third of metropolitan public school enrollments.

Second, the largest single component is the difference in the white/minority composition of central cities versus suburbs (36.9% of the total). Differences in the black/Hispanic/Asian composition of central cities versus suburbs contributes an additional 3.9 percent to the total, so equalizing the overall white/black/Hispanic/Asian composition of city versus suburban schools would reduce overall school segregation just over 40 percent (36.9% + 3.9%) in the average city.

Third, segregation within city school districts accounts for nearly one-quarter of all metropolitan school segregation (17.1% + 7.4%). Within central cities, most segregation lies within school districts, not across them. The opposite is true in the suburbs, where differences in racial composition across school districts are more important. Eliminating differences in racial composition across school districts in the suburbs would reduce school segregation in the average metropolitan area by an estimated 18.6 percent.

In short, decomposition work in the social sciences can be invaluable in pinpointing where to look for underlying causes, and in indicating where policy interventions have the greatest potential for change. The Reardon-Yun-Eitle decomposition of segregation, for example, indicates that racial segregation within school districts in suburban areas on average accounts for less than 10 percent of total metropolitan school segregation in the United States, whereas segregation within school districts in central cities accounts for nearly 25 percent of the total. On the basis of that decomposition, then, we know that policies to reduce segregation within school districts have a potentially greater payoff (for the reduction of total segregation) when applied to city school districts rather than to suburban school districts.

THE EFFECTS OF SOCIAL CONTEXT

One of the central notions of social science is that social context matters. Growing up in a crime-infested poor neighborhood, for example, surely is worse than growing up in a safe middle-class neighborhood. Note, critically, that this sort of effect is due to the child's neighborhood context, not to characteristics of the child or of the child's family. To determine the effects of neighborhoods, the telling comparison is not between poor children and middle-class children, but between poor children who grow up in poor unsafe neighborhoods and equally poor children who grew up in more affluent, safer neighborhoods.

Although it might seem virtually self-evident that children who grow up in bad neighborhoods will tend to fare worse in life than they would have had they grown up in better surroundings, that claim has proved devilishly difficult to demonstrate empirically. The major roadblock is selection bias, a problem we encountered before, in our discussion of causal inference (chapter 5). Because people self-select into neighborhoods, it is hard to determine whether differences we observe across neighborhoods are due to the neighborhoods themselves or to the way that people sort themselves into those neighborhoods. Returning to the example in the previous paragraph, suppose we find that poor children in unsafe neighborhoods fare worse than poor children in safe neighborhoods: That difference might reflect, not a neighborhood effect, but the effect of unmeasured family characteristics (such as differences in parental commitment to their children) that would induce some poor parents to sacrifice more than other poor parents do to live in a safer neighborhood for their children.

Context effects, then, are both important and contentious in the social sciences. There is, for example, the question of whether racial segregation (a contextual property) has negative consequences for minority groups—and, if so, what kinds of segregation lead to what kinds of harm. With respect to residential segregation, for example, Douglas Massey (2004) recently has claimed that the segregation of races leads to poorer health among African American adults. With respect to school segregation, there is longstanding interest in the effect of racial segregation on the academic achievement of minority students (Card and Rothstein 2006; Coleman et al. 1966; Charles, Dinwiddie, and Massey 2004; Hoxby and Weingarth 2005). Because some of the burning issues of our day turn on context effects, there has been a resurgence of interest lately in their estimation. This interest is welcome. We must "let method be the servant" when we fashion our methods to address issues of import, and there are few issues of more import in the social sciences than how human behavior is affected by social context.

Context Effects as Objects of Study

Let's begin by defining the term *context effect*. Social contexts vary on key social and economic characteristics, just like individuals do: Some neighborhoods have higher crime rates than other neighborhoods, some schools are better funded than other schools, some cities have higher levels of racial segregation than other cities, and so on. When we say that there is a context effect, what we mean is that there are one or more characteristics of contexts that matter for some individual-level outcome Y, independent of the characteristics of the individuals themselves. For example, there is a school context effect on high school completion if students in inner-city schools are more likely to quit high school than similar students in suburban schools.

More formally, consider $i = 1, 2, \ldots, N$ individuals nested in $j = 1, 2, \ldots$ J contexts (for example, neighborhoods, schools, cities). Let Y_{ij} denote the value on some outcome variable for the ith individual in the jth context, and X_j denote the value on some explanatory variable for the jth context (for example, average household income in a neighborhood). *A context effect exists when X_j has an effect on Y_{ij} independent of the individual-level causes of Y, including X_{ij} (if defined).* As Peter Blau (1960, p. 179) put it, "The individual's orientation undoubtedly influences his behavior; the question is whether the prevalence of social values in a community also exerts social constraints upon patterns of conduct that are independent of the influences exerted by the internalized orientations."[5]

In a classic study of the U.S. military, Samuel Stouffer and his colleagues (Stouffer et al. 1949) found numerous instances where the "prevalence of values in a community" influenced the attitudes and behaviors of American soldiers in World War II. They found, for example, that inexperienced soldiers in veteran units were less likely to say that they were ready for combat than inexperienced soldiers in inexperienced

---

[5] It is important to note the difference between the effect of social context and the effect of population *composition*. In the case of composition effects, differences between groups owe to differences in characteristics of the individuals making up the groups. If fertility rates are higher in country A than country B, for example, we would first want to know if the difference in fertility is due to difference in age composition: Perhaps a higher proportion of the women in country A are of child-bearing age.

units—an indication of the influence of the veterans (who believed the inexperienced soldiers were not ready for combat) on the inexperienced soldiers.

Interest in context effects among social scientists today centers on the effect of peers, schools, and neighborhoods on life chances, especially for the young (Borjas 1995; Cutler and Glaeser 1997; Hoxby and Weingarth 2005; Massey and Denton 1993; Mouw and Entwisle 2006). The intellectual forebear for much of this research is the so-called *Coleman Report* on the state of American education in the 1960s. In one of the largest and most influential social science studies ever (the sample consisted of more than 150,000 students), James Coleman and colleagues (1966) found that school effects on student achievement are relatively small compared to the effects of family background, and that disadvantaged black students profit from schooling in racially integrated classrooms. The surprising finding that school effects are relatively unimportant prompted a school-effects research literature (searching for such effects) that continues today. The finding that black students may benefit from school integration served as a catalyst for the implementation of busing to achieve racial integration. That conclusion also served to boost interest in research on the social consequences of residential and school segregation (research that continues to flourish today).

In thinking about the effects of social context, it is important to note that some characteristics of contexts have a counterpart at the individual level and some do not. A city, for example, can be characterized by average household income, or by the percentage of residents who are white or who are renters. We can call these *aggregative properties*. Other characteristics of contexts—integral or global properties, such as the jurisdictional boundaries in a city—are not formed by aggregating individual characteristics and have no obvious counterpart at the individual level (Selvin and Hagstrom 1963).

Context effects arising from aggregative properties can be classified as either *exacerbating* or *mitigating*. In the case of exacerbating effects, the context effect and the individual-level effect have the same sign. In the case of mitigating effects, the context effect and the individual-level effect have different signs.

Some of the most intriguing issues in social science involve the possibility of exacerbating versus mitigating context effects. We know, for example, that being rich confers certain advantages on individuals; but does associating with others who are rich confer *additional* advantage? And, at the other end of the spectrum, does disadvantage work in the same way, so that living in a poor neighborhood is harmful independent of the effect of one's own poverty? Or do the context effects instead mitigate the individual-level effects? Perhaps being poor in a neighborhood where most others are poor is less alienating than being poor in a neighborhood where others are not poor. Similarly, one might be better off to be middle class in a middle-class neighborhood than to be middle class in an upper-class neighborhood.

I use a study from economics to illustrate exacerbating context effects and a study from sociology to illustrate mitigating context effects.

EXACERBATING CONTEXT EFFECT

In addressing the question "Are ghettos good or bad?" David Cutler and Edward Glaeser (1997) begin by noting that the spatial separation of racial or ethnic groups could have either positive or negative effects on the groups in question. "Ghettos may have benefits as well as costs," they write (p. 827), "especially if they allow for mixing across income classes within a segregated group and for positive spillovers within that group." So the question of whether ghettos (used in the nonpejorative sense, referring to a racially separated community) are good or bad for their residents is an empirical question. On the basis of their analysis of census data for U.S. cities, Cutler and Glaeser conclude that segregation is bad for blacks, since blacks in more segregated cities are significantly worse off (in terms of schooling, employment, and single parenthood) than blacks in less segregated cities. Because blacks are also worse off at the individual level on these three outcomes (Cutler and Glaeser, table IV), the effect of social context (racial segregation) in this instance exacerbates the individual-level effect of being black.

MITIGATING CONTEXT EFFECT

James Davis's (1966) study "The Campus as a Frog Pond" provides a nice example of a mitigating context effect. The term "frog pond" here references the saying that it is better to be a big frog in a little pond than a big frog in a big pond. We expect frog pond effects where "success is judged by relative standing in the social group, not by standing in the total population" (Davis 1966, p. 25). The college campus, Davis suggests, is one such context, since student grades tend to be about the same across schools, regardless of selectivity. This tendency of colleges to grade on a curve has real-life consequences because it implies that a student will tend to obtain higher grades in a less competitive college, and grades affect career decisions.

Davis's central concept—that what matters is one's *relative rank on X* (for example, one's ability relative to others on the campus)—has been applied widely, from accounting for revolution (that revolution is fueled by relative, not absolute, deprivation) to explaining satisfaction with income (what matters is one's income relative to the income of one's peers). For our purposes here, the critical point is that X_{ij} (the individual value) and X_j

(the value for the context) have opposing effects. In Davis's example, career aspirations are boosted by high academic ability at the individual level but lowered by high academic ability among an individual's peer group.

Context Effects as Nuisance

In the last section we observed that, just as individuals can be distinguished on the basis of their values on some attribute X, so too neighborhoods and other social contexts can be distinguished on the basis of the prevalence of that attribute among those in each context. Because it could be said that these differing properties of social contexts put the "social" in *social research*, determining the effect of social context is fundamental to social research. Increasingly, social research is multilevel, measuring properties of contexts as well as properties of individuals. In many instances the goal of the research is to estimate context effects.

Unfortunately, data in the social sciences do not always permit us to separate context effects from individual-level effects. In those instances context effects can be a nuisance. Consider again the case of Governor George Wallace's bid for the presidency in the 1968 U.S. election (chapter 1). Because of Wallace's reputation as a segregationist, we would not expect Wallace to garner many votes among blacks. Yet, when we look at the vote in the 1968 election, we find that George Wallace received a greater share of the vote in regions with *higher* percentages of blacks. Across congressional districts in the South, for example, the correlation was $r=0.55$ between percent black and percent who voted for Wallace (Firebaugh 1978). We see the same pattern across larger regions in the United States. Wallace's strongest showing by far was in the South, where blacks constitute nearly 25 percent of the population. In the East, where blacks make up only about 10 percent of the population, Wallace fared much worse, capturing a much smaller share of the vote (less than 6 percent of the vote in the East versus more than 20 percent in the South).[6]

The naive explanation is that blacks must have been more inclined than other racial groups to vote for Wallace. This explanation is quickly ruled out by postelection survey data. In one postelection survey, the 1968 American National Election Study (ANES), we find that, of the 87 black respondents who said they voted, *not a single respondent* had voted for Wallace. Among the other respondents who voted, fully 1 in 8 said they had voted for Wallace. The GSS results for 1972 and 1973 confirm the ANES findings: Of the 237 black voters, *only 2* said they had voted for

---

[6] These figures are based on the 1972–73 General Social Survey. To complete the account, Wallace received less than 10 percent of the vote in the West and Midwest, where blacks constitute roughly 8–9 percent of the total N in the 1972–73 GSS.

Wallace. (In both surveys, 11.3 percent of respondents overall said they had voted for Wallace.)

The naive explanation is off the mark because of context effects. In the 1968 election, whites were more likely to vote for Wallace if they lived in heavily black districts. In other words, social context effects played a major role in that election. Although blacks themselves did not vote for Wallace, their presence affected the propensity of *whites* to do so. Thus, with the proper multilevel model we would find opposing signs for the effect of X_{ij} (race of respondent is black) and X_j (percent black for the region) on the odds of voting for Wallace.

The problem is that we cannot always separate the context effect from the individual-level effect because we do not always have access to data at both levels. In the case of elections, for example, the secret ballot means that we cannot observe how individuals actually vote; at best we can examine data aggregated by precincts, or we can (in some instances) rely on postelection surveys. For historical data we often are even more limited, since available data very often are aggregated, and we cannot go back in time to poll individuals.

Context effects are a nuisance when we do not have the appropriate data to estimate them (and thus must simply assume that they do not exist). In the most common occurrence of this problem, a researcher wants to draw inferences about individual behavior on the basis of aggregate data. Sometimes researchers ignore the possibility of context effects and draw conclusions about individuals from aggregate data anyway, committing what William S. Robinson (1950) called the *ecological fallacy*. That practice is called a fallacy because it makes the problematic assumption that relationships at the aggregate level mirror relationships at the individual level. If social context has an effect, however, there is said to be *aggregation bias*, and we should avoid drawing conclusions about individual-level effects from aggregate relationships. Indeed, as the 1968 presidential election results show, relationships at the individual and aggregate level may even be in *opposite directions*.

Aggregation bias is an issue in virtually all the social and behavioral sciences, but the problem is particularly acute in fields (such as history and epidemiology) where data often are not available for individuals. A growing technical literature (for example, King 1997) continues to seek solutions to the problem.

CRITICAL TESTS IN SOCIAL RESEARCH

In this book I have repeatedly emphasized the importance of multiple methods and multiple data sets in social research. In chapter 3, for example,

I cited a number of examples of multiple methods used as validity checks—testing the plausibility of the claim that Bush lost 10,000 votes in the Florida panhandle, using ethnographic data to interpret survey responses on race, using follow-up in-depth interviews to investigate abuse within families. In chapter 4, I extolled the virtues of identical analyses of parallel data sets.

In this section I want to return to the reality check rule and the replication rule to make the point that progress in social research is often a matter of progressively eliminating rival explanations by a series of critical observations or tests. In some instances a single critical test might suffice, as in the earlier example (chapter 5) of John Snow's classic investigation of how cholera is spread. More often, multiple causes are involved, and progress in sorting out those causes is often slow and halting. To illustrate the latter, consider the longstanding line of research on the black-white test score gap in U.S. schools. I begin with three observations: (1) The gap is real. (2) The gap is important. (3) The cause of the gap is the subject of a vigorous debate today in the social sciences.

First, the test score gap is real. Although the black-white gap has narrowed considerably in recent decades—the black-white reading gap was cut by almost one-half, and the math gap by one-third, from 1971 to 1996—the average black student in the United States still scores below three-fourths of white students in the United States on most standardized tests (Jencks and Phillips 1998a, p. 1). On some tests the gap is even greater, with more than half of black Americans scoring lower than 85 percent of white Americans. The black-white test score gap is no longer disputed, since it is found in study after study (for example, Bali and Alvarez 2003; Hedges and Nowell 1998; National Center for Education Statistics 2001). The gap appears early, even before children enter kindergarten (Fryer and Levitt 2004; West, Denton, and Reaney 2001), and it persists into adulthood. There are similar, though typically smaller, test score gaps between white students and Latino students. For our purposes here, it suffices to focus on the black-white gap.

The black-white test score gap is enormously important because "reducing the black-white test score gap would do more to move America toward racial equality than any politically plausible alternative" (Jencks and Phillips 1998b, p. 51). Scholars such as Christopher Jencks and Meredith Phillips believe that is the case because of pretty strong evidence that, in today's world, reducing cognitive inequality would go a long way toward reducing economic inequality. On the basis of recent data on test scores and earnings from the National Longitudinal Survey of Youth (NLSY), for example, we find that the black-white earnings ratio for men (black earnings as a fraction of white earnings for men in their thirties) increased for men with lower-than-average test scores, for men with average test scores, and for men with higher-than-average test scores. The increase was steepest for men with higher-than-average test scores, however, so that in 1993 black men who scored in the top half of the Armed Forces Qualification Test (AFQT) earned 96 percent as much as white men who scored in the top half of the test. This is in sharp contrast to the results thirty years earlier, when black men scoring above the national average on the AFQT earned only 65 percent as much as white men scoring above the national average on the AFQT. In today's world, then, equalizing test scores for blacks and whites should go a long way toward equalizing earnings for blacks and whites in the United States.[7]

The question of *how* to reduce the test score gap of course turns on the question of what is causing the gap. The cause of the gap, in turn, is the subject of a sometimes heated debate in the social sciences. The gap was first demonstrated in the testing of U.S. Army recruits for World War I, and since then empirical research on the subject has proceeded in fits and starts, as Jencks and Phillips (1998a, p. vii) explain:

> By now this cycle has become predictable. First someone claims that the black-white gap is largely innate. Then skeptics challenge the claim. The debate starts off largely unencumbered by evidence, but it eventually precipitates a number of useful empirical studies. The issue is not fully resolved, but the number of plausible explanations is smaller at the end of the debate than at the beginning. This happened in the 1920s. It happened again in the 1970s, after Arthur Jensen published "How much can we boost IQ and scholastic achievement?" in the *Harvard Educational Review* in 1969. It seems to be happening again.

Most likely there are multiple causes of the test score gap, and in that sense the test gap puzzle differs from the puzzle of how cholera is spread, as noted above. But the methodological principles are the same in both cases: Try to find critical tests of the predictions of various explanations. That is the approach that has been used with partial success in evaluating possible explanations for the test score gap:

- One hypothesis is that genetic differences account for the test score gap. If so, then racial differences in test scores should remain relatively constant over time, and there should be no difference in test scores for black students raised in black families and black students raised in white families. But neither is true. As noted earlier, the test

---

[7] Among students with the same twelfth-grade test scores, black students are *more* likely than white students to graduate from college. Thus, as Jencks and Phillips (1998b, p. 46) point out, equalizing test scores should reduce black-white disparities in educational attainment as well.

score gap has declined significantly in the United States in recent decades. Moreover, the preadolescent test scores of blacks are much higher for blacks raised in white families (Jencks and Phillips 1998a, p. 3), which is scarcely consistent with the genetic argument. Virtually all scholars now agree that the causes lie elsewhere.

- Another hypothesis locates the cause in the tests themselves: perhaps the tests are unreliable and biased against some groups. If so, then test scores should have little or no predictive ability of educational and occupational attainment. But test scores do predict later life chances for all racial groups, so for the most part researchers have turned elsewhere for explanations of the gap.
- Another explanation focuses on differences in school resources, as measured, for example, by spending per pupil. That explanation was more compelling during the "separate but equal" days of racial segregation, where schools for whites and blacks may have been separate but certainly were not equal. The explanation is less compelling today because per pupil spending (some glaring exceptions notwithstanding) on average is about the same for whites and blacks (Jencks and Phillips 1998a, p. 9). Equal spending does not necessarily translate into equal educational *quality*, however, so the test score gap may be due in large part to differences in the way money is spent—an important topic for further research.
- Other explanations focus on cultural differences. If cultural differences play a significant role, then black children raised in white families should score higher than black children raised in black families (as they do). Critical observations such as this strengthen the case for the role of culture, but they do not tell us what cultural differences matter. A particularly influential cultural explanation, based largely on ethnographic studies of minority students in schools (Fordham and Ogbu 1986; Ogbu 2003), argues that black adolescents are characterized by an "oppositional culture" that hinders their academic achievement. For example, in his classroom observations of students in Shaker Heights, Ohio (an affluent suburb of Cleveland), John Ogbu (2003) found that black students were more likely that white students to arrive late to class, come without materials, and disrupt lessons. Whatever the merit of the controversial claim that black adolescents exhibit an oppositional culture that undermines their academic achievement (Ainsworth-Darnell and Downey 1998; P. L. Carter 2005; Farkas, Lleras, and Maczuga 2002; Fryer and Torelli 2005; Mickelson 1990; Tyson, Darity, and Castellino 2005), differences in adolescent culture alone cannot account for the test score gap since, as noted earlier, the gap appears well before adolescence.

This brief summary scarcely does justice to the richness of the literature on the test score gap. My purpose, however, is not to provide an overview of research on this issue, but to illustrate how social researchers look for critical observations or tests to evaluate rival explanations, peeling off various explanations one by one as they fail to predict accurately across a variety of settings.

CONCLUSION

Even a cursory comparison of empirical work in the social science journals today with published work fifty years ago will show how far we have come in terms of the sophistication of our estimation methods. For the most part, the greater sophistication is good. There is the danger, however, that researchers will come to rely on estimation methods as substitutes for careful theorizing and conceptualization. An important theme of this chapter is that we cannot count on technical tricks to remedy defective theory or research design.

Another danger posed by increasing statistical sophistication is that the tools of research will overshadow the substance of research. "Let method be the servant, not the master" is meant to be a pointed reminder that the research problem should dictate the choice of the tool, not the other way around. Statistical methods should not be the motivators of our research.

Nor should statistical methods be an afterthought: Data design and estimation method go hand in hand. Sometimes researchers do not think much about estimation until the data have been collected. That is a big mistake because, generally speaking, estimation techniques are ill-suited for overcoming inadequacies in research design. Research design is about collecting the sort of data that enables you to estimate the right thing. Statistical estimation is about providing reliable and precise estimates. To ensure reliable and precise estimates of the right thing, we must not divorce research design and statistical estimation.

The secrets of the social world are not easily revealed, so we need to find all the levers and apply all the leverage we can. To advance in the social sciences, we need to hone our skills in the use of natural experiments and decompositions and critical observations to entice the social world to reveal its secrets. Regression analysis—the workhorse method in the social sciences for well more than a quarter century—should not be discarded, but used more thoughtfully, and applied strategically in conjunction with other approaches. Above all, what we need in social research today is more imagination.

Student Exercises on Rule 7

The lesson to be learned in this exercise is that, due to contextual effects, relationships observed at the aggregate level do not necessarily reflect relationships at the individual level. In fact, as this exercise demonstrates, individual-level and aggregate-level relationship can even be in opposite directions.

The more general point I wish to make, in line with rule 7, is that method without substance can be dangerous. In the 1968 election, regions with a higher percentage of blacks tended to vote at higher rates for George Wallace. Without an understanding of the issues of that day, you might be tempted to interpret that positive association to indicate that blacks voted disproportionately for Wallace. Yet, as you will see, black votes for Wallace were extremely rare.

The routine should be familiar by now. Go to the web site http://sda .berkeley.edu and follow the instructions below. The instructions should enable you to generate all the statistics you need to complete the assignments. Variable names are in **boldface**.

Note: If you did the prior exercises you should be able to do the assignment here. To avoid redundancy, the instructions below include only the key commands. Recall that the format in the SDA web site might have changed somewhat since these directions were written, so some of the specific directions below might be out of date. You nonetheless should be able to follow the logic of the instructions to obtain the tables you need to complete the assignments.

ASSIGNMENT 1: GEORGE WALLACE AND THE BLACK VOTE IN THE 1968
    PRESIDENTIAL ELECTION—RESULTS FROM THE ANES

The aim is to compare the individual-level versus regional-level association between race and vote for George Wallace in the 1968 presidential election. From the SDA Berkeley web site, choose the 1948–2000 cumulative ANES data set. There are five basic steps:

- First recode the ANES race variable **v106** into a variable called **black**, coded 1 for blacks and 0 for whites (everyone else). Currently, v106 is coded 1 = white, 2 = black, and 3 = other, and so you need to change these codes to 0 and 1. You also need to recode the voting variable **v704**, currently coded 1 = voted for Democratic party candidate, 2 = voted for Republican party candidate, 3 = voted for third-party candidate. Wallace was a third-party candidate, so create a variable called **thirdpartyvote** by recoding 1 for those who voted for a third-party candidate and 0 for those who voted Republican or Democrat. You will find that only 3.6 percent of voters say they voted for a third-party candidate. This figure, however, includes all elections from 1948 through 2000. The percentage is much higher for George Wallace (as you will see later, when you use "Selection filter" to isolate the 1968 election).

- The next step is to cross-tabulate **thirdpartyvote** (row variable) with **black**. Enter v4(1968) as "Selection filter" to isolate the 1968 election. Observe that, by isolating the 1968 election, **thirdpartyvote** is now vote for George Wallace. Choose "No weight" from the pull-down weighting menu, and otherwise choose the same default options as you did in prior assignments. You should find, of the 87 black voters in the sample, *not a single one* voted for George Wallace.

Question 1. Were blacks more likely or less likely than others to vote for George Wallace? Is the association statistically significant? Is it very strong?

- The third step is to cross-tabulate **black** (row variable) by **v112** (region of country—Northeast, North Central, South, and West). Again select "No weight" and insert **v4(1968)** in the selection filter, to isolate the year 1968. This cross-tabulation is needed to obtain percentage black in each of the four regions. We will use those percentages to create a new variable **regionblack**.
- Recode **v112** to create **regionblack** by inserting the percentages you obtained in the prior step. To illustrate: The Northeast region, which is coded "1" in **v112**, should be recoded as "6.8" in **regionblack**, since blacks constituted 6.8 percent of the respondents from the Northeast in the 1968 ANES.
- The final step is to cross-tabulate **thirdpartyvote** (row variable) with **regionblack**. Isolate the 1968 election by entering **v4(1968)**, **black(0-1)** as "Selection filter," and choose "No weight" from the pull-down weighting menu. Run the table. The number of cases should be 1,027, the same number as in the individual-level cross-tabulation of **black** and **thirdpartyvote**.

Question 2. (a) Note that the aggregate-level association is statistically significant. On the basis of the values for R (a measure of association), compare the aggregate-level association of race (blacks/nonblacks) and vote for George Wallace with the individual-level association you obtained previously.

(b) The context effect here is mitigating—explain what that means, substantively, in this case.

(c) Give one or two reasons why the vote of *whites* would be affected by the racial context of their region. That is, why would whites in a more heavily black region be more likely to vote for a segregationist candidate than would whites in a less heavily black region?

ASSIGNMENT 2: GEORGE WALLACE AND THE BLACK VOTE IN THE 1968 PRESIDENTIAL ELECTION—RESULTS FROM THE GSS

The second assignment is to examine George Wallace and the black vote again, this time using GSS data instead of data from the ANES. Because you can use the instructions for the ANES as your guide, the instructions below will be abbreviated.

- The 1968 election variable is called **pres68** in the GSS, coded 1 for vote for Hubert Humphrey (the Democratic candidate), 2 for vote for Richard Nixon (the Republican), 3 for vote for George Wallace, and 4 for vote for someone else. You should recode this variable, as before, as 1 for vote for Wallace and 0 otherwise. You can call this new variable **wallacevote**. You should find that 11.5 percent voted for Wallace, and 88.5 percent voted for Humphrey, Nixon, or some fourth-party candidate.

- Similarly, recode the GSS race variable, called **race**, to create a new variable **black** that is coded 1 for black and 0 for others. (You can see the codes for **race** by entering **race** in the "Selected" box and clicking on "View.") Of the 46,510 respondents in the 1972–2004 cumulative GSS, you will find that 6,399, or 13.8 percent, are black. (Note that this percentage is likely to be somewhat different in your subsequent tables that include **pres68**, since the use of **pres68** restricts the analysis to the 1968 election.)

- The GSS **region** has nine categories: 1–2 = Northeast; 3–4 = North Central; 5–7 = South; 8–9 = West. Use the recode command to create a new variable **region4_gss** that parallels the four-category region variable in the ANES.

- Cross-tabulate **black** (row variable) with **region4_gss** (the GSS region variable) to obtain the percentage black in each region. Insert **year (1972–1973)** as "Selection filter."

- Create **regionblack** from the percentages you obtained in the cross-tabulation of **black** with **region4_gss**.

- Do the cross-tabulations necessary to examine the individual-level and aggregate-level (four regions) association of race (black/non-black) with vote for Wallace.

Question 3. (a) Compare the GSS results with the results you obtained from the ANES. What are the individual-level and aggregate-level values of R for the GSS data? For the ANES data?
(b) Compare the values of R: Is the individual-level versus aggregate-level discrepancy roughly the same size in both data sets, or is the discrepancy notably larger in one of the data sets?

ASSIGNMENT 3. EXAMPLES OF NATURAL EXPERIMENTS

Table 1 in Angrist and Krueger (2001) lists fifteen economic studies that make use of natural experiments. From your reading of one of the studies, describe (in one or two paragraphs) the natural experiment that is used.

References

Abbott, Andrew. 2003. *Methods of Discovery: Heuristics for the Social Sciences.* New York: W. W. Norton.

Aghion, Philippe, Eve Caroli, and Cecilia García-Peñalosa. 1999. "Inequality and economic growth: The perspective of the new growth theories." *Journal of Economic Literature* 37:1615–60.

Agresti, Alan, and Barbara Finlay. 1997. *Statistical Methods for the Social Sciences.* Third edition. Upper Saddle River, NJ: Prentice Hall.

Ainsworth-Darnell, James W., and Douglas B. Downey. 1998. "Assessing the oppositional culture explanation for racial/ethnic differences in school performance." *American Sociological Review* 63:536–53.

Allison, Paul. 1978. "Measures of inequality." *American Sociological Review* 43:865–80.

———. 1990. "Change scores as dependent variables in regression analysis." Pp. 93–114 in *Sociological Methodology 1990*, ed. Clifford C. Clogg. Oxford: Basil Blackwell.

———. 2002. *Missing Data.* Sage University Paper Series on Quantitative Applications in the Social Sciences, 07-136. Thousand Oaks, CA: Sage.

———. 2005. *Fixed Effects Regression Methods for Longitudinal Data Using SAS.* Cary, NC: SAS Press.

Alwin, Duane F. 1996. "Coresidence beliefs in American society—1973 to 1991." *Journal of Marriage and the Family* 58:393–403.

Alwin, Duane F., and Robert M. Hauser. 1975. "The decomposition of effects in path analysis." *American Sociological Review* 40:37–47.

Amato, Paul R., and Joan G. Gilbreth. 1999. "Nonresident fathers and children's well-being: A meta-analysis." *Journal of Marriage and the Family* 61:557–73.

Amsden, Alice H. 2003. "Good-by dependency theory, hello dependency theory." *Studies in Comparative International Development* 38:32–38.

Angrist, Joshua D., and William N. Evans. 1998. "Children and their parents' labor supply: Evidence from exogenous variation in family size." *American Economic Review* 88:450–77.

Angrist, Joshua D., and Alan B. Krueger. 2001. "Instrumental variables and the search for identification: From supply and demand to natural experiments." *Journal of Economic Perspectives* 15:69–85.

Arrighi, Giovanni, Beverly J. Silver, and Benjamin D. Brewer. 2003. "Industrial convergence, globalization, and the persistence of the North-South divide." *Studies in Comparative International Development* 38:3–31.

Bali, Valentina A., and R. Michael Alvarez. 2003. "Schools and educational outcomes: What causes the 'race gap' in student test scores?" *Social Science Quarterly* 84:485–507.

Becker, S. O., and A. Ichino. 2002. "Estimation of average treatment effects based on propensity scores." *STATA Journal* 2:358–77.

Benabou, Roland. 1996. "Inequality and growth." *NBER Macroeconomics Annual* 11:11–74.

Bennett, Stephen, and Linda Bennett. 1987. "Political participation." *Annual Review of Political Science* 2:157–204.

Benson, Rodney, and Abigail C. Saguy. 2005. "Constructing social problems in an age of globalization: A French-American comparison." *American Sociological Review* 70:233–59.

Blake, Judith. 1989. *Family Size and Achievement*. Los Angeles: University of California Press.

Blau, Peter M. 1960. "Structural effects." *American Sociological Review* 25: 178–93.

Blinder, Alan S. 1973. "Wage discrimination: Reduced form and structural variables." *Journal of Human Resources* 8:436–55.

Bollen, Kenneth, and Robert W. Jackman. 1995. "Income inequality and democratization revisited: Comment on Muller." *American Sociological Review* 60:983–89.

Borjas, George. 1995. "Ethnicity, neighborhoods, and human capital externalities." *American Economic Review* 85:365–90.

Bourguignon, Francois, and Christian Morrisson. 2002. "Inequality among world citizens: 1820–1992." *American Economic Review* 92:727–44.

Bowles, Samuel, and Herbert Gintis. 1976. *Schooling in Capitalist America: Educational Reform and the Contradictions of Economic Life*. New York: Basic Books.

Bradatan, Cristina, and Glenn Firebaugh. 2007. "History, population policies, and fertility decline in Eastern Europe: A case study." *Journal of Family History* 32:179–92.

Brady, Henry E. 2004. "Data-set versus causal-process observations: The 2000 U.S. Presidential election." Pp. 267–71 in *Rethinking Social Inquiry: Diverse Tools, Shared Standards*, ed. Henry E. Brady and David Collier. Lanham, MD: Rowman and Littlefield.

Brady, Henry E., and David Collier, eds. 2004. *Rethinking Social Inquiry: Diverse Tools, Shared Standards*. Lanham, MD: Rowman and Littlefield.

Brewster, Karin L., and Irene Padavic. 2000. "Change in gender-ideology, 1977–1996: The contributions of intracohort change and population turnover." *Journal of Marriage and Family* 62:477–87.

Brown, B. W., Jr. 1972. "Statistics, scientific method, and smoking." Pp. 40–51 in *Statistics: A Guide to the Unknown*, ed. Judith M. Tanur, Frederick Mosteller, William H. Kruskal, Richard F. Link, Richard S. Pieters, and Gerald R. Rising. San Francisco: Holden-Day.

Bryk, Anthony, and Stephen Raudenbush. 1992. *Hierarchical Linear Models: Applications and Data Analysis Methods*. Thousand Oaks, CA: Sage.

Butterfield, Sherri-Ann P. 2004. " 'We're just black': The racial and ethnic identities of second-generation West Indians in New York." Pp. 288–312 in *Becoming New Yorkers: Ethnographies of the New Second Generation*, ed. Philip Kasinitz, John H. Mollenkopf, and Mary C. Waters. New York: Russell Sage Foundation.

Campbell, Donald T., and Julian C. Stanley. 1966. *Experimental and Quasi-Experimental Designs for Research*. Boston: Houghton-Mifflin.

Card, David, and Jesse Rothstein. 2006. "Racial segregation and the black-white test score gap." Cambridge, MA: National Bureau of Economic Research. NBER Working Paper no. 12078.

Carter, J. Scott. 2005. "Reassessing the effect of urbanism and regionalism: A comparison of different indicators of racial tolerance." *Sociation Today* 3 (web journal).

Carter, Prudence L. 2005. *Keepin' It Real: School Success Beyond Black and White*. New York: Oxford University Press.

Charles, Camille Z., Gniesha Dinwiddie, and Douglas S. Massey. 2004. "The continuing consequences of segregation: Family stress and college academic performance." *Social Science Quarterly* 85:1353–73.

Cherlin, Andrew, Linda M. Burton, Tera R. Hurt, and Diane M. Purvin. 2004. "The influence of physical and sexual abuse on marriage and cohabitation." *American Sociological Review* 69:768–89.

Clogg, Clifford C., and Aref N. Dajani. 1991. "Sources of uncertainty in modeling social statistics: An inventory." *Journal of Official Statistics* 7:7–24.

Coleman, James S., Ernest Q. Campbell, Carol J. Hobson, James McPartland, Alexander M. Mood, Frederic D. Weinfeld, and Robert L. York. 1966. *Equality of Educational Opportunity*. Washington, DC: United States Department of Education.

Collier, David, Henry E. Brady, and Jason Seawright. 2004. "Sources of leverage in causal inference: Toward an alternative view of methodology." Chapter 13 in *Rethinking Social Inquiry: Diverse Tools, Shared Standards*, ed. Henry E. Brady and David Collier. Lanham, MD: Rowman and Littlefield.

Conley, Dalton. 2004. *The Pecking Order*. New York: Pantheon Books.

Conley, Dalton, and Rebecca Glauber. 2005. "Parental educational investment and children's academic risk: Estimates of the impact of sibship size and birth order from exogenous variation in fertility." NBER Working Paper no. 11,302.

Cooper, Harris, and Larry V. Hedges, eds. 1994. *The Handbook of Research Synthesis*. New York: Russell Sage Foundation.

Cutler, David M., and Edward L. Glaeser. 1997. "Are ghettos good or bad?" *Quarterly Journal of Economics* 112:827–72.

Davis, James A. 1966. "The campus as a frog pond: An application of the theory of relative deprivation to career decisions of college men." *American Journal of Sociology* 72:17–31.

Deaton, Angus. 2005. "Measuring poverty in a growing world (or measuring growth in a poor world)." *Review of Economics and Statistics* 87:1–19.

Diekmann, Andreas, and Henriette Engelhardt. 1999. "The social inheritance of divorce: Effects of parent's family type in postwar Germany." *American Sociological Review* 64:783–93.

DiPrete, Thomas A., and David B. Grusky. 1990a. "The multilevel analysis of trends with repeated cross-sectional data." Pp. 337–68 in *Sociological Methodology 1990*, ed. Clifford C. Clogg. Oxford: Basil Blackwell.

———. 1990b. "Structure and trend in the process of stratification for American men and women." *American Journal of Sociology* 96:107–43.

Downey, Douglas. 1995. "When bigger is not better: Family size, parental resources, and children's educational performance." *American Sociological Review* 60:746–61.

Downey, Douglas, Beckett Broh, and Paul von Hippel. 2004. "Are schools the great equalizer? Cognitive inequality during the summer months and the school year." *American Sociological Review* 69:613–35.

Downey, Douglas, Brian Powell, Lala Carr Steelman, and Shana Pribesh. 1999. "Much ado about siblings: Change models, sibship size, and intellectual development (comment on Guo and VanWey)." *American Sociological Review* 64:193–98.

Duncan, Greg J., and Graham Kalton. 1987. "Issues of design and analysis of surveys across time." *International Statistical Review* 55:97–117.

Duncan, Greg J., W. Jean Yeung, Jeanne Brooks-Gunn, and Judith R. Smith. 1998. "How much does childhood poverty affect the life chances of children?" *American Sociological Review* 63:406–23.

Easterlin, Richard A. 1974. "Does economic growth improve the human lot?" In *Nations and Households in Economic Growth: Essays in Honour of Moses Abramovitz*, ed. P. A. David and M. W. Reder. New York: Academic Press.

———. 1996. *Growth Triumphant: The Twenty-first Century in Historical Perspective*. Ann Arbor: University of Michigan Press.

———. 2001. "Income and happiness: Towards a unified theory." *Economic Journal* 111:465–84.

Edwards, Ryan D., and Shripad Tuljapurkar. 2005. "Inequality in life spans and a new perspective on mortality convergence across industrialized countries." *Population and Development Review* 31:645–74.

Farkas, George, Christy Lleras, and Steve Maczuga. 2002. "Does oppositional culture exist in minority and poverty peer groups?" *American Sociological Review* 67:148–55.

Felson, Richard B. 2002. *Violence and Gender Reexamined*. Washington, DC: American Psychological Association Books.

Firebaugh, Glenn. 1978. "A rule for inferring individual-level relationships from aggregate data." *American Sociological Review* 43:557–72.

———. 1989. "Methods for estimating cohort replacement effects." Pp. 243–62 in *Sociological Methodology 1989*, ed. Clifford C. Clogg. Oxford: Basil Blackwell.

———. 1992. "Growth effects of foreign and domestic investment." *American Journal of Sociology* 98:105–30.

———. 1997. *Analyzing Repeated Surveys*. Sage University Paper Series on Quantitative Applications in the Social Sciences, 07-115. Thousand Oaks, CA: Sage.

———. 2003. *The New Geography of Global Income Inequality*. Cambridge: Harvard University Press.

Firebaugh, Glenn. In press. "Replication data sets and favored-hypothesis bias (Comment on Jeremy Freese and Gary King)." *Sociological Methods and Research*.

Firebaugh, Glenn, and Kevin Chen. 1995. "Vote turnout of Nineteenth Amendment women: The enduring effect of disenfranchisement." *American Journal of Sociology* 100:972–96.

Firebaugh, Glenn, and Kenneth E. Davis. 1988. "Trends in antiblack prejudice, 1972–1984: Region and cohort effects." *American Journal of Sociology* 94: 251–72.

Firebaugh, Glenn, and Jack P. Gibbs. 1985. "User's guide to ratio variables." *American Sociological Review* 50:713–22.

Firebaugh, Glenn, and Laura Tach. 2005. "Relative income and happiness: Are Americans on a hedonic treadmill?" Paper presented at the 100th annual meeting of the American Sociological Association, Philadelphia (August).

Fisher, Ronald A. 1959. *Smoking: The Cancer Controversy*. Edinburgh: Oliver and Boyd.

Fordham, Signithia, and John U. Ogbu. 1986. "Black students' school success: Coping with the 'burden of acting white.'" *Urban Review* 18:176–206.

Frank, Robert H. 1997. "The frame of reference as a public good." *Economic Journal* 107:1832–47.

———. 1999. *Luxury Fever: Money and Happiness in an Age of Excess*. Princeton: Princeton University Press.

Freedman, David. 1991. "Statistical models and shoe leather." Pp. 291–313 and 353–58 (rejoinder) in *Sociological Methodology 1991*, ed. Peter V. Marsden. Oxford: Basil Blackwell.

———. 1997. "From association to causation via regression." Pp. 113–61 in *Causality in Crisis? Statistical Methods and the Search for Causal Knowledge in the Social Sciences*, ed. Vaughn R. McKim and Stephen P. Turner. South Bend, IN: University of Notre Dame Press.

Fryer, Roland G., and Steven D. Levitt. 2004. "Understanding the black-white test score gap in the first two years of school." *Review of Economics and Statistics* 86:447–64.

Fryer, Roland G., Jr., and Paul Torelli. 2005. "An empirical analysis of 'acting white.'" Cambridge, MA: NBER Working Paper no. W 11,334 (May 1).

Galton, Sir Francis. 1874. *English Men of Science: Nature and Nurture*. London: Macmillan.

Garrett, Geoffrey. 2004. "Globalization's missing middle." *Foreign Affairs* (November/December): 84–96.

Ghosh, S., and C. R. Rao, eds. 1996. *Handbook of Statistics 13: Design and Analysis of Experiments*. Amsterdam: Elsevier Science.

Glaeser, Edward L., Bruce L. Sacerdote, and Jose A. Scheinkman. 2003. "The social multiplier." *Journal of the European Economic Association* 1:345–53.

Glass, Gene. 1976. "Primary, secondary, and meta-analysis of research." *Educational Research* 5:3–8.

———. 1977. "Integrating findings: The meta-analysis of research." *Review of Research in Education* 5:351–79.

Glenn, Norval D. 2005. *Cohort Analysis*. Second edition. Sage University Paper Series on Quantitative Applications in the Social Sciences, 5. Thousand Oaks, CA: Sage.

Goesling, Brian. 2001. "Changing income inequalities within and between nations: New evidence." *American Sociological Review* 66:745–61.

Groves, Robert M., Floyd J. Fowler Jr., Mick P. Couper, James M. Lepkowski, Eleanor Singer, and Roger Tourangeau. 2004. *Survey Methodology*. Hoboken, NJ: John Wiley and Sons.

Guo, Guang, and Leah K. VanWey. 1999. "Sibship size and intellectual development: Is the relationship causal?" *American Sociological Review* 64:169–87.

Haavelmo, Trygve. 1944. "The probability approach in econometrics." *Econometrica* 12 (Supplement):1–115.

Halaby, Charles N. 2004. "Panel models in sociological research: Theory into practice." *Annual Review of Sociology* 30:507–44.

Harding, David. 2003. "Counterfactual models of neighborhood effects: The effect of neighborhood poverty on dropping out and teenage pregnancy." *American Journal of Sociology* 109:676–719.

Harris, David R., and Jeremiah Joseph Sim. 2002. "Who is multiracial? Assessing the complexity of lived race." *American Sociological Review* 67:614–26.

Hedges, Larry V., and I. Olkin. 1985. *Statistical Methods for Meta-Analysis.* San Diego: Academic Press.

Hedges, Larry V., and Amy Nowell. 1998. "Black-white test score convergence since 1965." Pp. 149–81 in *The Black-White Test Score Gap*, ed. Christopher Jencks and Meredith Phillips. Washington, DC: Brookings Institution.

Ho, Daniel E., Kosuke Imai, Gary King, and Elizabeth A. Stuart. 2007. "Matching as nonparametric preprocessing for reducing model dependence in parametric causal inference." *Political Analysis* 15:199–236.

Hobcraft, John, Jane Menken, and Samuel Preston. 1982. "Age, period, and cohort effects in demography: A review." *Population Index* 48:4–43.

Holland, Paul W. 1986. "Statistics and causal inference." *Journal of the American Statistical Association* 81:945–70.

Hoxby, Caroline M., and Gretchen Weingarth. 2005. "Taking race out of the equation: School reassignment and the structure of peer effects." Manuscript, Department of Economics, Harvard University. Retrieved March 2006.

Hsiao, Cheng. 2003. *Analysis of Panel Data.* Second edition. Cambridge: Cambridge University Press.

Hummer, Robert A., Richard G. Rogers, Charles B. Nam, and Christopher G. Ellison. 1999. "Religious involvement and U.S. adult mortality." *Demography* 36:273–85.

Imai, Kosuke, and David A. van Dyk. 2004. "Causal inferences with general treatment regimes: Generalizing the propensity score." *Journal of the American Statistical Association* 99:854–66.

Jaccard, James, and Robert Turrisi. 2003. *Interaction Effects in Multiple Regression.* Second edition. Sage University Paper Series on Quantitative Applications in the Social Sciences, 07-72. Thousand Oaks, CA: Sage.

Jackman, Robert W. 1980. "Keynesian government intervention and income inequality (Comment on Stack, *ASR*, December 1978)." *American Sociological Review* 45:131–37.

Jacobs, Jerry A. 2005. "Multiple methods in *ASR*." *Footnotes* (December). Washington, DC: American Sociological Association.

Jencks, Christopher, with Marshall Smith, Henry Acland, Mary Jo Bane, David Cohen, Herbert Gintis, Barbara Heyns, and Stephan Michelson. 1972. *Inequality: A Reassessment of the Effect of Family and Schooling in America.* New York: Basic Books.

Jencks, Christopher, and Meredith Phillips, eds. 1998a. *The Black-White Test Score Gap.* Washington, DC: Brookings Institution.

Jencks, Christopher, and Meredith Phillips. 1998b. "America's next achievement test: Closing the black-white test score gap." *The American Prospect* (September/October) 41:44–53.

Jenkins, Stephen P. 1991. "The measurement of income inequality." Pp. 3–38 in *Economic Inequality and Poverty: International Perspectives,* ed. Lars Osberg. Armonk, NY: M. E. Sharpe.

———. 1995. "Accounting for inequality trends: Decomposition analyses for the U.K., 1971–86." *Economica* 62:29–63.

Kaldor, Nicholas. 1956. "Alternative theories of distribution." *Review of Economic Studies* 23:83–100.

Kalton, Graham. 1983. *Introduction to Survey Sampling.* Beverly Hills: Sage Publications.

King, Gary. 1997. *A Solution to the Ecological Inference Problem.* Princeton: Princeton University Press.

King, Gary, Robert O. Keohane, and Sidney Verba. 1994. *Designing Social Inquiry: Scientific Inference in Qualitative Research.* Princeton: Princeton University Press.

Kish, Leslie. 1965. *Survey Sampling.* New York: John Wiley and Sons.

———. 1987. *Statistical Design for Research.* New York: John Wiley and Sons.

Kitagawa, Evelyn M., and Philip M. Hauser. 1973. *Differential Mortality in the United States: A Study in Socioeconomic Epidemiology.* Cambridge: Harvard University Press.

Kleppner, Paul. 1982. "Were women to blame? Female suffrage and voter turnout." *Journal of Interdisciplinary History* 12:621–43.

Konow, James, and Joseph Earley. 2003. "The hedonic paradox: Is *Homo Economicus* happier?" Manuscript, Department of Economics, Loyola Marymount University. Retrieved December 2004.

Kozol, Jonathan. 1991. *Savage Inequalities: Children in America's Schools.* New York: Crown.

Kuh, Edwin, and John R. Meyer. 1955. "Correlation and regression estimates when the data are ratios." *Econometrica* 23:400–16.

Layard, Richard. 2005. *Happiness: Lessons from a New Science.* New York: Penguin.

Leamer, Edward E. 1983. "Let's take the con out of econometrics." *American Economic Review* 73:31–43.

Lesthaeghe, Ron, and Johan Surkyn. 1988. "Cultural dynamics and economic theories of fertility change." *Population and Development Review* 14:1–45.

Lieberson, Stanley. 1985. *Making It Count: The Improvement of Social Research and Theory.* Berkeley: University of California Press.

———. 1991. "Small N's and big conclusions: An examination of the reasoning in comparative studies based on a small number of cases." *Social Forces* 70: 307–20.

Liker, Jeffrey, Sue Augustyniak, and Greg Duncan. 1985. "Panel data and models of change: A comparison of first difference and conventional models." *Social Science Research* 14:80–101.

Little, R.J.A. 1992. "Regression with missing Xs: A review." *Journal of the American Statistical Association* 87:1227–37.

Lombard, Herbert L., and Carl R. Doering. 1928. "Cancer studies in Massachusetts: 2. Habits, characteristics, and environments of individuals with and without cancer." *New England Journal of Medicine* 198:481–87.

Lott, John R., Jr. 2000. "Gore might lose a second round: Media suppressed the Bush vote." *Philadelphia Inquirer*, November 14, p. 23A.

Luhman, Reid. 2002. *Race and Ethnicity in the United States: Our Differences and Our Roots.* Fort Worth: Harcourt.

Mannheim, Karl. 1927 [1952]. "The problem of generations." Pp. 276–322 in *Essays on the Sociology of Knowledge.* London: Rouledge and Kegan Paul.

McCloskey, Deirdre, and Stephen Ziliak. 1996. "The standard error of regressions." *Journal of Economic Literature* 34:97–114.

Manski, Charles F. 1993. "Identification and endogenous social effects: The reflection problem." *Review of Economic Studies* 60:531–42.

Massey, Douglas. 2004. "Segregation and stratification: A biosocial perspective." *DuBois Review* 1:7–25.

Massey, Douglas, and Nancy Denton. 1993. *American Apartheid: Segregation and the Making of the Underclass.* Cambridge: Harvard University Press.

Matthews, Robert. 2000. "Storks deliver babies ($p = .008$)." *Teaching Statistics* 22:36–38.

Mayer, Susan. 1997. *What Money Can't Buy: The Effect of Parental Income on Children's Outcomes.* Cambridge: Harvard University Press.

Melchior, Arne, and Kjetil Telle. 2001. "Global income distribution 1965–98: Convergence and marginalisation." *Forum for Development Studies* 1:75–98.

Merriam, Charles E., and Harold F. Gosnell. 1924. *Non-voting: Causes and Methods of Control.* Chicago: University of Chicago Press.

Mickelson, Roslyn Arlin. 1990. "The attitude-achievement paradox among black adolescents." *Sociology of Education* 63:44–61.

Middleton, Russell. 1976. "Regional differences in prejudice." *American Sociological Review* 41:94–117.

Milanovic, Branko. 2005. *Worlds Apart: Measuring International and Global Inequality.* Princeton: Princeton University Press.

Mirowsky, John, and Catherine E. Ross. 1999. "Economic hardship across the life course." *American Sociological Review* 64:548–69.

Moffitt, Robert. 2005. "Remarks on the analysis of causal relationships in population research." *Demography* 42:91–108.

Morgan, Stephen L. 2001. "Counterfactuals, causal effect heterogeneity, and the Catholic school effect on learning." *Sociology of Education* 74:341–74.

Morgan, Stephen L., and David J. Harding. 2006. "Matching estimators of causal effects: Prospects and pitfalls in theory and practice." *Sociological Methods and Research* 35:3–60.

Morgan, Stephen L., and Christopher Winship. 2007. *Counterfactuals and Causal Inference: Methods and Principles for Social Research.* Cambridge: Cambridge University Press.

Mouw, Ted, and Barbara Entwisle. 2006. "Residential segregation and interracial friendship in schools." *American Journal of Sociology* 112:394–441.

Muller, Edward N. 1995. "Economic determinants of democracy." *American Sociological Review* 60:805–21.

Myers, Scott M. 1996. "An interactive model of religiosity inheritance: The importance of family context." *American Sociological Review* 61:858–66.

National Center for Education Statistics. 2001. *The Condition of Education 2001*. Report 2001072. Washington, DC: NCES.

Norpoth, Helmut. 1987. "Under way and here to stay: Party realignment in the 1980s?" *Public Opinion Quarterly* 51:376–91.

Nuxoll, Daniel. 1994. "Differences in relative prices and international differences in growth rates." *The American Economic Review* 84:1423–36.

Oaxaca, Ronald. 1973, "Male-female wage differentials in urban labor markets." *International Economic Review* 14:693–709.

Ogbu, John U. 2003. *Black American Students in an Affluent Suburb: A Study of Academic Disengagement*. Mahway, NJ: Erlbaum.

Pager, Devah. 2002. "The Mark of a Criminal Record: The Consequences of Incarceration for the Employment Opportunities of Black and White Job Seekers." Ph.D. dissertation, University of Wisconsin, Madison.

Paukert, Felix. 1973. "Income distribution at different levels of development: A survey of evidence." *International Labour Review* 108:97–125.

Pearl, Judea. 2000. *Causality: Models, Reasoning, and Inferences*. Cambridge: Cambridge University Press.

Pearl, Raymond. 1938. "Tobacco smoking and longevity." *Science* 87:216–17.

Phillips, Meredith. 1999. "Sibship size and academic achievement: What we now know and what we still need to know (comment on Guo and VanWey)." *American Sociological Review* 64:188–92.

Raudenbush, Stephen. 2004. *HLM6: Hierarchical Linear and Nonlinear Modeling*. Lincolnwood, IL: Scientific Software International.

Ravallion, Martin. 2003. "Measuring aggregate welfare in developing countries: How well do national accounts and surveys agree?" *Review of Economics and Statistics*. 85:645–52.

Reardon, Sean F., and Glenn Firebaugh. 2002. "Measures of multi-group segregation." Pp. 33–67 in *Sociological Methodology 2002*, ed. Ross M. Stolzenberg. Boston: Blackwell.

Reardon, Sean F., John T. Yun, and Tamela McNulty Eitle. 2000. "The changing structure of school segregation: Measurement and evidence of multiracial metropolitan-area school segregation, 1989–1995." *Demography* 37:351–64.

Robinson, William S. 1950. "Ecological correlations and the behavior of individuals." *American Sociological Review* 15:351–57.

Rosenbaum, Paul R., and Donald B. Rubin. 1983. "The central role of the propensity score in observational studies for causal effects." *Biometrika* 76:41–55.

———. 1984. "Reducing bias in observational studies using subclassification on the propensity score." *Journal of the American Statistical Association* 79:516–24.

———. 1985. "Constructing a control group using multivariate matched sampling methods that incorporate the propensity score." *American Statistician* 39:33–38.

Rosenthal, Robert. 1979. "The 'file drawer problem' and tolerance for null results." *Psychological Bulletin* 86:638–41.

———. 1994. "Parametric measures of effect size." Pp. 231–44 in *The Handbook of Research Synthesis*, ed. Harris Cooper and Larry V. Hedges. New York: Russell Sage Foundation.

Rosenzweig, Mark R., and Kenneth I. Wolpin. 2000. "Natural 'natural experiments' in economics." *Journal of Economic Literature* 38:827–74.

Rubin, Donald B. 1973. "The use of matched samples and regression adjustment to remove bias in observational studies." *Biometrics* 29:185–203.

———. 1979. "Using multivariate matched sampling and regression adjustment to control bias in observational studies." *Journal of the American Statistical Association* 74:318–28.

———. 1987. *Multiple Imputation for Nonresponse in Surveys*. New York: John Wiley and Sons.

Rubin, Donald B., and Neal Thomas. 1996. "Matching using estimated propensity scores: Relating theory to practice." *Biometrics* 52:249–64.

———. 2000. "Combining propensity score matching with additional adjustments for prognostic covariates." *Journal of the American Statistical Association* 95:573–85.

Russett, Bruce M., Hayward R. Alker, Jr., Karl W. Deutsch, and Harold D. Lasswell. 1964. *World Handbook of Political and Social Indicators*. New Haven: Yale University Press.

Ryder, Norman B. 1965. "The cohort as a concept in the study of social change." *American Sociological Review* 30:843–61.

Sala-i-Martin, Xavier. 2006. "The world distribution of income: Falling poverty and . . . Convergence, period." *Quarterly Journal of Economics* 121:351–97.

Schafer, Joe L. 1997. *Analysis of Incomplete Multivariate Data*. London: Chapman and Hall.

Schultz, T. Paul. 1998. "Inequality in the distribution of personal income in the world: How it is changing and why." *Journal of Population Economics* 11:307–44.

Schwartz, Barry, and Howard Schuman. 2005. "History, commemoration, and belief: Abraham Lincoln in American memory, 1945–2001." *American Sociological Review* 70:183–203.

Seawright, Jason, and David Collier. 2004. "Glossary." Pp. 273–313 in *Rethinking Social Inquiry: Diverse Tools, Shared Standards*, ed. Henry E. Brady and David Collier. Lanham, MD: Rowman and Littlefield.

Selvin, Hanan C., and Warren O. Hagstrom. 1963. "The empirical classification of formal groups." *American Sociological Review* 28:399–411.

Sherman, Lawrence W. 1992. *Policing Domestic Violence: Experiments and Dilemmas*. New York: Free Press.

Sherman, Lawrence W., and Richard A. Berk. 1984. "The specific deterrent effects of arrest for domestic assault." *American Sociological Review* 49:261–72.

Smith, Herbert L. 1997. "Matching with multiple controls to estimate treatment effects in observational studies." Pp. 325–53 in *Sociological Methodology*, ed. Adrian E. Raftery. Boston: Blackwell.

Smith, Tom W. 1990. "Timely artifacts: A review of measurement variation in the 1972–1989 GSS." GSS Methodological Report no. 56. Chicago: National Opinion Research Center.

Snow, John. (1855) 1965. *On the Mode of Communication of Cholera*. Reprint. New York: Hafner.

Stack, Steven. 1978. "The effect of direct government involvement in the economy on the degree of income inequality: A cross-national study." *American Sociological Review* 43:880–88.

Stouffer, Samuel A., Edward A. Suchman, Leland C. DeVinney, Shirley A. Star, and Robin M. Williams. 1949. *The American Soldier: Adjustment During Army Life*. Volume 1. Princeton: Princeton University Press.

Sudman, Seymour, Norman M. Bradburn, and Norbert Schwarz. 1995. *Thinking about Answers: The Application of Cognitive Processes to Survey Methodology*. Jossey-Bass Social and Behavioral Science Series. San Francisco: Jossey-Bass.

Summers, Robert, and Alan Heston. 1991. "The Penn World Table (Mark 5): An expanded set of international comparisons, 1950–1988." *Quarterly Journal of Economics* 106:327–68.

Tourangeau, Roger, Lance J. Rips, and Kenneth Rasinski. 2000. *The Psychology of Survey Response*. Cambridge: Cambridge University Press.

Triplett, Jack E. 1997. "Measuring consumption: The post-1973 slowdown and the research issues." *Federal Reserve Bank of St. Louis Review* (May/June): 9–42.

Tuch, Steven. 1987. "Urbanism, region, and tolerance revisited." *American Sociological Review* 52:504–10.

Tufte, Edward R. 1983. *The Visual Display of Quantitative Information*. Cheshire, CT: Graphics Press.

Tyson, Karolyn, William Darity Jr., and Domini R. Castellino. 2005. "It's not 'a black thing': Understanding the burden of acting white and other dilemmas of high achievement." *American Sociological Review* 70:582–606.

Uggen, Christopher, and Jeff Manza. 2002. "Democratic contraction? Political consequences of felon disenfranchisement in the United States." *American Sociological Review* 67:777–803.

United Nations. 1993. *System of National Accounts*. Brussels: United Nations.

Uzzi, Brian, and Ryon Lancaster. 2004. "Embeddedness and price formation in the corporate law market." *American Sociological Review* 69:319–44.

Waite, Linda J., and Evelyn L. Lehrer. 2003. "The benefits from marriage and religion in the United States: A comparative analysis." *Population and Development Review* 29:255–75.

Waters, Mary C. 1998. "Multiple ethnic identity choices." Pp. 28–46 in *Beyond Pluralism: The Conception of Groups and Group Identities in America*, ed. Wendy F. Katkin, Ned Landsman, and Andrea Tyree. Urbana: University of Illinois Press.

———. 1999. *Black Identities: West Indian Immigrant Dreams and American Realities*. New York: Russell Sage Foundation.

———. 2002. "The social construction of race and ethnicity: Some examples from demography." Pp. 25–49 in *American Diversity: A Demographic Challenge for the Twenty-first Century*, ed. Nancy A. Denton and Stewart E. Tolnay. Albany: State University of New York Press.

———. 2004. "Race, ethnicity and immigration in the United States." Pp. 20–38 in *Social Inequalities in Comparative Perspective*, ed. Fiona Devine and Mary C. Waters. Malden, MA: Blackwell.

Weeden, Kim, Kim Young-Mi, Matthew Di Carlo, and David B. Grusky. 2007. "Social class and earnings inequality." *American Behavioral Scientist* 50: 702–36.

West, Jerry, Kristin Denton, and Lizabeth Reaney. 2001. *The Kindergarten Year: Findings from the Early Childhood Longitudinal Study, Kindergarten Class of 1998–99* (NCES 2001–03). U.S. Department of Education, National Center for Education Statistics. Washington, DC: U.S. Government Printing Office.

White, Kevin M. 2002. "Longevity advances in high-income countries, 1955–96." *Population and Development Review* 28:59–76.

Winship, Christopher, and Stephen L. Morgan. 1999. "The estimation of causal effects from observational data." *Annual Review of Sociology* 25:659–706.

Zajonc, Robert B. 1975. "Birth order and intelligence: Dumber by the dozen." *Psychology Today* 8:37–43.

Ziliak, Stephen, and Deirdre McCloskey. 2004. "Size matters: The standard error of regressions in the *American Economic Review*." *Economic Journal Watch* 1:331–58.

Index